COLT

COLT

THE REVOLVER OF THE AMERICAN WEST

The Autry Collection

Jeffrey Richardson

**CHARTWELL
BOOKS**

CONTENTS

For Giovanna

PREFACE

Lieutenant General William M. Keys, USMC (Retired)
President and CEO, Colt's Manufacturing LLC

As a lifetime admirer of Gene Autry, Western entertainment, and the captivating saga of the West—and as a keen arms collector—it is a pleasure to offer this preface to *Colt: The Revolver of the American West.*

Combining craftsmanship, history, mechanics, adventure, and romance, *Colt: The Revolver of the American West* strikingly demonstrates that Colt firearms are an extremely popular theme in the American experience. In many respects, Colt repeaters are the ultimate collectible, exotic treasures of history and of decorative and industrial art. In the world of collecting, Colts are indisputably No. 1—the Blue Chips of the firearms field.

Teaming the extraordinary Autry National Center Colt Collection (as featured in the Greg Martin Colt Gallery) with the distinguished publisher Rizzoli New York—with the text by Gamble Curator Jeffrey Richardson—this beautiful new book stands as a landmark in the study and appreciation of Colt firearms. How fitting it is—considering Gene Autry's unique stature, and that of the remarkable museum named after him—that the foremost Colt collection in the world is at the Autry National Center, a museum devoted to the history of the American West.

Not only is Colt's Manufacturing LLC pleased with the creation of this 200th anniversary salute to Samuel Colt's birthday, we are also equally delighted with its showcasing a breathtaking array of historic, handsome, and intriguing arms from our extensive and multifaceted legacy as gun inventors, designers, and manufacturers.

Here at Colt's we are very proud of our many firsts, dating back to our founder. Colonel Samuel Colt was hailed as one of the leading industrialists and entrepreneurs of his day—in his own way, a Steve Jobs—and was the first industrial tycoon in American history. It is fitting that our predecessor as the pioneer Colt collector was the inventor and founder himself. And fittingly, that Mrs. Elizabeth Hart Jarvis Colt carried on, becoming the second.

The publication of *Colt: The Revolver of the American West* not only adds significantly to the literature and culture of Samuel Colt and his repeaters, but also provides important new avenues for Colt studies, for all who share a deep appreciation of this very esteemed, captivating, and quintessentially American theme.

We at Colt's Manufacturing LLC are pleased to have the opportunity to endorse this beautiful and informative book in every way, and look forward to enjoying the elegant and comprehensive displays at the Autry that add to the ever-increasing fascination of the public with the magic of Colonel Colt and his firearms, and their role in history and the decorative and industrial arts.

FOREWORD

Beverly Haynes, Historian
Colt's Manufacturing LLC

A s Colt's Historian, it was my pleasure to attend the 2011 dedication of the exhibition *The Colt Revolver in the American West* in the Autry's Greg Martin Colt Gallery, and to present on behalf of Colt's Manufacturing LLC a 175th Anniversary Colt Single Action Army. That occasion offered an opportunity for us to contribute to the wonderful collection of Colt firearms at the Autry National Center.

With the publication of *Colt: The Revolver of the American West*, it is yet another pleasure to have this opportunity to add some background to Lieutenant General Keys's preface. When honored with the appointment to succeed Kathleen Hoyt on her retirement in 2011, I already had served several years as the company's Archivist. In developing and refining our Historical Department, many fresh insights and previously unknown historic facts have been recorded, adding to Colt's ever-evolving legacy.

Well aware of his place in history, Samuel Colt had created a private museum display in his home, Armsmear, and maintained a reference collection at the factory, which was termed in his own writings and in ledger records as a "museum." After his death in 1862, his widow, Elizabeth Colt, further enhanced his private exhibit at Armsmear, and also published the first Colt book: *Armsmear: The Home, the Arm, and the Armory of Samuel Colt; A Memorial* (1866). Created with her direct involvement and personal funding, Elizabeth Colt also commissioned special leather and Charter Oak bindings, all designed to further consecrate the published tribute to her late husband. Despite the flowery prose, the heart of *Armsmear* provided contemporary documentation of his pioneer role in American industry, as well as in entrepreneurial business—at which his genius was revealed in classic 19th-century empire building. Colonel Samuel Colt had the flair of the ultimate promoter, setting the stage for such masters as William F. "Buffalo Bill" Cody and Enzo Ferrari (who had a liking for firearms, and used a prancing horse logo with similarities to our own Rampant Colt).

Samuel Colt's timing couldn't have been better: he was there when the international stage was ready for his brilliantly designed and manufactured product line. In this enterprise, he was in sync with an array of dramatic events: the Texas Revolution, the Mexican-American War, the California Gold Rush, the Crimean War, America's westward pioneer migration, the Civil War, cattle drives from the Southwest up to the Kansas railheads, and epic conflicts with Indian populations.

Creating the Autry National Center Colt Collection

We at Colt's feel a solid bond with the Autry National Center. The Autry's superior Colt holdings originated principally from two remarkable figures who shared a love of firearms and of the West:

Gene Autry, "America's Favorite Singing Cowboy," and George A. Strichman, Chairman of the Board, Colt Industries.

The link between them was through a mutual friend: author and antiquarian R. L. Wilson. When Gene Autry, already owning a collection of 100 firearms (most of them Colt revolvers, particularly the Single Action Army), decided to create the Autry National Center—with his collaborators as cofounders, wife Jackie and their dear friends Joanne and Monte Hale—he arranged for Wilson to come to California to appraise his guns.

Fortunately, some 10 years earlier, Wilson had been commissioned by Strichman to organize the Colt Industries Museum Collection for display in the corporate offices at Park Avenue and 54th Street in the city of New York. Since Colt's had generously donated its 1,250-piece company museum to the state of Connecticut in 1957, it was Strichman's wish to organize a carefully and logically selected replacement, and to employ that display as Samuel Colt had done—promoting the Colt name and much-expanded product line. Under Strichman's leadership, by 1970, Colt Industries had become one of the leading international corporations in the industrial sector. Timing proved auspicious, and thus it was that on the retirement of Strichman as chairman in 1982, the Autry National Center was invited to view this collection. Here was the opportunity to acquire a museum-quality selection not only of firearms, but also of memorabilia, patent papers, and a reference library.

Further aiding the Autry was the availability a few years later of Strichman's private Colt collection of some 170 pieces. Strichman's collection contained a rich group of modern engraved and gold-inlaid Colts, and specially serial-numbered, special-issue handguns. The idea for Strichman to collect was an accident of a casual mention to him that Samuel Colt was the first Colt collector.

Also assisting in the assembly of the Colt Industries corporate museum and the Strichman collection were Colt Firearms Division Presidents Paul A. Benke, C. E. Warner, and Gary French, as well as Kathleen Hoyt, and Colt Custom Shop Manager for many years, Al DeJohn. That collaboration made it all the more fitting that Colt's presented the 175th Anniversary Single Action Army to the Autry in 2011.

At the Autry over the years, a litany of achievements—like the endowing of the Greg Martin Colt Gallery, the addition of the Gamble Firearms Gallery in 2013, and donations from collectors like Dennis A. LeVett, as well as the purchase by the Autry family of John E. Bianchi Jr.'s Frontier Museum—has created what is now recognized as one of the finest museum collections of Colt firearms in the world.

I look forward to returning to the Autry as often as possible. It is always rewarding to view the wonderful displays, which feature our beloved Colt firearms in a special setting, visited by hundreds of thousands of people from around the world every year.

G. Catlin Pinx.t Day & Son, Lith.rs to The Queen On Stone by J.M. Baley City Wall Theatre

CATLIN THE ARTIST SHOOTING BUFFALOS WITH COLT'S REVOLVING PISTOL.

He writes: I gave five shots to the right and left, four of which were fatal to the heart, and all in less than half a minute.

To capitalize on the connection between his revolvers and the American West, Samuel Colt commissioned George Catlin in 1851 to create a series of images showing the artist using the revolver on the frontier. (90.183.4.5)

THE COLT REVOLVER IN THE AMERICAN WEST

Jeffrey Richardson, Gamble Curator of Western History, Popular Culture, and Firearms, Autry National Center

Firearms were key tools in the settlement of the American West. Part of a larger technological revolution that transformed the United States from an isolated agricultural nation into the world's leading industrial and military power, firearm manufacturing and expertise came of age when Western expansion was at its peak. More than two million people flooded into the West in the last four decades of the 19th century, and almost all of them relied on firearms in one way or another. The two firearms that are commonly cited as "the gun that won the West" are the Winchester Model 1873 Rifle and the Colt Single Action Army Model Revolver.

The Colt revolver was the handgun of choice on the frontier because it was the first practical revolving firearm capable of firing more than one shot without having to be reloaded. It revolutionized the firearms industry and was the first truly global manufacturing export in American history. The Colt revolver had a dramatic impact around the world, but its greatest influence was in the American West in the second half of the 19th century. The revolver was used by just about everyone on the frontier, from settlers and Native Americans to law-enforcement officers and outlaws. Even today, the Colt revolver remains extremely popular in the region. As a result of their shared history, the Colt revolver and the American West will forever be connected.

The history of the American West is chronicled at the Autry National Center in Los Angeles. Entertainer Gene Autry was born and raised in the West, and he owed his fabulous success to the region. Autry was also an avid collector of Western Americana throughout his life. Wanting to give back to the community that had given so much to him, Autry sought "to build a museum which would exhibit and interpret the heritage of the West and show how it influenced America and the world." In 1988, he established the Gene Autry Western Heritage Museum, now the Autry National Center, in Los Angeles's Griffith Park. Autry understood that the history of the West was a combination of fact and fiction, so he wanted the museum to explore both the historic and mythic Wests, two equally important aspects of Western history. Because the Colt revolver played such an important role in the history of the West, it is an integral part of the museum. Over its 25-year

history, the Autry has compiled one of the finest collections of Colt revolvers and related artifacts in the world. The collection is the result of several key acquisitions. In 1987, the Autry acquired the corporate collection of Colt's—then called Colt Industries—and in 1990, the museum obtained the personal collection of former Colt Industries Chairman George A. Strichman. These two acquisitions, along with firearms from John E. Bianchi Jr.'s Frontier Museum and the personal collection of Gene Autry, account for a sizable portion of the Autry Collection. The Autry has also benefited from the donation of Colt revolvers and related artifacts from museum trustees and supporters such as Greg Martin, Dennis A. LeVett, and George Gamble.

The Autry has more than 500 Colt revolvers in its collection. For this book, 100 of the finest and most important examples were selected. The revolvers include pieces of historical significance, opulently engraved specimens, and extremely rare models. Each of the revolvers in this book is described in detail. These descriptions range from the revolver's production history and specifications to the individual who used it and its provenance. Countless other artifacts are also featured to help put the revolvers in their proper historical context. The majority of these artifacts were produced by or for Samuel Colt's companies: the Patent Arms Manufacturing Company and Colt's Patent Fire Arms Manufacturing Company (whose corporate name has changed over the years to include Colt Industries, Colt's Manufacturing Company, and Colt's Manufacturing LLC). Everything in this book, from the revolvers to the related artifacts, is part of the Autry's permanent collection.

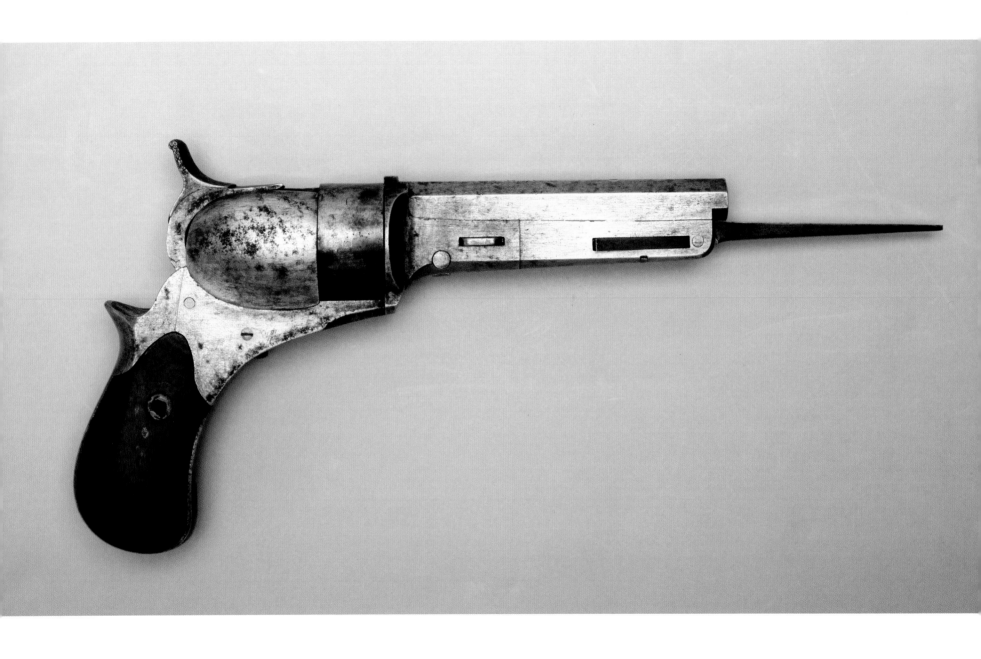

Samuel Colt designed this prototype revolver, which was manufactured by John Pearson in 1835. (90.183.1.1)

PROTOTYPE COLT REVOLVER

A Revolutionary Invention

Samuel Colt did not invent the revolver, and he was not the first person to patent a handgun with a mechanically rotating cylinder. For centuries, gunsmiths had attempted to design a handgun capable of firing several shots without having to be reloaded. Various methods were employed, from harmonica guns that used a slide to pepperboxes with multiple barrels, but these firearms did not have a single rotating cylinder so they were not revolvers. Finally, in 1818, Elisha H. Collier patented a multishot handgun with a single rotating cylinder. The cylinder was designed to rotate mechanically, but the revolver Collier actually manufactured required the user to manually rotate the cylinder. As a result, a revolver with a mechanically rotating cylinder did not exist when Colt first sought patent protection in 1835. Colt is thus credited with inventing the first practical revolver (i.e., a revolver with a mechanically rotating cylinder).

According to legend and the official history of Samuel Colt and his supporters, Colt came up with the basic design for his revolver when he was a 16-year-old seaman in 1830. He supposedly found inspiration in the ship's wheel turning and locking into position. Colt believed the action could be translated to firearms, so he carved a simple wooden model made up of three pieces that became the basis for his mechanically rotating cylinder. Critics dismissed the story of divine inspiration as the product of shrewd promotion. They claimed, both then and now, that Colt was more likely inspired by Collier's revolving mechanism, which Colt likely came across while out at sea. Countering this accusation, Colt professed to be completely unaware of Collier's revolvers until years later, giving further credence to his official story. Exactly what Colt knew and when will continue to be debated, but even if Colt was aware of Collier's revolver, it is important to note that he did not copy its features. Colt's revolver was truly revolutionary, and when he returned from sea, he was determined to turn his dream into reality.

From 1831 to 1836, Colt worked with several gunsmiths, most notably John Pearson of Baltimore, Maryland, to manufacture prototypes. Pearson was a clockmaker prior to becoming a gunsmith, and his mechanical skills were instrumental in the early development of Colt's revolver. Approximately nine rifles, one shotgun, and 16 handguns were made in those early years.

Only a few of the prototype handguns still exist, and the Pearson prototype in the Autry Collection dates from 1835. The revolver has a case-hardened finish and walnut grips. The barrel is four inches long, and it is chambered in .30 caliber. Unlike the revolvers that were later mass-produced, a flash plate and enlarged recoil shield cover most of the cylinder. The bayonet swiveling at the muzzle end of the barrel enabled users to defend themselves even if the revolver was out of ammunition. The Pearson prototypes clearly show that Colt continued to perfect his invention prior to seeking patent protection. With several working prototypes, Colt finally patented his revolver around the world over several months in 1835 and 1836.

Colt initially patented his revolver in Great Britain on October 22, 1835, and a month later, he patented the revolver in France. He secured an American patent for his invention on February 25, 1836. Colt filed in Europe before applying for a patent in the United States because of the peculiarities of international patent laws. Although an American patent would have precluded the filing of a patent in England or France, no such stipulation prevented him from filing in the United States after securing his foreign patent rights. Colt's copies of the British and American patents, two of the most important documents in the history of firearms, are part of the Autry Collection. With these patents in place, Colt set about mass-producing his revolver.

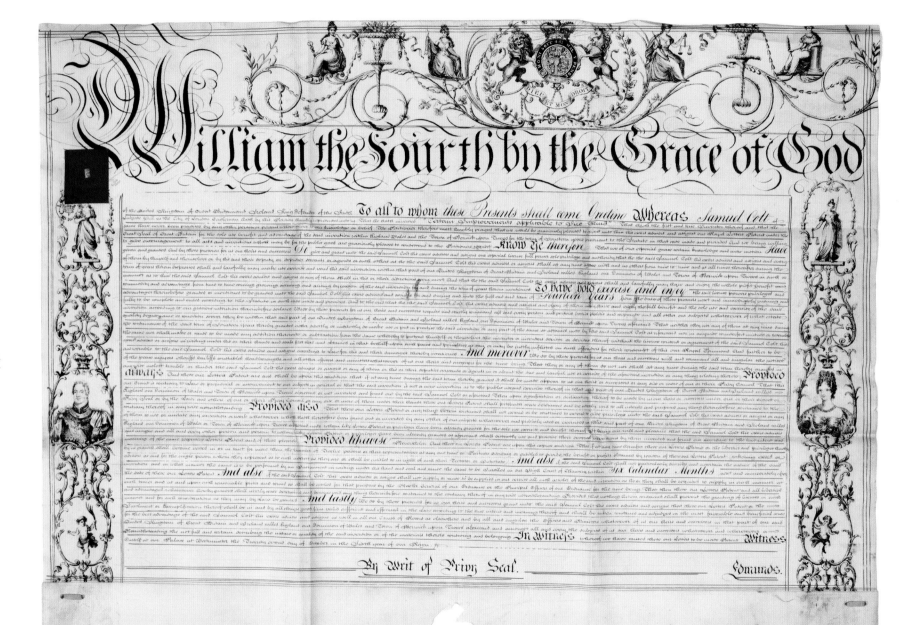

William the Fourth by the Grace of God

To all to whom these Presents shall come Greeting Whereas Samuel Colt

By Writ of Privy Seal.   Edmunds.

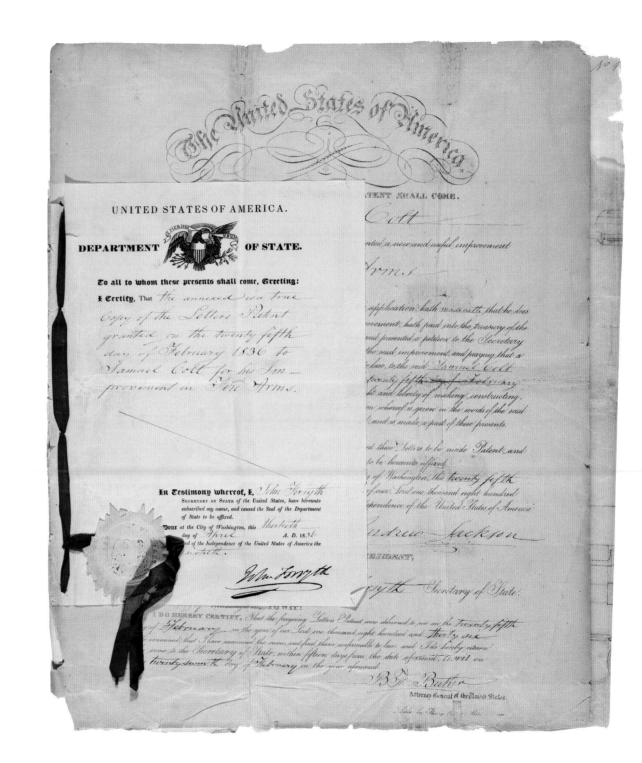

Opposite:
Samuel Colt's first patent, for "Certain Improvements Applicable to Fire Arms," was granted in 1835 by His Majesty's Patent Office in Great Britain. (90.183.53)

Right:
The first American patent issued to Samuel Colt in 1836 was bound with a detailed description and drawings of the revolutionary invention. (90.183.54)

The smallest revolving handgun produced by the Patent Arms Manufacturing Company was the No. 1 Pocket Model. (2012.38.1; the Dennis A. LeVett Collection)

CASED NO. 1 POCKET MODEL

Establishing a Corporation

I n 1836, with patents filed around the world, Samuel Colt set about incorporating a company and setting up a production facility to mass-produce his revolvers. Colt was a gifted salesman and self-promoter, two qualities that ultimately helped set him apart from his rivals, so he had very little trouble finding financial backing for his endeavor, especially from rich and well-connected friends and relatives. The lure of quick and substantial profits also helped. With enough capital on hand—estimates range from $230,000 to $300,000—Colt chartered the Patent Arms Manufacturing Company in the state of New Jersey in March 1836. The company was headquartered in the manufacturing town of Paterson, with a showroom and sales office in the city of New York. (The revolvers produced by the company are often referred to as Patersons in deference to their place of manufacture.)

Images of the armory in Paterson are exceptionally rare, and the Autry Collection includes what may be the only original period photograph. Embossed "Photo by J. Reid Paterson, N.J." in the lower right corner of the mat, the photograph shows the city of Paterson with the Patent Arms Mfg. Co. building visible on the far right. A handwritten notation dates the photograph to circa 1850. The company was established with Thomas Addis Emmet serving as president and Dudley Seldon serving at times as both secretary and treasurer. Seldon was Colt's cousin, and he was instrumental in raising capital for the company through the sale of corporate stock. The only surviving stock certificate for the Patent Arms Mfg. Co., 50 shares issued to Ferris Pell in 1837, is also in the Autry Collection. It was warranted by President Emmet and Secretary Seldon, and the seal features a colt standing above two crossed pistols. Colt was another shareholder, and he was officially employed by the company as a salesman, consultant designer, and engineer. Colt was given an annual salary, a commission for every revolver sold, and an expense account. In return, Colt assigned his patent rights to the company.

The No. 1 Pocket Model, or Baby Paterson, was the first and smallest revolving handgun made by the Patent Arms Mfg. Co. Approximately 500 were produced from circa 1837 to 1838. The model had a small frame and the barrel length ranged from two and a half inches to four and three-quarters inches. It was available in .28 and .31 caliber. Serial number 127 in the Autry Collection is .28 caliber with a four-inch barrel. The revolver has a blued finish, and the grips are made of rosewood. Four German silver bands are inlaid on the barrel and two are inlaid on the recoil shield. It has a standard five-shot cylinder that is roll engraved with a scene of a centaur. (A similar scene is also roll engraved on the No. 2 Belt Model and the No. 3 Belt Model, but due to the fact that the Belt Model cylinders have a larger circumference, an additional centaur is much more visible.) The extra cylinder in the case is also serial number 127. Given the fact that the No. 1 Pocket was the first model revolving handgun produced, some examples were modified by the company in later years as new features and design elements were introduced.

Sales were slow for the No. 1 Pocket and the other revolvers produced by the Patent Arms Mfg. Co. Although they were made of the highest quality, Colt's revolvers were prone to malfunction. The dirty black powder needed to fire the revolvers often fouled the barrels, and small parts tended to break. As a result, multiple discharges were frequent and extremely dangerous. The high cost of revolvers also hurt sales. Colt was confident that his revolvers would be positively received by both the military and civilians, but reviews were generally negative. Despite this early and mounting criticism, Colt continued to promote his revolvers and the company. The key was finding the right promotional idea.

The stone building on the right with bell tower,
is the place where Col. Samuel Colt first
began making fire arms in 1836.
The tower burned in 1862, and was not rebuilt.
This photograph was taken in 1850.
                    Paterson, N.J.

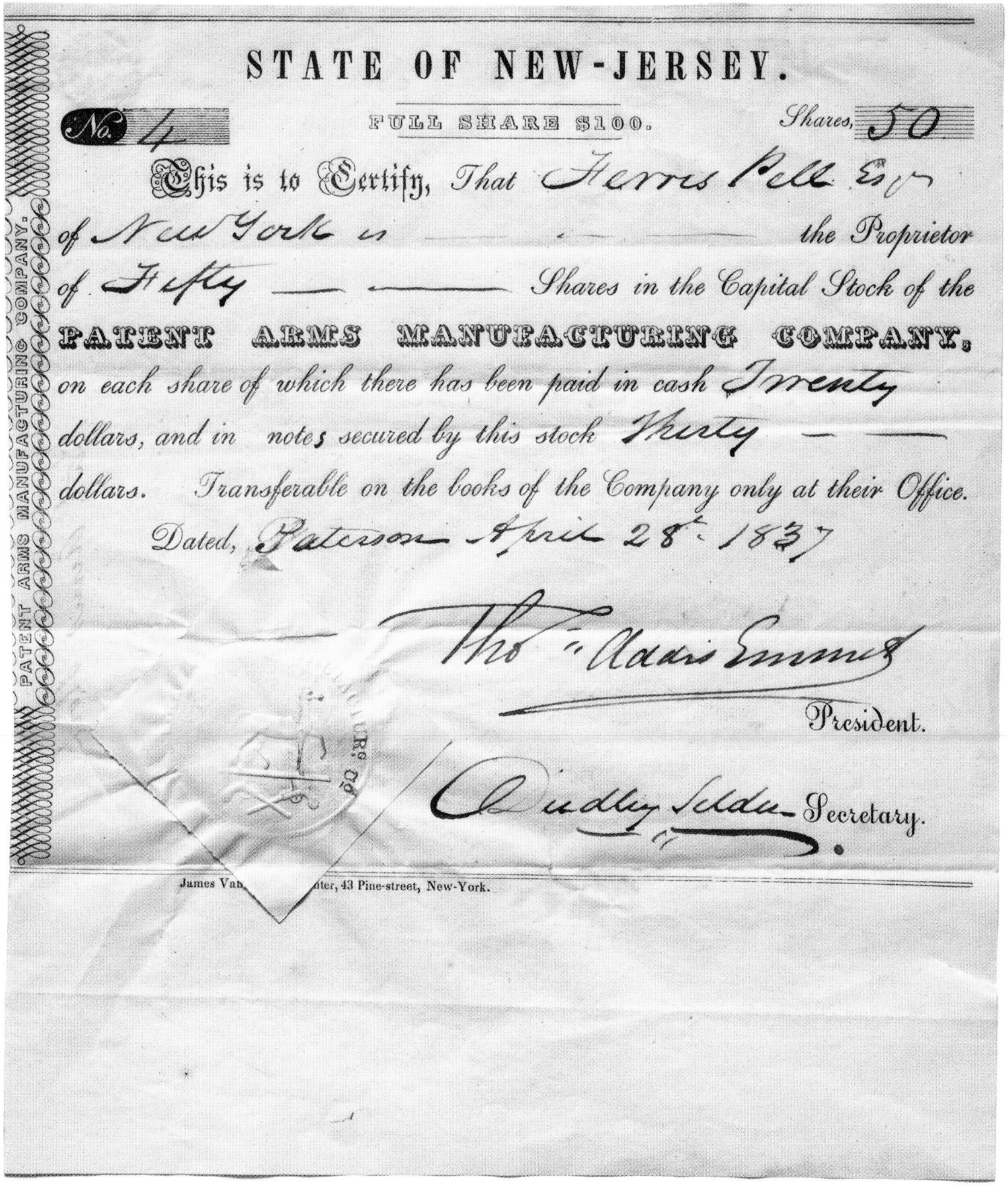

STATE OF NEW-JERSEY.

No. 4 FULL SHARE $100. Shares, 50

This is to Certify, That Ferris Pell Esqr of New York is the Proprietor of Fifty Shares in the Capital Stock of the PATENT ARMS MANUFACTURING COMPANY, on each share of which there has been paid in cash Twenty dollars, and in notes secured by this stock Thirty dollars. Transferable on the books of the Company only at their Office.

Dated, Paterson April 28th 1837

Thos Addis Emmet President.

Dudley Selden Secretary.

PATENT ARMS MANUFACTURING COMPANY.

James Van[...]nter, 43 Pine-street, New-York.

Opposite:
Housed in the building at the far right, the Patent Arms Manufacturing Company was located in Paterson, New Jersey, one of the first industrial cities in America. (2012.42.1; donated by Petra and Greg Martin)

Right:
The Patent Arms Manufacturing Company was chartered in the state of New Jersey in 1836, and the only surviving stock certificate is dated April 28, 1837. (90.183.57)

The No. 1 Model Ring Lever Revolving Rifle was the first firearm mass-produced by the Patent Arms Manufacturing Company. (87.118.129)

NO. 1 MODEL RING LEVER REVOLVING RIFLE

Mass Production

T he name Colt is commonly associated with revolving handguns, but the first firearm mass-produced by Samuel Colt was actually a rifle. The No. 1 Model Ring Lever Revolving Rifle was manufactured by the Patent Arms Manufacturing Company from circa 1837 to 1838. The company produced only 200 of the rifles, making it the rarest firearm made in Paterson. The rifles shared many similarities, both internal and external, with the revolvers depicted in the drawings accompanying Colt's first patents. Given the revolutionary and complex nature of the revolving rifle, Colt personally wrote out detailed directions for using it circa 1838. The original handwritten directions, now part of the Autry Collection, were later condensed for a printed version distributed by the company. A close inspection of the No. 1 rifle in the Autry Collection, serial number 164, reveals that it was hand fitted. Since the parts were not interchangeable, almost every piece on the rifle was numbered.

Colt knew that government patronage was essential to the success of his company, and he believed his revolving rifles were ideally suited for the military. The United States government disagreed, as initial reports found Colt's revolving rifles to be unacceptable for military purposes. Colt felt that his revolving rifles were not given a fair test. While the Ordnance Department and other key individuals in the military historically were slow to adapt to change, the unreliability of Colt's revolvers was a key factor in their decision. Colt's revolving rifles, like all the revolvers produced by the Patent Arms Mfg. Co., were prone to malfunction. The difficulty of repairing the revolving rifle and its high cost were also issues for the military.

Colt finally secured a military contract, albeit a small one, when the United States government ordered 50 No. 1 rifles in 1838 for use in Florida during the Second Seminole War. The war, fought from 1835 to 1842, was one of many attempts by the government to forcibly relocate Florida's native populations to Indian Territory in the West. The conflict was expensive for the military, both in terms of lives and resources expended, due in part to the Seminole's proficiency with rifles. When Colt personally showed up in Florida to promote his revolving rifles, he was warmly welcomed by Colonel William S. Harney, a key figure in the war. Harney was familiar with Colt's revolvers, and desperate to find some sort of advantage against the Seminole, he persuaded the government to try Colt's revolving rifles.

The revolving rifles performed admirably, although there were significant malfunctions. Unfortunately for Colt, the conflict ended before the revolving rifles really had the opportunity to make a serious impact. Making matters even worse, on his way home from Florida, Colt was involved in a boating accident. When his boat capsized, he was forced to tread water for several hours before help arrived. Colt's entire luggage was lost, including the $6,250 check the government gave him for the revolving rifles and a second $25 check for 25,000 percussion caps. He waited impatiently by the shore in hopes that the luggage would wash up, but it never reappeared. At a time when the Patent Arms Mfg. Co. was struggling to survive and desperately needed capital, Colt had lost a significant amount of money. He spent the next three months trying to get new checks issued.

Colt sent several letters to the relevant government officials asking for duplicate checks. A draft letter written by Colt, now in the Autry Collection, discussed his attempts. Dated May 22, 1838, and addressed to Major Henry Whiting, quartermaster for the Army in Florida, Colt asked in the letter for assurances that the original checks had not been cashed. He also noted that he was waiting on the necessary paperwork proving the sale of 50 revolving rifles actually took place. Although Colt encountered significant bureaucracy, military officials in Florida did provide him with the documentation needed and duplicate checks ultimately were issued. Colt finally had his money, but the problems facing him and the Patent Arms Mfg. Co. were just beginning.

Patent Arms Manufacturing Co. Paterson, NJ

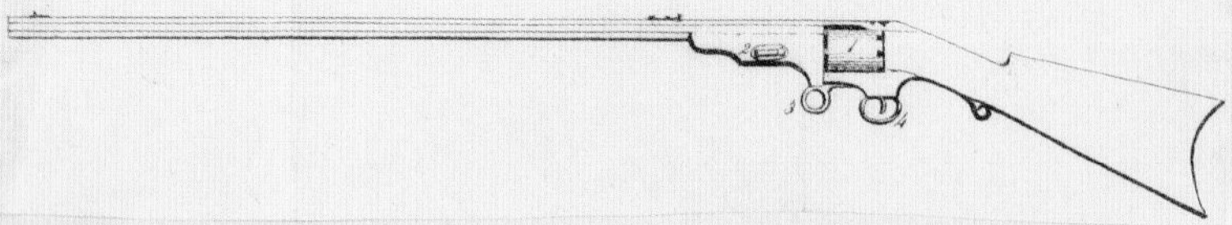

Directions for using Colts Rifle

~~To load the Amunition flask it is reproved in the ~~

To load the Rifle. First place the Percussion Caps on the tubes. Next place the Reciver on the Arbor with the Ketch of the Index entering its smallest notch. Next place the powder end of the Amunition flask over the Chambers of the Reciver then by turning the valve & raising the flask a charge of Powder will fawl into each Chamber. Next place the Ball end of the Amunition flask over the Reciver, & by turning the valve a charge of Balls will fall into the ~~the~~ mouths of the Chambers. which are to be prest by the lever below the surface of the Reciver

To put the Rifle togeather. Place the Reciver on the Arbor with the ketch of the Index entering its depest notch. then place their Barrel on the end of the Arbor & press the Connecting Key into the Mortaces of the

Barrel & Arber lightly light enough to bring the Barrel in contact with the ~~surface of the~~ Reciver without creating so much friction as to prevent it from turning freely

To Discharge the Rifle. Pull down the Lock untill a chamber is turned oppo-site the barrel, & pull the Triger in the ordenary manner.

Avoid snapping the lock without Percusion Caps on the cones

The Rifle should be thuraly cleaned & Oiled after it has been used.

Reference to the Drawing

No 1. Is the Reciver containing Chambers for the Charges
. 2. " Key for connecting the Barrel with the Reciver
. 3. " Lock to opperate the Lock.
. 4. " Triger to discharge the Gun.
The Index is that part which turnes the Reciver when the Lock is opperated
The Arber is that part on which the Reciver turns

Saml Colt. Patentee

Mr

Bought of Patent Arms Manfg Co
One Colts Patent Rifle & Appendages complete — $125.
Received Payment.

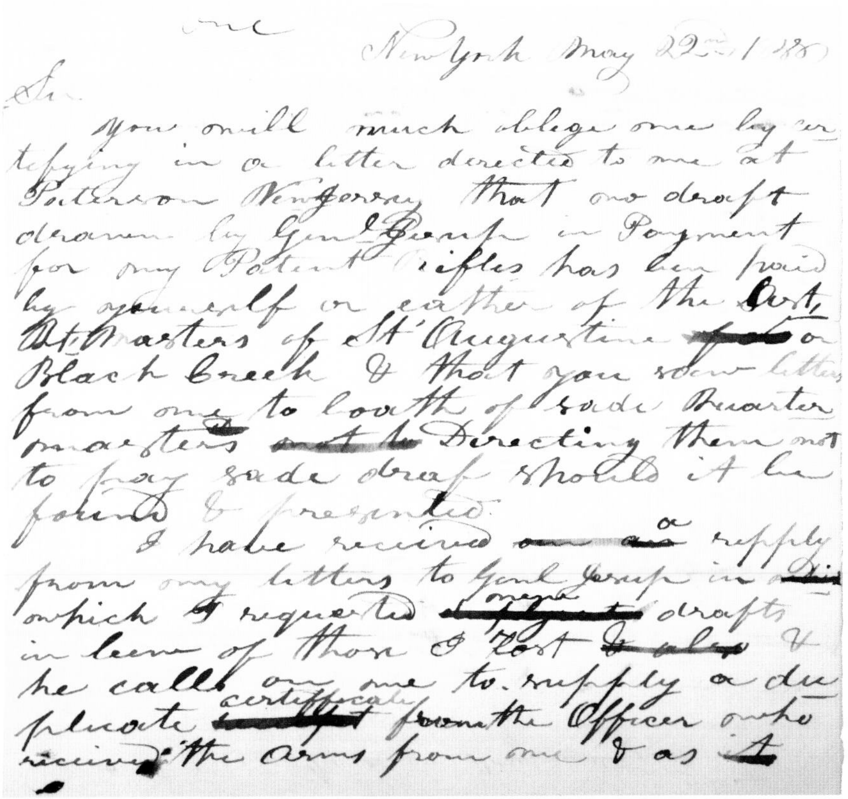

New York May 22d 1838

Sir

You will much oblige me by certifying in a letter directed to me at Paterson New Jersey that the draft drawn by Genl Jesup in payment for my Patent Rifles has been paid by yourself or either of the Act. Qt Masters of St Augustine or Black Creek & that you saw letters from me to both of said Quarter masters ... directing them not to pay said draft should it be found & presented.

I have received a reply from my letters to Genl Jesup in which I requested ... drafts in lieu of those I lost & he calls on me to supply a duplicate certificate from the Officer who received the arms from me & as ...

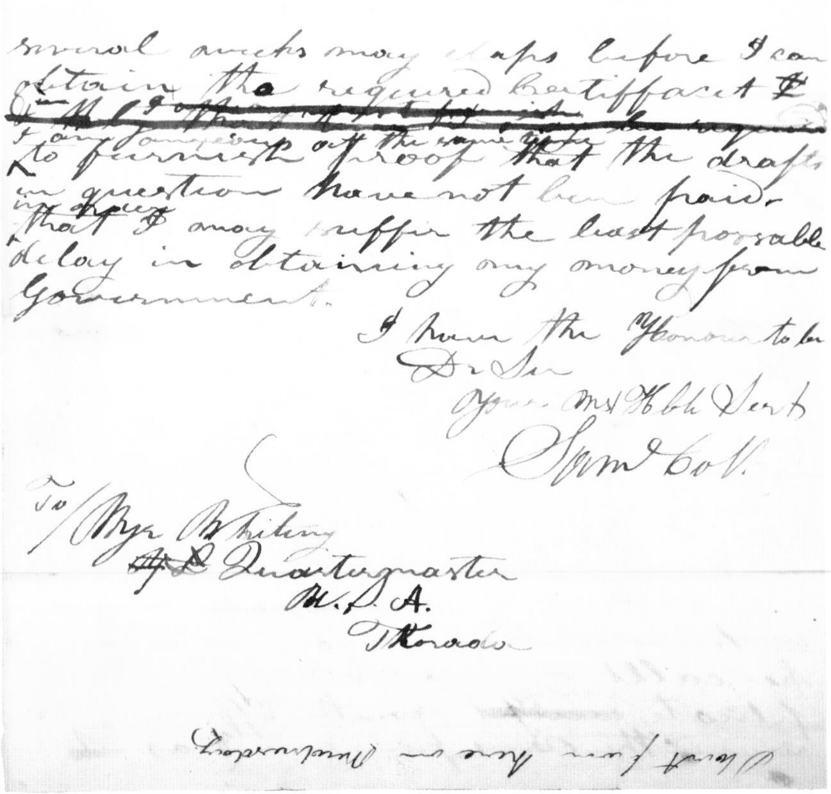

several weeks may ... laps before I can obtain the required certificate ...

... to furnish proof that the drafts in question have not been paid ... that I may suffer the least possable delay in obtaining my money from Government.

I have the Honour to be
Dr Sir
Your most Hbl Servt
Saml Colt.

To Major Whiting
Quartermaster
U.S.A.

23

Opposite:
Samuel Colt's detailed directions for using the revolving rifle, handwritten by the inventor circa 1838, are accompanied by a receipt at the bottom right for the sale of one rifle and appendages. (2012.42.2; donated by Petra and Greg Martin)

Above:
After losing a check for 50 revolving rifles sold to the military, Samuel Colt documented his struggles to get reimbursed in this letter written to Major Henry Whiting in 1838. (2010.57.4; donated by Petra and Greg Martin)

The No. 2 Belt Model came with straight grips;
in this rare instance, they are made of ebony
rosewood with German silver bolsters.
(2012.38.2; the Dennis A. LeVett Collection)

CASED NO. 2 BELT MODEL

Revolving Handgun Classifications

Samuel Colt's long-term success as a gunmaker was due in large part to the use of state-of-the-art machinery and interchangeable parts. The revolvers produced by the Patent Arms Manufacturing Company, however, were not entirely machine manufactured. The individual parts were machined, but a significant amount of hand fitting was required for each revolver. After the parts had been manufactured, they were passed down an assembly line, where skilled workers personally fitted an individual piece or section. The unfinished revolvers were then passed down the line to the next workman until completed.

Firearms had traditionally been made one gun at a time by a single worker, so the process used in Paterson was rather modern for the period. It resulted in savings in time and money, but the hand fitting meant the individual parts of each revolver were not necessarily interchangeable. In other words, a cylinder taken off one revolver might not fit on a different revolver of the same model. Mismatched parts were dangerous, as they could lead to misfires. Whereas Colt recognized early on the potential of interchangeable parts, he would not be able to achieve it until many years later.

The Patent Arms Mfg. Co. produced revolving longarms and revolving handguns. The revolving handguns came in three different sizes—Pocket, Belt, and Holster. Internal company documents referred to the revolving handguns as the No. 1, No. 2, No. 3, and No. 5 Models. Although some have speculated that the company closed before the No. 4 could be introduced, no reference to the No. 4 is known to exist. Almost universally, the small-frame Pocket Model is referred to as the No. 1, the medium-frame Belt Model is referred to as the No. 3, and the large-frame Holster Model is referred to as the No. 5. The No. 1 Pocket came in .28 and .31 calibers, the No. 3 Belt in .31 and .34, and the No. 5 Holster in .36.

The classification of the No. 2 is where scholars sometimes disagree, even within their own work. The fact that variations to the generally accepted rules exist makes things even more confusing. The No. 2 is referred to by some as a Pocket Model and by others as a Belt Model. Research indicates that Colt referred to the No. 2 Model as a .31-caliber Belt pistol with straight grips. (Colt called all of his handguns pistols as opposed to revolvers.) Colt's classification thus used the size of the frame, the caliber, and the shape of the grips as determining factors. As such, most scholars and collectors describe both the No. 2 and No. 3 as Belt Models, with the key differentiating feature being the shape of the grips. Other variations within the Belt Model are known to exist, but again, the shape of the grip is the key for classification. (Despite the fact that Colt described the No. 2 Belt Model as a .31 caliber, some examples also came in .34 caliber.)

Serial number 897 in the Autry Collection is an example of a rather unique No. 2 Belt Model. Manufactured circa 1840, the revolver appears to be the highest serial number known for a No. 2 Belt. The defining feature of serial number 897 is its silver-plated frame and back strap. Less than 10 such examples have been documented. The ebony rosewood grips with German silver bolsters are also rare. The revolver's more standard characteristics include its four-and-a-half-inch barrel and .31 caliber. Like most Paterson revolvers, "Patent Arms M'g Co Paterson N-J Colt's Pt." is stamped on the top of the barrel. The mahogany case is lined with dark velvet and features an extra cylinder with a matching serial number.

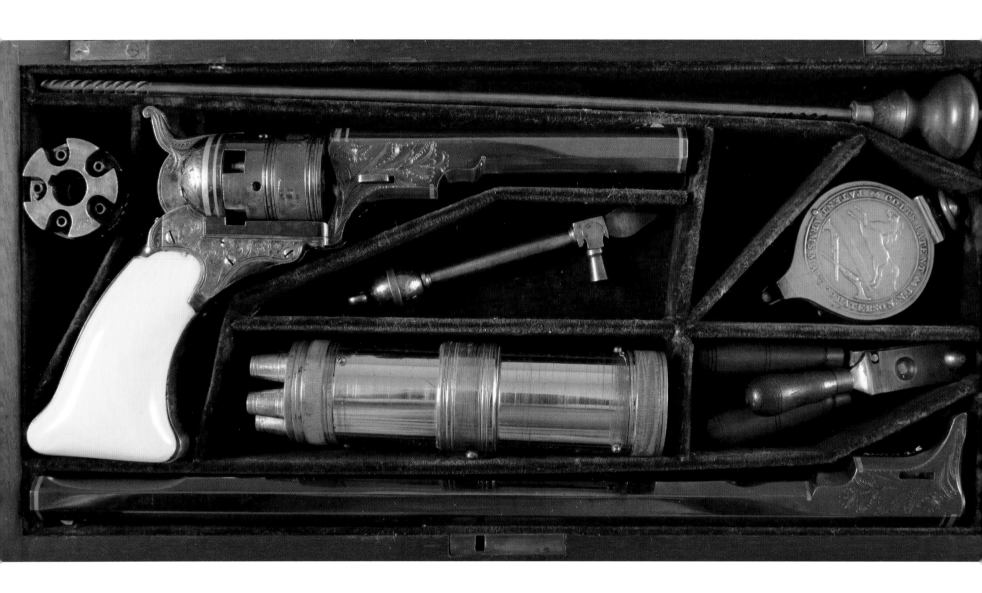

The revolvers of the Patent Arms Manufacturing Company often came cased with a full complement of accessories, such as this No. 3 Belt Model with an additional 12-inch barrel and a Rampant Colt capper. (2012.2.2; the George Gamble Collection)

CASED NO. 3 BELT MODEL

Works of Art

Samuel Colt recognized early on that his revolvers were more than just tools. In the hands of master craftsmen, Colt saw the revolver as a canvas upon which beautiful art could be created. Although Colt was not the first firearm manufacturer to engrave and embellish his creations, he certainly was one of the most successful, not only in the quality of engraving, but also in the promotion of engraved pieces. During his lifetime, Colt employed the finest engravers to decorate revolvers for people ranging from the president of the United States to cowboys roaming the American frontier. Engraving came in a variety of styles and coverage, and although it could be done inside or outside of the factory, factory engraving has always held a unique appeal with users and collectors.

Colt also made sure that the cases that housed his revolvers were equally as impressive as the guns themselves. Cases were necessary because a variety of tools and accessories were needed to fire and maintain the weapons. All of the revolvers produced during Colt's lifetime employed the percussion system. Unlike modern firearms, which use metallic cartridges that are fully self-contained, percussion revolvers required the user to individually load the primer (a percussion cap), powder charge, and bullets. In order to keep all of these essential items readily available, the Patent Arms Manufacturing Company sold most of its revolvers with fully equipped cases.

A standard case was made of varnished mahogany with a beveled lid. A rectangular plaque made of silver, German silver, or brass was affixed to the top of the case. Although the plaques were capable of being inscribed, contemporary inscriptions were rare. The interior of the case was lined with dark velvet. The exact contents of an individual case varied, but commonly featured were an extra cylinder, multipurpose tool, bullet mold, cleaning rod, combination flask and charger, and a capper. Although cases were standard, unique variations exist. The beautifully engraved cased No. 3 Belt Model in the Autry Collection, serial number 548, is one of the finest Paterson revolvers extant. It is engraved with a floral and leaf decoration and features eight inlaid bands of German silver. The grips are made of ivory. The case has an inscription that reads "Joseph A. Voison" and includes an additional 12-inch barrel. The revolver was manufactured circa 1838–1840.

The capper was the first product mass-produced by Colt that used the Rampant Colt logo. Colt traced his ancestry to Essex, England, where his family's coat of arms was adorned with a "rampant colt," a horse with a broken spear in its mouth standing on its hind legs with its forelegs in the air. Horses were traditionally used on English coats of arms to symbolize a willingness to serve king and country. For the Colt family, the use of a horse or colt was also a direct reference to their name. The oldest known depiction of the Colt coat of arms in America is a watercolor with ink calligraphy and gold leaf in the Autry Collection. Done in a primitive, folk-art style, records indicate it was made by Elizabeth Colt Clapp, a relative of Samuel, circa 1835.

The Rampant Colt itself eventually became the trademark for Colt's Patent Fire Arms Manufacturing Company, Samuel Colt's second business founded after the failure of the Patent Arms Manufacturing Company. A sculpted pattern in the Autry Collection is one of the only large representations of the Rampant Colt that survives from Colt's lifetime. Made of two pieces, the inside of the sculpture is stamped "S. Colt" and "G. Allge," an individual who is presumed to have been the maker. It appears to have been commissioned circa 1855 as a model or maquette for a much larger Rampant Colt that stood atop the dome on the main factory building at the Colt armory in Hartford, Connecticut. The Rampant Colt has been a powerful symbol used by the company for various promotional purposes for more than 150 years.

Left:
The Rampant Colt first appeared in America on the Colt coat of arms, a watercolor painted by a relative of Samuel Colt circa 1835. (2010.57.1; donated by Petra and Greg Martin)

Opposite:
Samuel Colt commissioned this Rampant Colt sculpture sometime around 1855, the year the successor to the Patent Arms Manufacturing Company was officially incorporated. (2007.76.1; donated by Petra and Greg Martin)

The Model 1839 Revolving Shotgun was not successful, mechanically or commercially, despite Samuel Colt's best promotional efforts. (87.118.130)

MODEL 1839 REVOLVING SHOTGUN

An Agent of the Company

Samuel Colt traveled extensively promoting himself and the various revolvers produced by the Patent Arms Manufacturing Company. Initially, Colt did not distinguish between himself and the company. Willing to do whatever it took to sell his revolvers, Colt gave shooting exhibitions and visited gun stores. He published trade cards and price lists. He passed out his business card to anyone he thought could be of benefit to himself or the company. An example of one of his earliest business cards is in the Autry Collection. Colt also doggedly pursued government and military officials in hopes that they would test and ultimately adopt his revolvers. To help spur acceptance, Colt occasionally presented revolvers to key officials.

Colt wrote off the presentations as expenses, which he charged to the company, infuriating stockholders such as Treasurer Dudley Seldon. Seldon was also enraged when Colt appeared to suggest that a military contract might be had by bribing a key government official. Colt's use of alcohol as a promotional tool further upset Seldon. In addition to his expenses, Colt borrowed heavily from the company so he could present an image of prosperity in hopes of inducing further sales. Seldon, one of Colt's earliest supporters, quickly became one of his biggest critics. With the backing of other stockholders, Seldon forced Colt to relinquish his position as an employee of the Patent Arms Mfg. Co. Colt was thus reduced to an agent of the company, responsible for his own expenses.

Through it all, Colt continued to have confidence in his revolvers. He was especially convinced that his revolving longarms would be successful. Besides the revolving rifle, the Patent Arms Mfg. Co. also produced revolving shotguns and revolving carbines. The Model 1839 Revolving Shotgun was made in 16-gauge smoothbore with caliber dimensions ranging from .61 to .62. The standard barrel lengths were 24 and 32 inches. Approximately 225 revolving shotguns were manufactured from circa 1839 to 1841. The 1839 Revolving Shotgun in the Autry Collection, serial number 138, is .62 caliber and has a 32-inch barrel. The barrel lug profile has one rounded and one scalloped corner, whereas some examples have two scalloped corners. The 1839 Revolving Shotgun also came in a revolving carbine variation. The Model 1839 Revolving Carbine had a standard caliber of .525, a shorter cylinder than the revolving shotgun, and a 24-inch barrel usually with an attached loading lever. Approximately 950 revolving carbines were made.

The revolving shotgun was not successful, despite Colt's best efforts to promote it, as evidenced by a posting in the Autry Collection from the August 19, 1839, edition of the *New York Times and Commercial Intelligencer*. The posting lists all of the revolvers being sold by the Patent Arms Mfg. Co., but the emphasis is clearly on the revolving shotgun. Unfortunately, like the revolving handguns produced by the company, revolving shotguns were prone to malfunctions and multiple discharges. It was especially dangerous for a user to place a steadying hand on the barrel while firing. A failure in the United States, Colt even tried to sell the revolving shotgun to European markets to no avail. Several years after the demise of the Patent Arms Mfg. Co., when Colt's new business was flourishing, he attempted to revive the revolving shotgun. It once again proved unsuccessful.

32

As Samuel Colt set about promoting his revolving shotguns, he passed out business cards with an engraved facsimile of his flamboyant signature but no information about his company or profession. (88.53.1)

N. B. All these mills are easily transported to any section of the country. Communications (post-paid) will be promptly attended to.

j5 3 mos.   WM. H. SHAY-

COLT'S REPEATING FIRE ARM.—The Patent Arms Manufacturing Company inform the public that they have just received from their manufactory a number of Repeating Shot Guns, of six charges each, which they confidently recommend to he notice of Sportsmen, as equal in workmanship and finish to any thing imported, and, from repeated experiments, they are satisfied they will throw shot superior to any gun ever manufactured.

Also—Carbines, for balls or shot; Rifles, of different sizes; and Pistols, from pocket to holster size. All of which are offered at greatly reduced prices.

je29   Z. B. ZABRISKIE, Agent, 155 Broadway.

SAMUEL W. BENEDICT, Watchmaker, has removed to the New Exchange, on the corner of Wall and William streets, one door east of his former stand, where he pas just opened a splendid assortment of every descrip-

Heralded as superior to anything on the market, the revolving shotgun was advertised in this 1839 posting from the *New York Times and Commercial Intelligencer*. (2012.38.22; the Dennis A. LeVett Collection)

33

The No. 5 Holster Model is commonly called the Texas Paterson because of its association with the famed Texas Rangers. (2012.38.4; the Dennis A. LeVett Collection)

CASED NO. 5 HOLSTER MODEL PAIR

Success in the Field

The best patron of the Patent Arms Manufacturing Company was the Republic of Texas, a sovereign state that existed from March 2, 1836, when the country declared its independence from Mexico, to February 19, 1846, when Texas joined the United States. The Republic of Texas was established in response to the dictatorial regime of Mexican President Antonio López de Santa Anna. When Santa Anna abolished the Mexican constitution and gave himself enormous powers, Anglo-American colonists and Tejanos (Texans of Spanish or Mexican descent) concluded Mexican republicanism was dead. Armed conflict between Texas and Mexico began in October 1835, and when it became clear to Texans that the two sides would not be able to resolve their differences, formal independence was declared.

As Texans were fighting the Mexican army, they also found themselves facing off against Native Americans. Anglo-Americans and Native Americans had been at odds since Europeans first arrived in North America. The two groups initially sought to negotiate issues such as landownership and commerce, but broken promises and acts of unspeakable violence committed by both sides quickly led to armed conflict. The United States responded by attempting to move Native Americans from their ancestral homelands to reservations in the West. Movement was supposed to be voluntary, but American policy often led to forced removal and further conflict. Hostilities between Anglo-Americans and Native Americans were not limited to the borders of the United States, as Texans also found themselves at odds with Native Americans.

The relationship between the Republic of Texas and Native Americans fluctuated between periods of negotiation and open warfare. Although the Republic of Texas fought with several Native American tribes, the major conflict was with the Comanche, a powerful tribe whose ancestral homeland included most of northwest Texas. Determined to defeat their enemies, the Republic of Texas sought to establish a strong army and navy. A special force known as the Texas Rangers was also created. Unofficially founded in 1823, the Rangers were formally constituted in 1835. The main mission of the Rangers was to combat hostile Native Americans, especially the Comanche and the Cherokee. The Republic of Texas sought to arm all of its troops, including the Rangers, with the best weapons. This included Samuel Colt's revolutionary revolvers.

From 1839 to 1841, the republic ordered approximately 100 Ring Lever Revolving Rifles, 180 Model 1839 Revolving Carbines, and 180 No. 5 Holster Model Revolvers. (The republic also ordered customized accessories, such as the powder flask in the Autry Collection made specifically for the revolving carbines.) Popular beyond the borders of Texas, the No. 5 Holster was the most abundant revolving handgun manufactured in Paterson. Approximately 1,000 were produced from circa 1838 to 1840. Chambered in .36 caliber, it was also the company's largest and most powerful revolving handgun. The rarest examples of the No. 5 Holster are cased pairs, as only about half a dozen are known to exist. Two of the cased pairs have revolvers with nine-inch barrels, including serial numbers 582 and 600 in the Autry Collection. In addition to the nine-inch barrels, both revolvers also have square-backed cylinders.

The No. 5 Holster proved its worth in the hands of the Rangers at the Battle of Walker's Creek in the summer of 1844. Ranger Captain John Coffee "Jack" Hays and 14 other Rangers fought off a large contingent of approximately 80 Comanche using the model. Hays and the other Rangers immediately became vocal advocates for the Colt revolver. Word of the incident spread, due in part to Colt's own promotion, and the model came to be known thereafter as the Texas Paterson. Colt later immortalized the battle by roll engraving a scene of it on the cylinders of two future models, the Walker and the Dragoon. A proof plate of the "Ranger and Indian" cylinder scene is part of the Autry Collection.

The powder flasks made for the Republic of Texas featured the Lone Star Flag on the right and two crossed No. 5 Holster Models at the bottom. (2012.38.23; the Dennis A. LeVett Collection)

A scene of the Texas Rangers using the No. 5 Holster Model, as seen on this proof plate, was featured on the cylinder of two Colt models. (87.118.165)

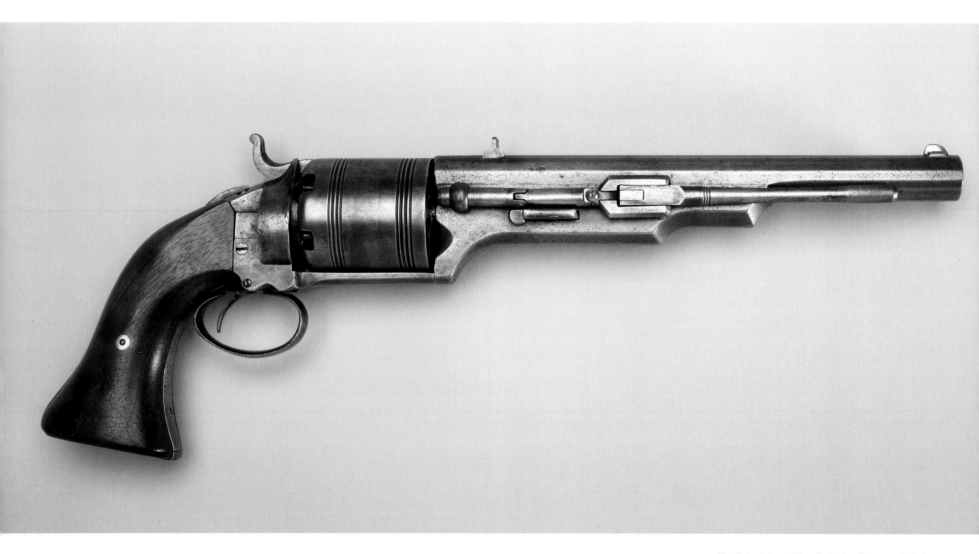

The Patent Arms Manufacturing Company failed, but the potential of large-caliber revolvers was evident in longarms converted into pistols outside the factory, such as this Model 1839 Revolving Carbine Pistol. (2012.38.10; the Dennis A. LeVett Collection)

MODEL 1839 REVOLVING CARBINE PISTOL

Corporate Failure

Despite the success of the No. 5 Holster Model with the Texas Rangers, the Patent Arms Manufacturing Company was in serious trouble. Revolvers simply were not selling the way Samuel Colt and company executives had anticipated, due in large part to mechanical problems and a high selling price. Significant government patronage, essential to the revolver's success, was also not forthcoming. After a trial at West Point in June 1837, the government deemed the revolver to be unsuitable for military service. The government's declaration in many ways sealed the fate of Colt's initial revolvers. Although minor orders from the government took place after the tests, such as the 50 No. 1 Model Ring Lever Revolving Rifles sold for use in the Second Seminole War, large government orders never materialized.

Colt nevertheless continued to promote his revolvers, especially to key military officers and individuals in Washington, D.C. He sought and publicized endorsements, such as the one in the Autry Collection from Lieutenant John McLaughlin, commander of a schooner fleet during the Second Seminole War. Nothing seemed to work, and by almost all accounts, the Paterson revolvers were a failure. Despite promises of significant profits, many shareholders took their losses and simply abandoned the company. A stock transfer in the Autry Collection, giving Treasurer Dudley Seldon the right to sell stock on behalf of shareholder Ferris Pell, shows that investors were trying to leave the company as early as 1837. However, a few key shareholders were determined to recoup as much as possible from the venture. With the approval of the company's board of directors, the Patent Arms Mfg. Co. closed in 1842 and its assets were liquidated.

Several factors besides the mechanical problems and high selling price should be cited for the demise of the company. While Colt was a mechanical genius and a prodigious inventor, he did not have the expertise or even the basic understanding of what it took to manufacture firearms on a large scale. Pliny Lawton, the company's superintendent in charge of production, had a background in woolens manufacturing, and he too seemed to lack the appropriate skills. The task of inventing and constructing the necessary equipment was underestimated and never fully perfected. Some revolvers actually were sold for less than their manufacturing cost. The financial climate of the period was yet another factor that led to slow sales. The Panic of 1837 and the five-year depression that followed led to the closing of countless banks and a record high unemployment rate. With so many obstacles, it is somewhat amazing that the company survived as long as it did.

The Patent Arms Manufacturing Company ultimately was in business from 1836 to 1842. During that time, approximately 2,350 revolving handguns in various models and sizes were manufactured. The company also produced approximately 1,375 revolving rifles, shotguns, and carbines. Interestingly, some of the revolving longarms manufactured in Paterson were converted into revolving pistols outside of the factory by skilled gunsmiths. These revolving pistols, likely customized in the early 1840s, revealed the demand for large-caliber revolving handguns at a time when they did not exist. They can also be considered forerunners of the powerful Walker Model, the revolver that revived Samuel Colt's fortunes after the failure of the Patent Arms Mfg. Co. The Model 1839 Revolving Carbine Pistol in the Autry Collection is serial number 919. The barrel was shortened to $10\frac{1}{6}$ inches and pistol grips were added. The revolving pistol is chambered in .525 caliber and a loading lever is positioned on the right side. Serial number 919 and other revolving longarm pistols showcased the potential of Colt's revolvers at a time when the inventor's future as a gunsmith was certainly in question.

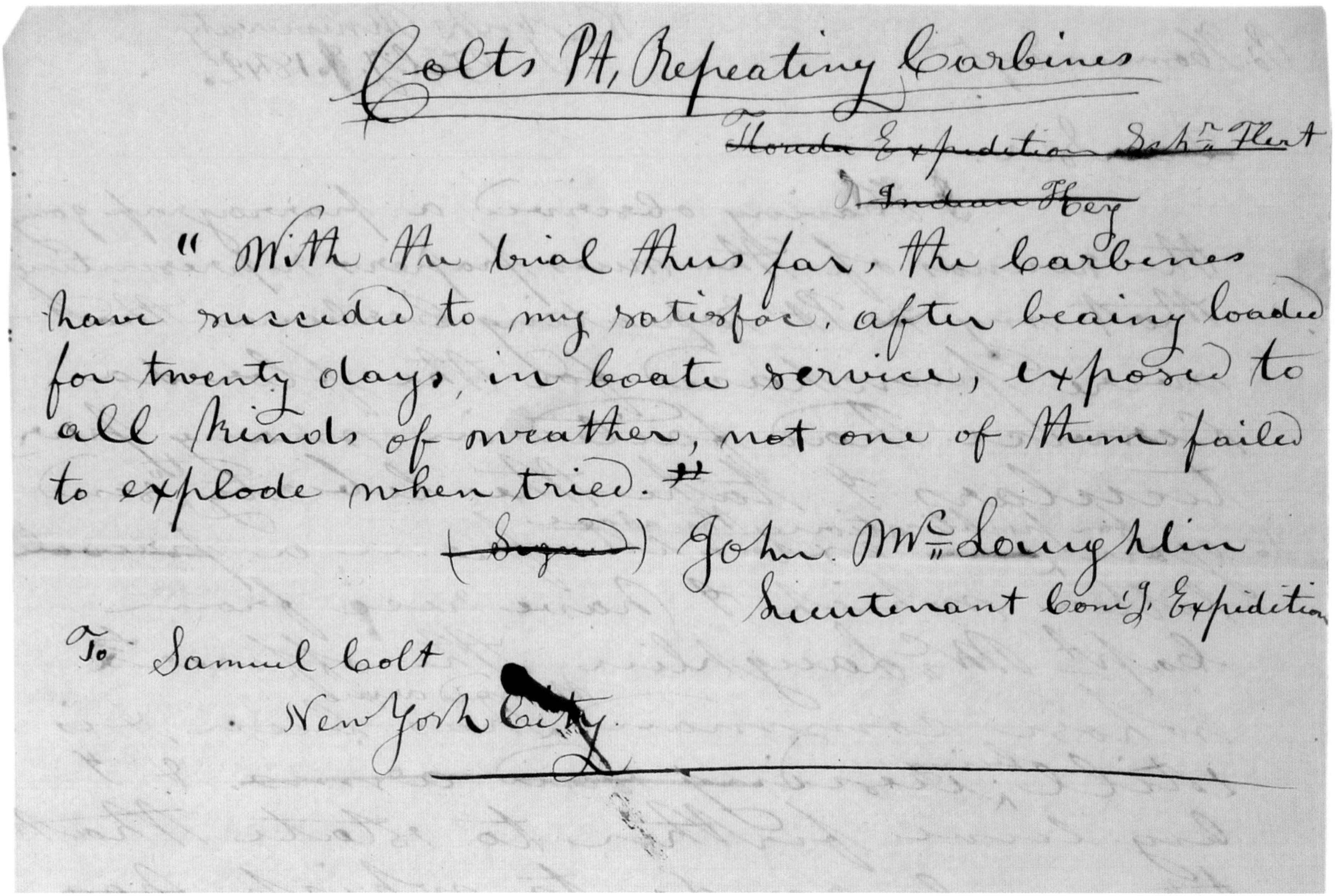

Colts Pt, Repeating Carbines

~~Florida Expedition Sch'r Fleet~~

~~Indian Key~~

" With the trial thus far, the Carbines have misceded to my satisfac, after beaing loaded for twenty days, in boate service, exposed to all kinds of weather, not one of them failed to explode when tried. #

(~~Signed~~) John. Mc. Loughlin

Lieutenant Com'g Expidition

To Samuel Colt

New York City

Above:
The revolvers of the Patent Arms Manufacturing Company were not adopted by the military, despite endorsements from key officers such as Lieutenant John McLaughlin. (2010.57.3; donated by Petra and Greg Martin)

Opposite:
Shareholders of the Patent Arms Manufacturing Company quickly became disillusioned with the company, as evidenced by this stock transfer dated 1837, a year after the company was founded. (90.183.56)

⑤

Know all Men by these Presents, THAT

I, *Ferris Pell* ———— of the *City of New York*

do hereby constitute and appoint *Dudley Selden* of said *City*

to be *my* true and lawful Attorney, for *me* and in *my* name and behalf, to sell,

assign, and transfer to *himself or any other person or persons*

———————————————— the whole or any part

of *Fifty Shares* ——— ——— ~~Shares~~ in the Capital Stock of

the *Patent Arms Manufacturing Company* — and for

that purpose to make and execute all necessary acts of Assignment and Transfer.

In Witness whereof, *I* have hereunto set *my* hand and seal

this *twelfth* day of *August* ——— 183*7*

Sealed and delivered in the presence of

Ferris Pell

41

The Ehlers Fifth Model takes its name from
John Ehlers, an individual who found himself in
conflict with Samuel Colt as both a corporate
officer and creditor of the Patent Arms
Manufacturing Company. (2012.38.6; the
Dennis A. LeVett Collection)

CASED EHLERS FIFTH MODEL

A Bitter End

Prior to the closing of the Patent Arms Manufacturing Company, hardware merchant John Ehlers was elected as the company's treasurer in 1840. Ehlers replaced Dudley Seldon, who resigned after repeatedly finding himself at odds with Samuel Colt. From the moment Ehlers took the position of treasurer, it was clear the company was in serious financial trouble. Like his predecessor, Ehlers blamed Colt's promotional tactics for the company's problems, and he too found himself at odds with the inventor. Besides being a corporate officer, Ehlers also owned approximately 10 percent of the company and was its largest creditor. With the backing of fellow shareholders, Ehlers sought to seize and sell Colt's patent rights. Legal wrangling ensued, but Ehlers was able to take possession of more than 800 finished revolvers (carbines, rifles, and handguns). After the company closed in 1842, Ehlers was also able to acquire machinery and parts to more than 500 unfinished revolvers.

Ehlers sold many of the finished revolvers he acquired, despite attempts by Colt to stop him. Ehlers also assembled the unfinished revolvers, and he even went so far as to "improve" them, primarily through the addition of a loading lever. (Colt seemingly planned to add a loading lever to all models, but was unable to do so prior to the closing of the Patent Arms Mfg. Co.) An advertisement in the Autry Collection, most likely from *Doggett's New York Business Directory* for 1845–1846, listed five agents selling Colt's revolvers "with the latest improvements" on behalf of Ehlers. Commonly referred to as an Improved No. 2 Belt Model, the Ehlers Fifth Model in the Autry Collection, serial number 37, is an exceptional example. In addition to its fine condition and brilliant casing, serial number 37 is also a rare example of an Ehlers Model chambered in .34 caliber. Ehlers sold a sizable number of "improved" revolvers to the United States Navy in 1845, and he continued to sell the revolvers as late as 1846. It is not known exactly how much money Ehlers made from the sales, but if anyone profited from the short-lived company, it was Ehlers.

Samuel Colt, the inventor of the revolver and the founder of the Patent Arms Manufacturing Company, seemed to be the biggest loser in the company's failure. Not only was he removed from the company in a rather humiliating manner, Colt's name and the reputation of his revolvers were severely tarnished. Instead of examining his own failings, Colt placed almost all of the blame on John Ehlers. When all revolvers were found to be unsuitable for military use, Colt blamed Ehlers for the production defects and negative publicity because many of Ehlers's "improved" revolvers had been acquired by the government. (Interestingly, the only known contemporary photograph of a soldier armed with a revolver made by the Patent Arms Mfg. Co. is part of the Autry Collection, and it features a Fifth Model Ehlers.) Colt also viewed the closing of the company as an attempt by Ehlers to seize control of his invention.

By placing all of the blame on Ehlers, Colt overlooked the fact that many of the Paterson revolvers malfunctioned prior to Ehlers's association with the company. The initial negative tests by the military also took place prior to Ehlers's involvement. Regardless of who was to blame, Colt's first attempt at mass production was a disaster. The failure, however, provided Colt with a great deal of information about manufacturing and the intricacies of running a business. It also taught him valuable lessons about promotion and marketing. The revolver had even shown great potential in places like Texas. While Colt's future as a firearm manufacturer seemed bleak after the failure of the Patent Arms Mfg. Co., it was just the beginning of an amazing journey. Luckily for Colt, one influential Texas Ranger was aware of the revolver's potential, and he was determined to see it on the battlefield. The individual was Captain Samuel Hamilton Walker.

COLT'S REPEATING PISTOLS,
With the latest Improvements of 1844 & 1845.

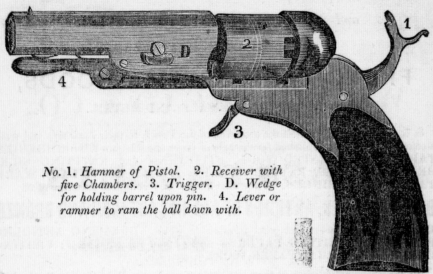

No. 1. *Hammer of Pistol.* 2. *Receiver with five Chambers.* 3. *Trigger.* D. *Wedge for holding barrel upon pin.* 4. *Lever or rammer to ram the ball down with.*

The Pistols have 5, Carbine and Shot Guns 6, and Rifles 8 chambers. Pocket Pistols with 2 inch to 3½ inch barrel, Belt pistol 2½ inch to 6 inches, and holster or Ship pistol 5 to 12 inch barrel. The pocket pistol will carry from 40 to 50 yards, belt pistol 50 to 60, and the holster or ship pistol 80 to 100, with a very small quantity of powder; and the pocket pistol with ball and cap only, without any powder, from 12 to 15 yards point blank; pistols in Mahogany cases, from $16, $20, $30, to $100.

The above is a true representation of the COLT's PATENT REPEATING PISTOL; which is acknowledged to be superior in every respect to any other Pistol manufactured in this country or Europe. The Emperor of Russia, the Emperor of Austria, the King of Prussia, the Prince de Joinville of France, the Imaum of Muscat, all have them, and speak in the highest terms of them. The Texan Army and Navy are supplied with them, and the U. S. Navy has been supplied with them to some extent, and the officers have given a most favorable report of Colt's repeating fire-arms. *Great impositions have lately been practised upon the Public by representing and selling the Six Barrel or Self Cocking Pistol as Colt's Patent Pistol.* The Colt's Repeating Pistols, Carbines, and Shot Guns are sold for Cash at reduced prices, at

No. 2 Barclay-street, Astor-house, New-York, by

JOHN EHLERS, *Proprietor.*

W. H. HORSTMANN & Co., *Maiden-lane.*
HYDE & GOODRICHE, *Chartres-street, New-Orleans.*
H. E. BALDWIN & Co.,   "   "
B. DAFFIN, *Ba timore.*
MULFORD & WENDELL, *Broadway, Albany.*

JUDD'S WAREHOUSE,
CORNER MARKET AND SOUTH STREETS.
GOODS STORED AT REASONABLE RATES.
FOR PARTICULARS
APPLY ON THE PREMISES,
OR TO
SAMUEL JUDD'S SONS,
139 Front-street.

44

Left:
Although Colt's patent is referenced frequently, the inventor of the revolver is never directly mentioned in this advertisement posted on behalf of John Ehlers, circa 1845–1846. (2012.38.19; the Dennis A. LeVett Collection)

Opposite:
The unidentified solider in this tintype has a Fifth Model Ehlers tucked into his belt on the right side of the image. (2012.38.20; the Dennis A. LeVett Collection)

45

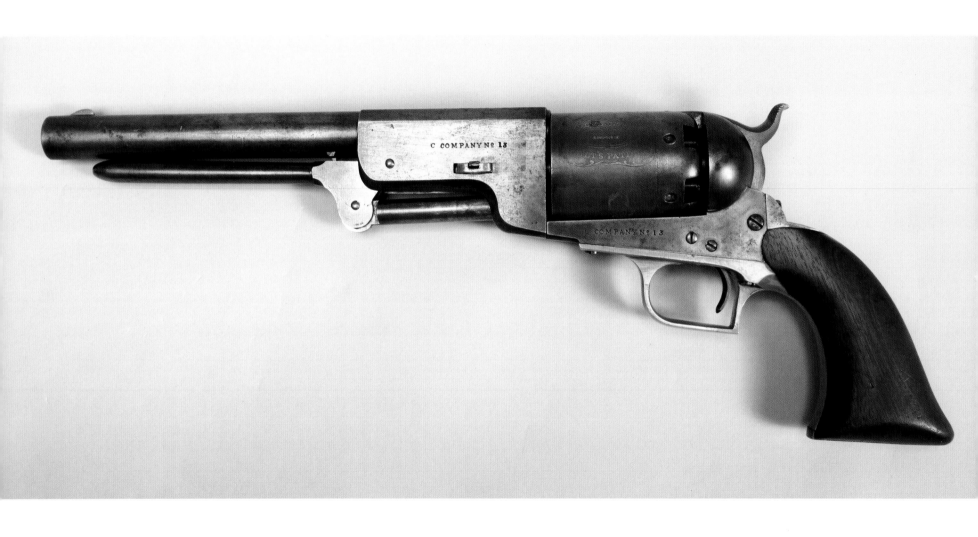

The Walker Model, designed for use in the Mexican-American War, revived Samuel Colt's fortunes as a gunmaker. (2012.2.1; the George Gamble Collection)

MILITARY WALKER MODEL

A Triumphant Return

Samuel Colt spent the years after the failure of the Patent Arms Manufacturing Company in the city of New York working on various projects. Colt's greatest passion at the time was a system that used electrical charges to detonate strategically placed underwater mines. Colt believed the mines could protect America's shores and harbors, so he set about selling the idea to the government. Several successful demonstrations were held, including the detonation of a large schooner sailing down the Potomac River, but government officials saw little value in the system. Colt also experimented in telegraph communications, and he actually made a profit designing waterproof powder cartridges. Although these projects took up a significant amount of Colt's time, he did not abandon the revolver. He constantly improved upon his greatest invention, and he continued to seek out endorsements that he hoped could be used to revive production.

One of the endorsements Colt sought was from Captain Samuel Hamilton Walker, a Texas Ranger and a newly appointed captain of the United States Mounted Rifles. A national hero from his exploits fighting Native Americans and Mexicans along the Texas border, Walker was familiar with Colt's revolver, having used it as a Ranger. In his reply to Colt's inquiry, Walker credited the revolver with giving the Rangers a distinct advantage over their adversaries. Walker also said the revolver could be the ideal weapon for mounted troops if several changes were implemented. Colt understood that Walker's input could dramatically improve his invention and help induce future government contracts, so Colt worked closely with Walker on the design of a new model. Confident in their improvements, Walker was able to secure an order from the United States military in 1847 for 1,000 revolvers for use in the Mexican-American War, which had begun a year earlier. Colt scrambled to get them manufactured quickly, and within a few months, the latest Colt revolvers were being used in battle.

The newly improved Colt revolvers, the Walker Models as they later came to be known, were shipped to the government in the summer of 1847 for use in the war. The revolvers were marked with serial numbers corresponding to companies A through E. Each company was issued approximately 220 revolvers, except for E Company, which was issued around 120.

Serial numbers began at 1 for each company. The first 220 revolvers delivered went to Walker's C Company. Initially, it was intended that a pair of revolvers would be issued to each mounted soldier, but a single revolver was deemed sufficient. Performing admirably during the war, the Walker Model played a pivotal role in several battles. Ruptured cylinders were a problem, but this was due in some part to the improper loading of a new conical-shaped bullet.

The Military Walker in the Autry Collection is serial number C Company 13. It is 100 percent original and is certainly one of the finest Walkers extant. The revolver is in such remarkable condition because it remained in the possession of the family of Aaron Pulhamus, an employee who worked on the model's manufacture, for more than 90 years. Pulhamus worked at the Patent Arms Mfg. Co., and at the urging of Colt, he helped oversee the manufacture of the Walker at the Whitneyville Armory in Connecticut. Serial number C Company 13 probably failed some sort of inspection and thus was never shipped to the military. Instead, it was likely given to Pulhamus by Colt in appreciation for his work. Pulhamus later used the revolver as a model and demonstrator. Because of the revolver's unique pedigree, it is often referred to as the Pulhamus Walker.

The success of the Walker Model ultimately led to the incorporation of Colt's Patent Fire Arms Manufacturing Company, an offshoot of which continues to operate to this day. (87.118.3)

CIVILIAN WALKER MODEL

Birth of an Empire

The Walker Model was the largest and most powerful black powder revolver ever made. It weighed four pounds, nine ounces, with a nine-inch part round, part octagonal barrel. It was chambered in .44 caliber and was capable of firing six shots. (The revolvers produced by the Patent Arms Manufacturing Company were all five-shot.) The cylinders of the Walker were roll engraved with a scene depicting Captain Jack Hays and his Texas Rangers fighting the Comanche with the No. 5 Holster Model, or Texas Paterson. The "Ranger and Indian" scene was engraved by Waterman Lilly Ormsby, a renowned bank-note engraver and a specialist in the art of engraving on steel plates. The cylinder also read "Model U.S.M.R." (United States Mounted Rifles) and "Colt's Patent," with the serial number in between.

Besides the 1,000 Walkers manufactured for the government, commonly called Military Walkers, an additional 100 were manufactured in 1847 for presentation to important personnel Samuel Colt hoped could help secure future sales. A few were also offered to the general public. As a result, these 100 examples were often referred to as Civilian Walkers. The civilian series was numbered from 1001 to about 1100. Recipients of these revolvers included Captain Samuel Hamilton Walker, codesigner and champion of the model; Captain Jack Hays, the Texas Ranger immortalized on the cylinder scene; Colonel William S. Harney, the officer responsible for the order of 50 No. 1 Model Ring Lever Revolving Rifles in 1838; Major General Winfield Scott, the hero of the Mexican-American War; and Major General Zachary Taylor, the future president of the United States. Serial number 1004 in the Autry Collection is also from the series, although for whom the revolver was originally intended is unknown.

The Walker, either military or civilian, is considered the Holy Grail of Colt revolvers. The model is held in such high esteem because it was instrumental in proving the effectiveness of Colt's mechanically rotating cylinder. The model's scarcity adds to its significance. Fewer than 200 of the original 1,100 Walkers are known to still exist. Almost every Walker was subject to rough use in the Mexican-American War and on the American frontier, so those that have survived are usually in no better than good or fair condition.

They often have modern restorations and replacement parts, unlike serial number 1004, which is completely original and in fine condition. No matter its appearance, the Walker is highly prized by collectors and historians. As a result, more fake Walkers exist than any other Colt model. Many reproduction Walkers have also been produced.

The success of the Walker allowed Colt to establish a new enterprise and return to gunmaking full time. Incorporated as Colt's Patent Fire Arms Manufacturing Company (commonly shortened to Colt's) in 1855, Samuel Colt's second attempt at mass production was an unqualified success. The revolvers produced by the company had a tremendous impact around the world, and Colt became one of the most successful and recognizable industrialists in the United States. Colt was so well known that his likeness was used for promotional purposes. A gelatin silver print of Colt in the Autry Collection was distributed by the company circa 1895. The company's Rampant Colt trademark quickly grew to be one of the most respected and recognizable corporate symbols in American history. Besides firearms, Colt used the trademark on a variety of his personal items, including his custom-made sterling-silver cigar stand. Part of the Autry Collection, the cigar stand was finely crafted by New York silversmith William Adams with an engraved Rampant Colt on the bulbous center section. More than 150 years after the founding of the company, Colt's continues to be a leader in its field.

Left:
Samuel Colt became so successful that his likeness was used for promotional purposes during and after his lifetime, as evidenced by this gelatin silver print distributed circa 1895. (85.1.603; acquisition made possible in part by John E. Bianchi Jr.)

Opposite:
Samuel Colt's wealth (and appreciation of cigars) was evident in his custom-made, sterling-silver cigar stand engraved with a Rampant Colt, the symbol of his industrial empire. (87.118.155)

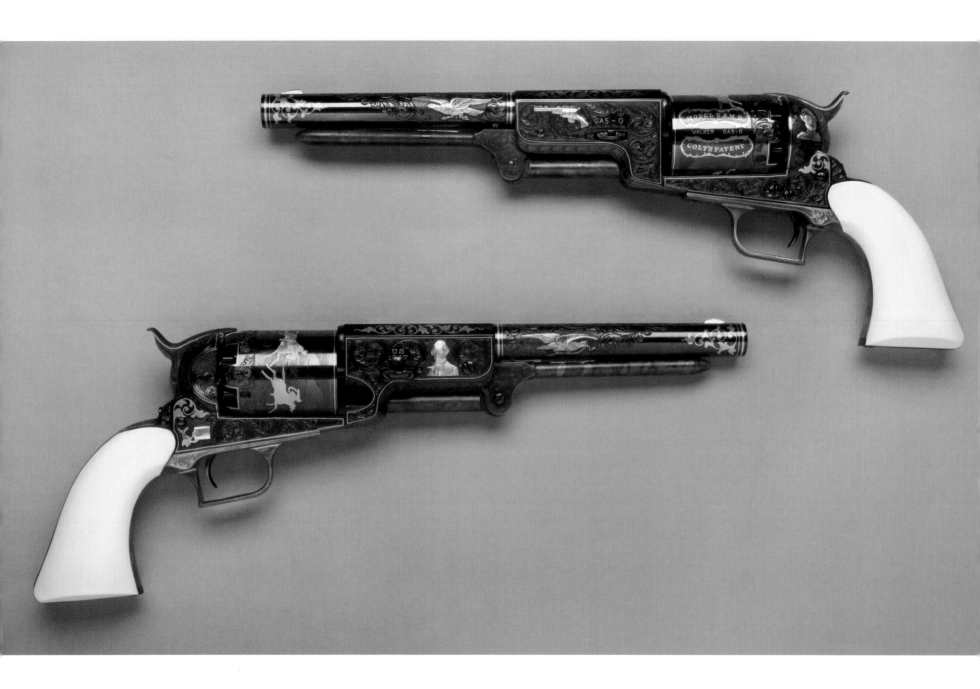

The finest modern Walker Models ever made feature gold-inlaid iconography documenting the history of the pivotal model. (90.183.6)

MODERN WALKER MODEL PAIR WITH GOLD INLAY

Celebrating the Past

R are and historically important Colt revolvers can be found in the best museums in the world and the finest private collections. For the general public, however, these guns are virtually unattainable. As a result, Colt's introduced commemorative guns in 1961 in an attempt to allow all collectors the opportunity to own historic models. The Colt Custom Gun Shop, launched in 1976, took it a step further by allowing individuals to custom order revolvers by choosing the grade and style of the engraving. Other personal touches, such as inlay, finish, grips, and inscriptions, could also be added. On some rare occasions, custom-ordered revolvers are arguably more beautiful than the originals. A notable example is the pair of modern Walker Models in the Autry Collection.

The revolvers, crafted circa 1980, depict the development of the Walker. They feature factory engraving with ivory grips. The relief and flush inlay is done in 18- and 24-karat gold. Both revolvers feature gold-inlaid cylinder scenes and scrolls. Serial number GAS-0 has a gold-inlaid bust of Samuel Colt on the recoil shield and a gold-inlaid image of the prototype Walker on the left side of the frame. The prototype was built by Blunt & Syms, a firearm manufacturer in New York. The right side of the modern Walker includes a gold-inlaid reproduction of Colt's signature and an image from a George Catlin promotional lithograph commissioned by Colt. The locking mechanism used on the Paterson revolvers, one of the most important features of Colt's invention, is also depicted in gold inlay.

Serial number GAS-00 has a gold-inlaid bust of Captain Samuel Hamilton Walker and an image of the Walker Model's improved locking mechanism on the right side. The left side includes Walker's signature in gold. Although Walker was the codesigner and champion of the model, he never had the chance to see its success. Walker was killed in action on October 9, 1847, fighting at the Battle of Huamantla in the Mexican-American War. Walker supposedly died carrying two Civilian Model Walkers that were presented to him by Colt. A gold-inlaid image of Eli Whitney Jr.'s armory is also featured on the left side of the frame. When the order for 1,000 revolvers was placed in 1847, Colt did not have a factory of his own, so he arranged for the Walkers to be manufactured at Whitney's armory in Whitneyville, Connecticut. Whitney was a prominent industrialist and the son of the inventor of the cotton gin.

Designed by master engraver Alvin A. White, the modern Walkers were made on special order for George Strichman, chairman of the board and later chairman emeritus of Colt Industries. An inscription on the back strap of both revolvers reads "George A. Strichman / Chairman of the Board / Colt Industries." Strichman was instrumental in amassing a vast collection of historic Colt firearms and artifacts for Colt Industries, with author R. L. Wilson serving as his personal consultant. The collaboration also led to Strichman's amazing private collection, the majority of which were opulently engraved modern revolvers featuring the finest embellishments. The inspiration for Strichman's personal collection was Samuel Colt. Besides being the inventor of the revolver, Colt was also the first collector of his revolvers.

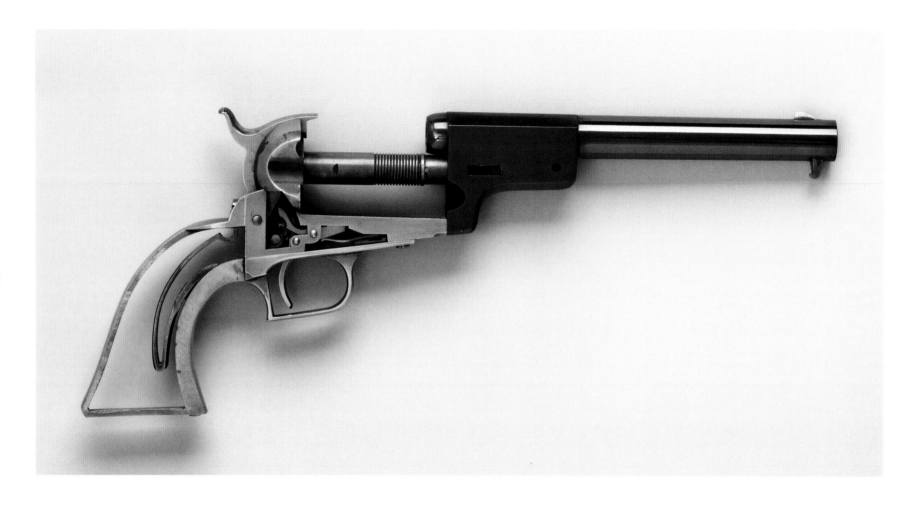

The first cutaway or skeleton arm machined to show the inner workings and special features of the revolver was this Second Model Dragoon. (87.118.4)

CUTAWAY SECOND MODEL DRAGOON

Advertising Perfection

The initial order of 1,000 Walker Models was followed by an additional order for another 1,000 revolvers. With the funds provided by the two orders, Samuel Colt had the necessary resources to return permanently to gunmaking. For the rest of his life, Colt devoted himself completely to the manufacture of firearms and related accessories. To fill the latest government contract, Colt purchased the machinery and tools used at the Whitneyville Armory to manufacture the Walker. Additional machinery came from the Ames Manufacturing Company, well known for its specialty swords. Colt also leased a building in Hartford, Connecticut, his hometown. Colt's decision to return to Hartford was based primarily on money. He still needed capital, and having exhausted all of his resources in the New York–New Jersey area, he found several financial backers in the Hartford area. The new company came to be known as Colt's Patent Fire Arms Manufacturing Company.

The Walker had proven effective in the Mexican-American War, but there were some complaints, including the model's barrel length and weight. Colt continued to modify the revolver's design, and late in 1847, he released a new transitional model that used leftover Walker parts. The following year, Colt released an entirely new line of revolvers called Dragoons. Unlike the revolvers produced by the Patent Arms Manufacturing Company, the parts that composed the individual Dragoon revolvers were interchangeable. Colt was not the first gunmaker to adapt the system of interchangeable parts to mass-produce firearms, but he quickly perfected the technique. Colt's factory and the products it produced were at the forefront of the American Industrial Revolution and the American system of manufacturing.

To demonstrate that his revolvers were perfectly machined, Colt introduced cutaway or skeleton arms to highlight the revolver's mechanics and special features. Very few cutaways were produced, and they were never marketed. The earliest known revolver to receive such treatment was a Second Model Dragoon in the Autry Collection. Manufactured in 1850 with no serial number, records indicate that it may have been used by Colt in a lecture he gave before the Institution of Civil Engineers in London in 1851. Colt's lecture highlighted the ingenuity of his revolvers and the advanced techniques used to manufacture them. The lecture was so successful that Colt was elected as an associate member of the institution. The cutaway revolver was also exhibited at the Great Exhibition of the Works of Industry of All Nations, commonly called the Crystal Palace Exhibition, which also took place in London in 1851. The exhibition was a showcase for industrialization from around the world, and Colt's revolvers were a popular attraction.

The inner workings of the revolver also were showcased on the first broadside released by Colt's Hartford operations. Accompanied by a testimonial from Colt, the broadside featured images of an early transitional Dragoon and an experimental revolving rifle. The parts that composed the revolvers were individually numbered, and additional images illustrated the distinct parts of the Dragoon. All of the images featured on the broadside were taken from a patent caveat that Colt filed on August 28, 1848. This important document is now part of the Autry Collection. It includes written descriptions of the Dragoon and revolving rifle, along with several detailed images. Records indicate that Colt only applied for eight caveats—an official notice of an intention to file a patent application at a later date—and, given its use as an advertisement, the caveat for the Dragoon is arguably the most significant. Whether it was a cutaway arm, a patent caveat, or a broadside, Colt was determined to emphasize the inner workings of his revolutionary revolvers.

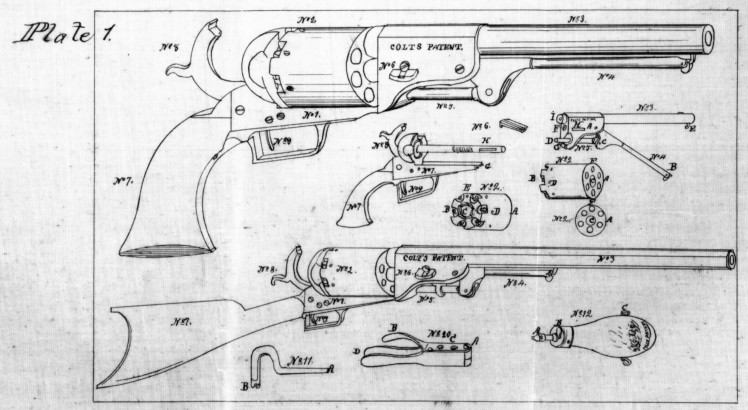

Plate 1.

COLTS PATENT.

COLT'S PATENT.

Colt's Patent Repeating Firearms.

Opposite:
The parts that made up the Dragoon were illustrated in a drawing accompanying a patent caveat Samuel Colt filed in 1848. (2010.57.6.5; donated by Petra and Greg Martin)

Right:
Along with the patent caveat drawing, Colt provided a description of the parts and information on their functions. (2010.57.6.3; donated by Petra and Greg Martin)

Colt's Patent Repeating Fire arms.

Plate. 1. Figure N.º 1 is the base or lock frame with which all parts are connected. N.º 2 is the receiver containing chambers for six or more charges N.º 3 is the barrel. N.º 4 & N.º 5 the lever and rod for forcing the balls into the chambers. N.º 6 the key to connect the barrel with the receiver N.º 7 the stock or handle within which the lock is located. N.º 8 the hammer N.º 9 the trigger for operating the lock in firing.

The pistol being loaded by drawing back the hammer, its first action is to relieve a bolt which holds the Cylinder in place, a hand attached to the hammer then operates on the receiver and forces it forward until the second charge is brought in line with the hammer, the bolt is then again relieved and holds the receiver in position until by pulling the trigger the 2.ª chamber is fired, repeating the same action another chamber is brought in position and the same result follows, until all the Chambers are discharged.

This principle of a combination of Charge in a receiver applies equally well to rifles carbines, muskets and shot guns with but slight difference in arrangement.

After one of these arms has been fired too much care Cannot be observed in cleaning and oiling all parts of it, particularly the receiver & the axis on which it turns to prevent rust

Sam.ˡ Colt,

A rare factory-engraved bust of President George Washington is featured on the barrel lug of this Third Model Dragoon. (87.118.5)

ENGRAVED THIRD MODEL DRAGOON

American Ingenuity

Cutaway arms were an effective way to promote the revolver, but Samuel Colt knew that engraved examples were even more powerful. A small portion of the revolvers produced by the Patent Arms Manufacturing Company were engraved, and Colt resumed the practice when he returned to gunmaking. Although the number of engraved revolvers and the quality of the engraving increased dramatically during the production of the Dragoon series, engraved revolvers continued to be a small portion of the overall number produced. Approximately 20,000 Dragoons were manufactured from 1848 to 1861, and only a few hundred were engraved. An even smaller number were displayed around the world as exhibition showpieces. Third Model Dragoons were commonly used for such purposes.

The Third Model was the final design in the Dragoon series. The model was manufactured from 1851 to 1861, and approximately 10,500 were produced. The Third Model was distinguishable from earlier models by its oval trigger guard and rectangular cylinder stops. The Third Model was the only Dragoon to feature multiple barrel lengths, seven and a half inches and eight inches, and it also was designed to fit three standard variations of detachable shoulder stocks. The Third Model was well liked by civilians, and a significant number of the revolvers saw use in the American West. The model was also popular with troops in the field, but individuals at the Ordnance Department were slow to recognize the revolver's potential, despite earlier success. While almost half of the total production was ordered by the military, Colt certainly expected a higher number.

The lowest serial number in the Third Model Dragoon series and certainly one of the most striking examples is serial number 10222 in the Autry Collection. It was manufactured in 1851. Prior to its discovery, it was commonly assumed by Colt experts that the Third Model series began approximately with serial number 10700. Serial number 10222 is also the lowest serial number of the Dragoon series engraved in the so-called donut style. Only used briefly from approximately 1851 to 1852,

the donut style featured spirals with thick inner and outer leaves. The engraving may be the work of Waterman Lilly Ormsby, the individual responsible for the roll-engraved cylinder scenes found on many percussion revolvers. Other rare or unusual aspects of the engraving on serial number 10222 include the design on the top of the hammer, a leaf device encircling the muzzle, the decorative treatment to the recoil shield, extensive scrollwork on the back strap, and a serpent design on each side of the hammer. The most remarkable feature, however, is the engraved bust of George Washington.

Only two Colt revolvers from the percussion period are known to have an engraved bust of Washington, America's first president. The first revolver is serial number 10222 and the second is serial number 12406, a gold-inlaid Third Model Dragoon presented by Colt to the sultan of Turkey. The engraved bust of Washington on serial number 10222 is located on the left side of the barrel lug. Due to the revolver's superior quality and unique design, one can assume that it was made on Colt's direct order for use as a showpiece. The revolver most likely was featured at London's Crystal Palace Exhibition in 1851 and other exhibitions around the world. Colt probably spotlighted Washington as a way to further highlight the superiority of American ingenuity in the manufacturing of firearms.

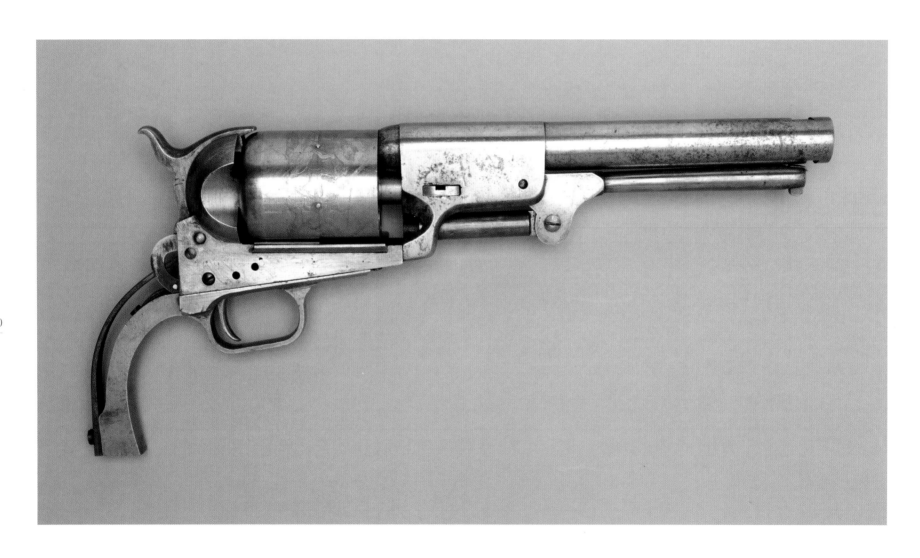

The experimental locking mechanism on this Third Model Dragoon is one of many features that were never incorporated into the revolvers that were mass-produced. (87.118.6)

EXPERIMENTAL THIRD MODEL DRAGOON

The Locking Mechanism

Cutaways and showpieces were a great way for Samuel Colt to promote his revolvers. Endorsements from troops in the field were also extremely important. Just as the Walker Model had proven effective in the Mexican-American War, the Dragoon series was quickly accepted by troops stationed across North America. This was especially true in the West, as firearms were the primary tools for hunting and for defense against hostile elements on the American frontier. Initially, the efficiency of firearms was severely limited by the fact that the majority had to be reloaded after each shot. The introduction of the multishot Colt revolver, however, gave the military a new and distinct advantage. Unfortunately, while troops recognized the superiority of the revolver, the military brass was slow to adopt the new weapon.

The revolver's multishot capacity, the primary reason it was popular with troops, was one of the things that concerned the Ordnance Department. The military brass was worried that troops armed with multishot weapons, be they revolvers or repeating rifles, would waste more ammunition, resulting in higher costs. The Ordnance Department also objected to the supposed fragility of the moving parts on the revolver and the tendency for gas to escape, resulting in misfires or even explosions. Pressure from key military personnel and congressmen, many of whom were directly lobbied by Colt, along with growing public recognition, finally forced the Ordnance Department to adopt the revolver. The revolver was especially popular with mounted troops who were often issued pairs, which they carried in large holsters attached to their saddles. The use of the Colt revolver by mounted troops led early Colt collectors to call the post-Walker series Dragoons, the name commonly used for mounted troops in the mid-19th century. (The term cavalry ultimately replaced dragoon around the time of the Civil War.)

Despite its increased use and acceptance, Samuel Colt and Colt's Patent Fire Arms Manufacturing Company continued to refine and improve the revolver. Even the revolving locking mechanism, the most revolutionary and important aspect of the revolver, was reexamined, as evidenced in an experimental Third Model Dragoon now in the Autry Collection. The revolver was manufactured circa 1855 with no serial number. The revolver's experimental locking mechanism is extremely unorthodox and complex. When the hammer is engaged, a curved rectangular plate beneath the cylinder is pushed forward by an arm attached to the hammer, part of which is visibly protruding from the rear of the frame. Grooves on the sliding plate ultimately engage pins on the cylinder, causing it to rotate. Although this particular design was deemed impractical and never patented, it illustrates an active research and development program at Colt's.

A careful inspection of the revolver reveals that it has several other notable features. The trigger is unique, and the barrel lug is rounded at the top. The front sight and the rammer latch are missing, but the barrel is machined for their attachment. Several extra holes are visible in the frame, and the grips and back strap are missing entirely. The revolver's cylinder is especially interesting. While it is roll engraved with the "Ranger and Indian" scene, the nipple cutouts at the breech, an essential part of the percussion system, are completely absent. The revolver is unfinished, or "in the white," and machine markings are visible on several parts. Given all of the special features, it would appear that the revolver was used for experimentation beyond just the revolving mechanism.

Samuel Colt presented E. K. Root, his company's superintendent, with a Third Model Dragoon cased with an exceptionally rare mirrored top. (2012.2.3; the George Gamble Collection)

COLT SUPERINTENDENT E. K. ROOT'S CASED PRESENTATION THIRD MODEL DRAGOON

The Man behind the Machines

The individual who designed and patented most of the equipment used at Colt's armory was Elisha King (E. K.) Root. He was also responsible for laying out the entire factory floor. It is said that Samuel Colt invented the revolver, but E. K. Root figured out how to make it. Born in Belchertown, Massachusetts, in 1808, Root spent his youth working in a textile mill and apprenticing at a machine shop. He spent several years working as a machinist at several different locations, and in 1832, he joined the Collins Axe Company. Made superintendent of the company in 1845, Root devised a system that used automated machinery to produce axes. That same year, Root was offered the position of master armorer at the Springfield armory, one of the most important firearm manufacturers in the United States. He turned it down, but in 1849, he accepted Colt's offer to become the superintendent and chief engineer of Colt's Patent Fire Arms Manufacturing Company.

According to legend, Root first met Colt on July 4, 1829. Colt was a 15-year-old student at a private school in Amherst, Massachusetts, at the time, and he was fascinated with underwater explosives. Much like his experiments years later, Colt sought to detonate a mine from shore using electrical current. Colt distributed a handbill across town inviting people to witness an explosion scheduled to take place at a local pond. The experiment was a success, but the explosion was so powerful it doused the onlookers with water, many of whom were in their finest clothes for the holiday. The furious crowd converged upon Colt, presumably to throw him in the pond to make sure he got as wet as they did, but a 20-year-old local machinist stepped in to protect him. The machinist was E. K. Root. Root was fascinated with Colt's invention, and the two spent hours discussing machines and technology.

Years later, as superintendent and chief engineer, Root revolutionized Colt's operations. Adapting the system he had perfected at the Collins Axe Company, Root designed special-purpose machines to manufacture revolvers. An example of one of these machines can be seen in a series of patent documents in the Autry Collection. Dated November 28, 1854, the documents relate to a machine for boring the chambers in the cylinders of firearms. Root carefully placed all of his machines on the factory floor in a

layout that would fully maximize efficiency without sacrificing quality. Years before Henry Ford and the Model T, Root perfected the assembly line for the mass production of interchangeable parts. Root also surrounded himself with the best and brightest inventors, machinists, and mechanics. The Colt armory under Root turned out some of the best industrial minds of the 19th century. Given all that he did and the quiet, dignified manner in which he did it, Root's contribution to the success of the revolver and Colt's cannot be overstated.

Samuel Colt certainly recognized Root's contributions. Root was one of the highest-paid workers in the state of Connecticut, and when Colt's was officially incorporated in 1855, Root was given a symbolic ownership stake in the company. Colt also lavished gifts on Root, including firearms. One of the most spectacular examples is the cased Third Model Dragoon, serial number 16461, in the Autry Collection. The engraving, executed by Gustave Young, is fine and extremely rich. An inscription on the case reads "Presented to / E. K. Root / by Col. Saml Colt / Prest. Colts Pt. F. A. Mfg Co. / May 16th 1857." The importance of the set is evident in the case's mirrored top. Only one other factory case set is known to have such a top, and it was a Model 1851 Navy that was also presented to Root by Colt on May 16, 1857. (The 1851 Navy is also part of the Autry Collection.)

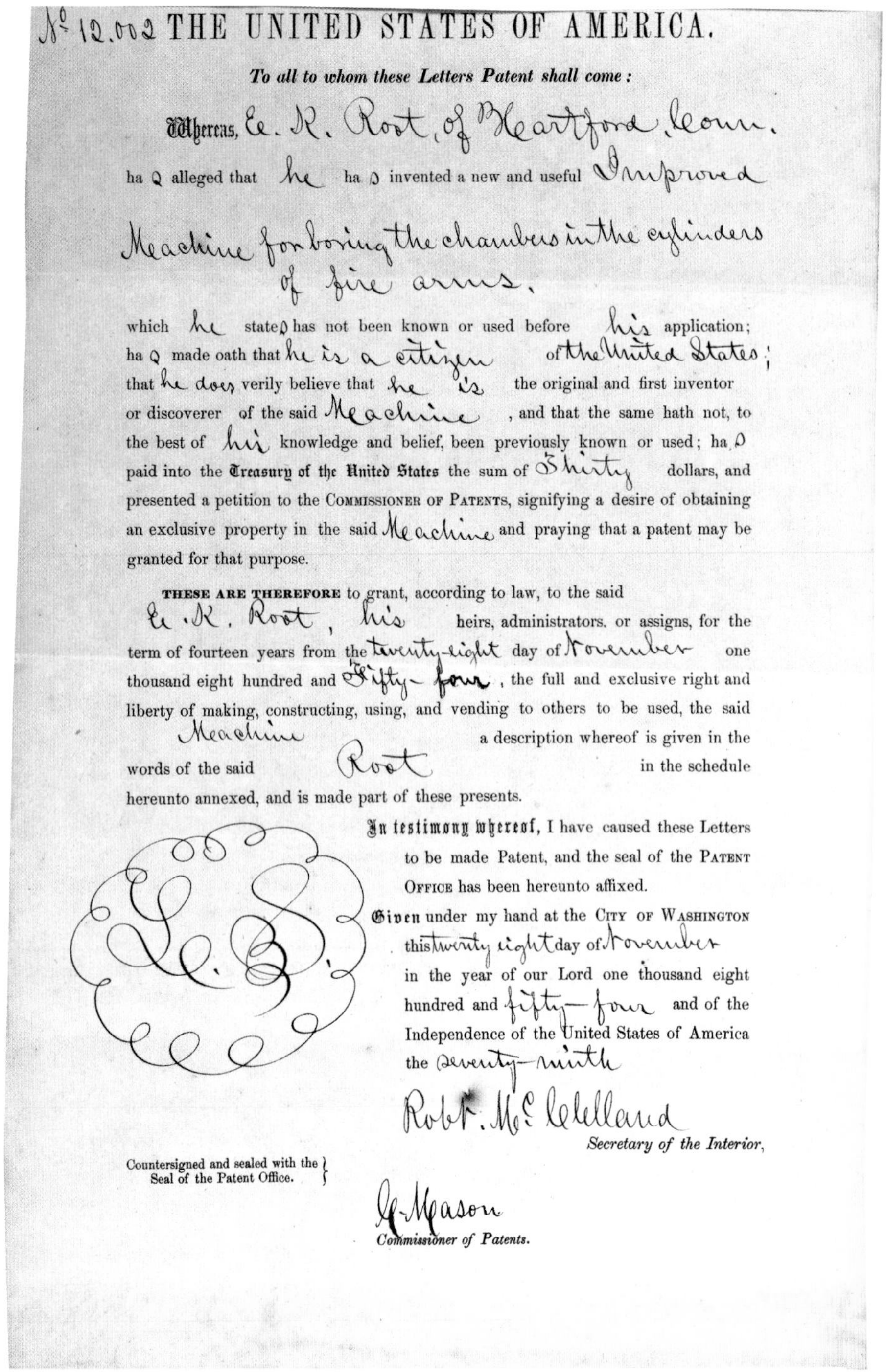

THE UNITED STATES OF AMERICA.

To all to whom these Letters Patent shall come:

Whereas, E. K. Root, of Hartford, Conn. ha_ alleged that *he* ha_ invented a new and useful *Improved*

Machine for boring the chambers in the cylinders of fire arms,

which *he* state_ has not been known or used before *his* application; ha_ made oath that *he is a citizen* of the United States; that *he does* verily believe that *he is* the original and first inventor or discoverer of the said *Machine*, and that the same hath not, to the best of *his* knowledge and belief, been previously known or used; ha_ paid into the Treasury of the United States the sum of *Thirty* dollars, and presented a petition to the COMMISSIONER OF PATENTS, signifying a desire of obtaining an exclusive property in the said *Machine* and praying that a patent may be granted for that purpose.

THESE ARE THEREFORE to grant, according to law, to the said *E. K. Root, his* heirs, administrators. or assigns, for the term of fourteen years from the *twenty-eight* day of *November* one thousand eight hundred and *Fifty-four*, the full and exclusive right and liberty of making, constructing, using, and vending to others to be used, the said *Machine* a description whereof is given in the words of the said *Root* in the schedule hereunto annexed, and is made part of these presents.

In testimony whereof, I have caused these Letters to be made Patent, and the seal of the PATENT OFFICE has been hereunto affixed.

Given under my hand at the CITY OF WASHINGTON this *twenty eight* day of *November* in the year of our Lord one thousand eight hundred and *fifty-four* and of the Independence of the United States of America the *seventy-ninth*

Robt. McClelland

Secretary of the Interior,

Countersigned and sealed with the }
Seal of the Patent Office. }

C. Mason

Commissioner of Patents.

Left:
E. K. Root filed a patent in 1854 for an "improved machine for boring the chambers in the cylinders of fire arms." (87.118.399)

Opposite:
Root submitted this drawing as part of the patent application process in 1854 for his machinery for cylinder chambers used at Colt's. (87.118.406)

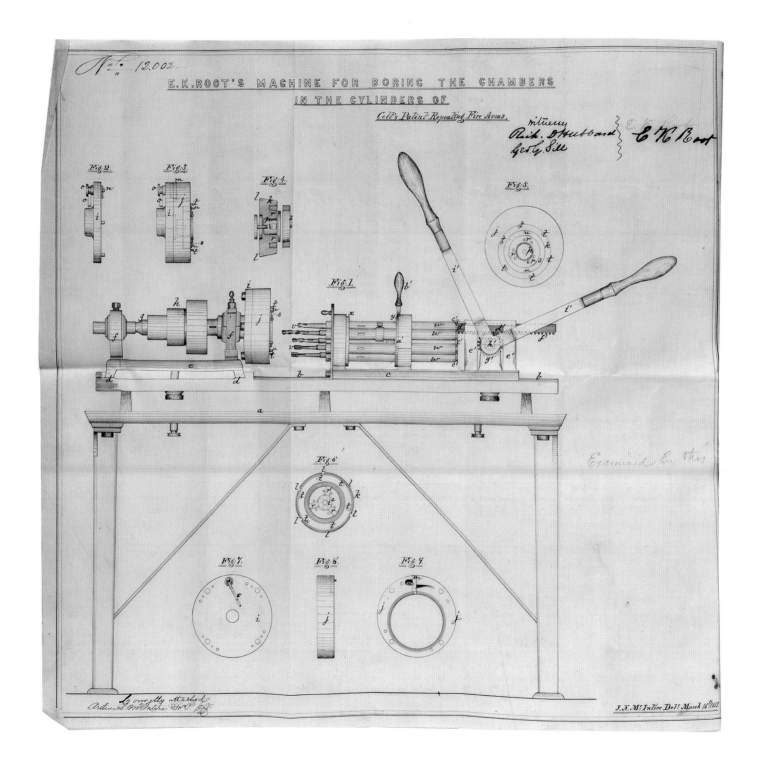

Nº 12.002

E.K. ROOT'S MACHINE FOR BORING THE CHAMBERS
IN THE CYLINDERS OF
Colt's Patent Repeating Fire Arms.

witnesses
Rich. D Hubbard
Geo. G. Sill

E. K. Root

Fig. 2   Fig. 3   Fig. 4   Fig. 5

Fig. 1

Fig. 6

Fig. 7   Fig. 8   Fig. 9

Correctly attached
Arthur L. McEntire SoL.P. Off

J. N. McIntire Del: March 16ᵗʰ 1855

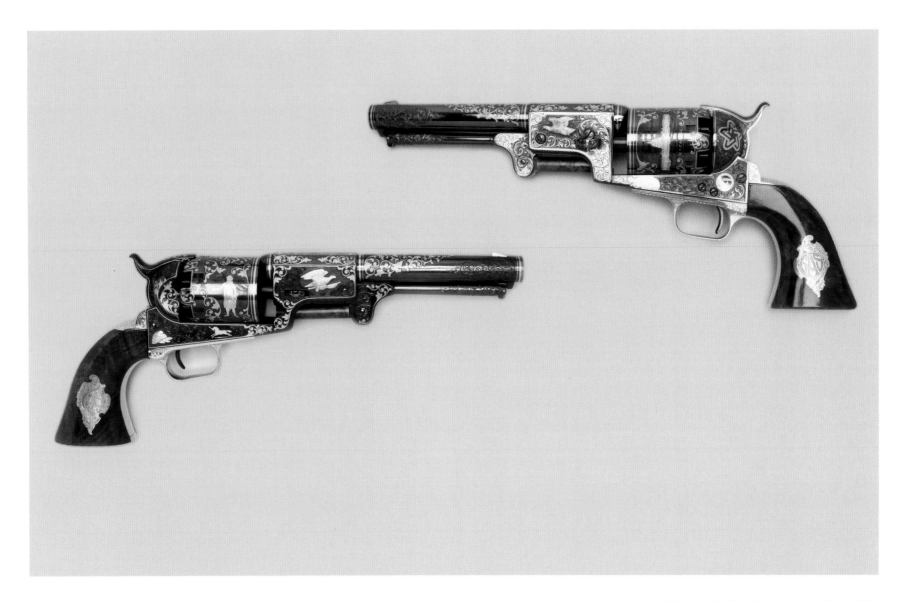

Modeled after historic presentations Samuel Colt made in 1854, this exceptionally rich and detailed pair of Third Model Dragoons represents two of the finest modern percussion revolvers ever made. (90.183.5)

MODERN THIRD MODEL DRAGOON PAIR WITH GOLD INLAY

Historic Presentations

The history and significance of Colt percussion revolvers is recognized in modern re-creations of some of the company's most important models. Many of these opulently engraved and richly decorated revolvers are based on historic presentation arms, whereas others celebrate key moments in the history of the company. Modern percussion revolvers combine old-world craftsmanship with state-of-the-art technology. A notable example is a pair of modern Third Model Dragoons, serial numbers GAS-1/1776 and GAS-2/1776, in the Autry Collection. Two of the most richly decorated modern percussion revolvers ever made, the pair is modeled after revolvers that Samuel Colt presented to Sultan Abdülmecid I of the Ottoman Empire and Russian Czar Nicholas I.

Overseas sales were an important aspect of Colt's business, and he traveled to Europe on several occasions to promote his revolvers. In 1849, on his first sales trip overseas, Colt visited the Ottoman Empire and was given the rare opportunity to meet with Sultan Abdülmecid I. Colt presented the sultan with a pair of beautifully engraved Dragoon revolvers. The sultan in return presented Colt with a gold snuffbox, and he placed an order for an unknown number of revolvers. Colt continued to maintain relations with the sultan's empire for several years. It is believed that Colt made an additional presentation to the sultan, albeit not in person, of a Third Model Dragoon with gold inlay sometime around 1854. The sultan's Third Model Dragoon was very similar to another revolver that Colt presented to Czar Nicholas I of Russia.

Colt visited Russia for the first time in 1854 when he met with Czar Nicholas I at the Winter Palace. Russian interest in the Colt revolver dated back to the Patent Arms Manufacturing Company, when a group of Russian navy officers visited the Paterson factory. When meeting the czar in 1854, Colt presented him with three revolvers, including a Third Model Dragoon. All of the revolvers featured gold inlay and had been used previously by Colt across Europe as promotional pieces. Czar Nicholas I later responded with the presentation of a diamond ring, but more importantly, his government

ordered 5,000 revolvers. A few years later, in 1858, Colt visited Russia again for the coronation of Alexander II, Nicholas's son, as czar. Colt presented a broad array of revolvers to Alexander and his brothers Grand Dukes Michael and Constantine.

The modern Third Model Dragoons in the Autry Collection were modeled after the Dragoons Colt presented to Sultan Abdülmecid I and Czar Nicholas I in 1854. Crafted circa 1981, they are profusely engraved and covered with gold-inlaid scrolls, bands, and borders. The gold inlay, engraving, and walnut grips are all the work of Alvin A. White, one of the finest firearm engravers of the 20th century. Serial number GAS-1/1776 features a gold-inlaid portrait of George Washington on the cylinder, based on the famed painting by Gilbert Stuart, and a bust of the Marquis de Lafayette on the frame. A Rampant Colt, similar in appearance to those depicted on the Colt coat of arms, is also depicted in gold inlay on the frame. The cylinder of serial number GAS-2/1776 has a gold-inlaid image of the United States Capitol Building with a gold-inlaid Lady Justice on the frame. "Saml Colt" is scripted in gold inlay on the top of each revolver, and gold medallions inscribed "GAS" (for Colt Industries Chairman George A. Strichman) are affixed to the grips of both revolvers on opposite sides. Although not as historically significant, the re-creations are arguably more beautiful than the originals.

The "Wells Fargo" was a rare variation of the Model 1849 Pocket, a popular revolver with miners and other individuals in the American West. (87.118.10.1)

PROTOTYPE "WELLS FARGO" MODEL 1849 POCKET

A Model in Name Only

The hiring of E. K. Root and the first sales trip overseas were only two of the significant events that took place in the life of Samuel Colt in 1849. For more than a decade, Colt's patents protected him from serious competition. Colt understood the importance of his patent rights, and he guarded vigilantly against infringement. When his American patent protection was scheduled to expire in 1849, he successfully petitioned the government for an extension that effectively gave him a monopoly on revolvers until 1857. Colt's patent rights were legally recognized when he successfully sued the Massachusetts Arms Company, the manufacturer of Wesson and Leavitt revolvers, for infringement in 1851.

The year 1849 was also noteworthy because it solidified the importance of the Colt revolver in the American West. From their initial offering, Colt revolvers saw extensive use on the American frontier. The efficiency of the No. 5 Holster Model in Texas, the success of the Walker Model in the Mexican-American War, and the popularity of the Dragoon series with Western troops were all key moments in the early history of the revolver. The turning point, however, came with the discovery of gold in California. Although gold was initially discovered in 1848, word of the discovery did not spread around the world until 1849. A total of 300,000 people, commonly called forty-niners, eventually made their way to the California gold fields. Approximately half of these fortune hunters traveled across the North American continent. Whether it was on the arduous journey west or in the raucous gold towns, forty-niners recognized the importance of firearms, especially Colt revolvers. Demand increased substantially, and in the West, Colt revolvers sold for several times their asking price.

The revolver that was particularly popular with gold miners was the Model 1849 Pocket. Like most Colts, early collectors in the 20th century gave the model its name. The revolver was actually first manufactured in 1850, but collectors inaccurately believed it was released in 1849, hence its name. Production of the diminutive revolver ceased in 1873 with a total of more than 325,000 manufactured, making it the best-selling model of all of Colt's

percussion line. The 1849 Pocket was also popular as a defensive weapon on the American frontier. It was carried by pioneer families, gamblers, prostitutes, businessmen, and soldiers. The 1849 Pocket came in many variations. One of the rarest and most sought after variations was the "Wells Fargo" series. The "Wells Fargo" was designed for easy concealment, and the most noticeable feature was the lack of a loading lever.

The series got its name from the banking and express firm Wells, Fargo & Company, one of the most important businesses in the history of the American West. In the early 1850s, Wells Fargo inquired with Colt's about a short-barreled 1849 Pocket without a loading lever intended for use by the company's stagecoach agents. Colt's manufactured approximately 6,000 such revolvers, but there is no conclusive evidence proving that Wells Fargo ordered any of the revolvers or issued them to their agents. The "Wells Fargo" 1849 Pocket in the Autry Collection is serial number 1, a unique prototype manufactured circa 1850. Keeping with company tradition, prototypes often were numbered in their own serial number range. If a decision was made to move forward with mass production, serial numbers recommenced with 1, unless the series was considered a variation of an existing model. The first specimen produced for any model, whether it is a prototype or the beginning of mass production, is extremely important and highly collectible.

Nineteenth-century gold-inlaid percussion revolvers were used for the finest presentations, and this spectacular Model 1849 Pocket is linked to Italian nationalist leader Giuseppe Garibaldi. (2012.2.4; the George Gamble Collection)

ITALIAN NATIONALIST LEADER GIUSEPPE GARIBALDI'S CASED PRESENTATION MODEL 1849 POCKET WITH GOLD INLAY

Exhibition Showpiece

The Model 1849 Pocket was one of the most popular models produced by Colt's Patent Fire Arms Manufacturing Company during Samuel Colt's lifetime. In numbers manufactured, it was the most successful model. It was also the most commonly engraved, although engraved specimens are still considered rare and highly collectible. The most sought after examples of the 1849 Pocket are presentation pieces and those that feature gold inlay. Serial number 63303 in the Autry Collection is believed to be both. Manufactured in 1853, it was one of only five 1849 Pockets to feature gold inlay. Research indicates that it may have been presented to Italian nationalist leader Giuseppe Garibaldi. A general and politician, Garibaldi played an important role in the unification of Italy in the 19th century.

Interestingly, Colt also played a role in Italian unification. In 1859, a delegation from the Italian Committee of New York met with Colt to seek his assistance in arming Garibaldi's troops. Colt agreed to their request by giving 100 arms at no cost to the Italian cause. As with all his presentations, Colt hoped the gesture would garner good publicity and result in future orders. A year later, Colt's gesture paid off when Garibaldi directly ordered 23,500 firearms from Colt's. In another show of generosity, Colt discounted the price of the firearms. Colt received a personal letter of thanks from Garibaldi, and in return, he may have presented Garibaldi with serial number 63303, a revolver of the highest quality.

Like other presentations to European leaders, serial number 63303 was originally used by Colt as an exhibition showpiece, as it clearly illustrated the craftsmanship of its manufacture and the artistry of its engraving. Cased in a rosewood box lined with rich burgundy velvet, the revolver is profusely engraved. Almost every surface of the revolver is decorated in elaborate intertwined scrolls, accentuated with finely detailed designs, including animal and bird motifs. Rare gold inlay is used throughout. A gold-inlaid border can be found on the barrel, frame, cylinder, loading lever, and hammer. The barrel features "Saml Colt" scripted in gold-inlaid Old English letters, while the frame has an unusual gold-inlaid "Colt's Patent" marking. Gold inlay was also used for the serial and patent markings on the cylinder. The cylinder scene features rare hand engraving. The decoration was the work of Gustave Young.

As previously employed on the revolvers produced by the Patent Arms Manufacturing Company, almost all of the revolvers manufactured by Colt's featured a roll-engraved cylinder scene. The scene depicted on the 1849 Pocket was called the "Stagecoach Holdup." It shows bandits attempting to rob a stagecoach, but they are thwarted by passengers armed with Colt revolvers. The scene appears on several models other than the 1849 Pocket, including the Model 1848 Pocket, the Model 1855 Sidehammer Pocket, and some Model 1862 Police and Pocket Navy conversions. Whereas most cylinder scenes were roll engraved, some deluxe revolvers such as serial number 63303 feature hand-engraved cylinder scenes.

The European-style engraving employed on the London Model 1849 Pocket was an attempt by Colt's to overcome English apprehension toward American firearms. (87.118.12)

LONDON MODEL 1849 POCKET

Overseas Expansion

Samuel Colt's revolvers originally were made in Paterson, New Jersey, and then in Hartford, Connecticut. From 1852 to 1857, Colt revolvers were also manufactured in London. Colt's association with Great Britain dated back to the beginnings of the revolver. He first visited the area as a young seaman on the voyage that supposedly led to the inspiration for the revolver. Colt returned in 1835 to seek his first patent. He made several subsequent trips to London, including a tour in 1851 that included triumphant stops at the Institution of Civil Engineers and the Crystal Palace Exhibition. Colt's frequent visits to the region were due in part to the importance of Great Britain to the international firearms market. A likely acquisition of Colt while in London included a set of cutlery made by the English firm Harrison Bros & Howson, "Cutlers to Her Majesty." A table knife from the set, now part of the Autry Collection, features a bone handle engraved with the Rampant Colt logo.

Colt's revolvers were well received in London, but a general skepticism existed for all American products. Colt nevertheless knew his revolvers were superior to any British handguns on the market, and he was convinced that they would sell accordingly. In 1852, he established a London production facility on the River Thames, the only Colt factory located outside the United States. It was also the first factory established by an American manufacturer outside his home country. Colt employed a combination of American and British labor. He initially wanted to buy the machinery in London, hoping it would make a favorable impression, but he was unable to find anything in the region that was up to his high standards. The machinery was thus imported from the Hartford factory.

The first guns made entirely at the London armory came off the line in 1853. They were the same as those produced in Hartford, with the exception of British proof stamps on the cylinder and barrel lug and a British address on the top of the barrel. On the other hand, British engraving and cases, the work of local artisans, were noticeably different than their American counterparts. The use of British labor and styles was designed to make the product more appealing to British and European consumers. The London armory garnered tremendous press in Great Britain and in America. For the British public, the notion of manufacturing firearms by

machine with interchangeable parts was truly revolutionary. The factory saw a parade of notable visitors, including author Charles Dickens, who wrote a glowing review of the armory in 1855. Dickens noted, among other things, that the technology in use at Colt's London factory "cannot be seen under one roof elsewhere in all of England."

An excellent example of a revolver manufactured in London is the Model 1849 Pocket, serial number 7755, in the Autry Collection. It has a five-inch barrel, five-shot cylinder, and is .31 caliber. Manufactured in 1855, the revolver has a blue and case-hardened finish with silver plating. The barrel is stamped "Address Col. Colt / London," and British proof marks of a crown over the letters GP and a crown over the letter V are located on the cylinder and barrel lug. The grips are a deluxe walnut, and the grip straps are made of steel. It was engraved by the staff at the London armory in a scroll style similar to other British firearms from the period. A dot accompanying the serial number indicates that it was given special treatment throughout its manufacture. Like the 1849 Pockets manufactured in Hartford, the "Stagecoach Holdup" scene is roll engraved on the cylinder. The scene is clearly depicted on a proof plate in the Autry Collection that was made in the early 20th century using the original roll die, the only such die still in existence.

Samuel Colt likely acquired this table knife, made in England and custom engraved with the inventor's Rampant Colt logo, during one of his many trips to London. (2012.38.18; the Dennis A. LeVett Collection)

The Model 1849 Pockets manufactured at the
London armory featured the same "Stagecoach
Holdup" cylinder scene as the revolvers produced
in Hartford. (87.118.162)

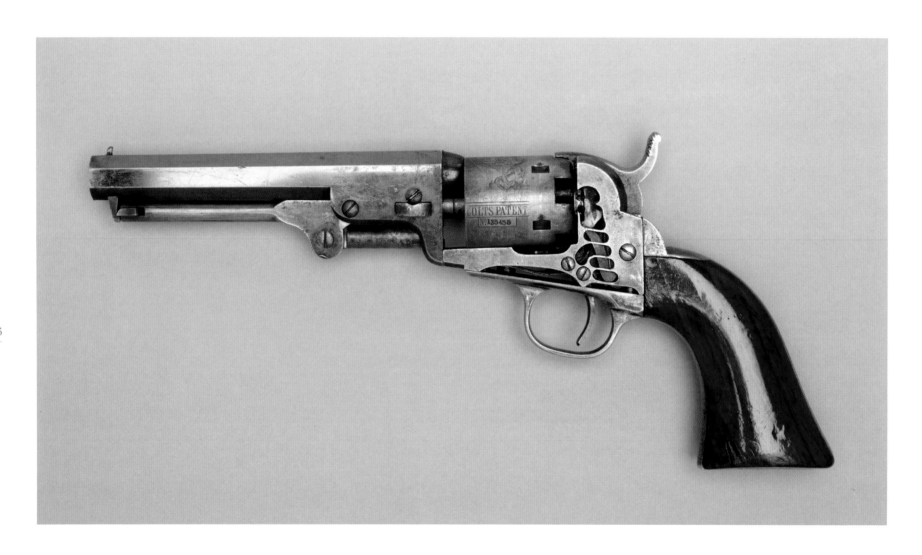

Samuel Colt waited several years after the manufacture of the first cutaway revolver to reintroduce the practice with this Model 1849 Pocket. (87.118.11)

CUTAWAY MODEL 1849 POCKET

The Inner Workings

The establishment of the London armory was one of many notable things happening for Samuel Colt in the 1850s. As the decade progressed, Colt's Patent Fire Arms Manufacturing Company became the most profitable and busiest private armory in the United States. Thanks to factory superintendent E. K. Root, it was the best organized and most efficiently run. Colt also made sure it was the most widely publicized and heavily promoted armory in the world. In spite of his success, Colt continued to perfect his revolver, eliminating any problems that arose through extensive research and development. Models were constantly improved. Colt wanted the superiority of his revolvers to be clearly evident, so he reintroduced cutaway or skeletal arms in 1857.

The earliest known cutaway revolver was a Second Model Dragoon manufactured in 1850. (The Dragoon is part of the Autry Collection.) Colt appears to have used the revolver for several key promotional ventures, including a lecture he gave to the Institution of Civil Engineers in London in 1851. The talk was very successful, but for unknown reasons, Colt's did not manufacture any additional cutaways for several years. When they were finally reintroduced, cutaways were used for various promotional activities. They were also seen as a way to induce future sales. During Samuel Colt's lifetime, cutaway arms were produced for the Second Model Dragoon, the Model 1849 Pocket, the Model 1851 Navy, and the Model 1855 Sidehammer series. Although the tradition continues to this day, cutaway arms are exceptionally rare.

Out of a total production run of more than 325,000 Model 1849 Pockets manufactured in Hartford, only one is known to have been a cutaway. (An additional example was cut away at the London armory, but given the fact that only 11,000 London Model 1849 Pockets were manufactured, the Hartford cutaway is of much greater significance and rarity.) Manufactured in 1857, it was the second cutaway arm ever produced. The revolver is serial number 135455 in the Autry Collection. It has a five-inch barrel and a five-shot cylinder. It has been cut away on the left and right side of the frame to expose the inner workings, including the hammer, hand, trigger, cylinder stop, and the trigger-cylinder stop spring. Almost every mechanical function of the frame is evident, and even the screws entering the frame from the left side and through the trigger guard are visible. Despite its apparent widespread use for demonstration and promotional purposes, the revolver retains a high percentage of finish, the cylinder scene is sharp, and the bore is in perfect condition.

In addition to Colt's, other American firearm manufacturers produced cutaway arms in the 19th and early 20th century, although Colt's was the most proficient in exploiting them. The Winchester Repeating Arms Company was probably second to Colt's in the number of cutaway arms produced. Other manufacturers include Smith & Wesson, Iver Johnson, Remington, and Harrington and Richardson. Like Colt's, all of these companies used cutaways to showcase mechanics and special features. Cutaway arms were also requested by the military for instructional purposes. All of the manufacturers produced very few cutaways, so they comprise a unique subset for collectors and historians. Especially prized are 19th-century cutaway Colt revolvers.

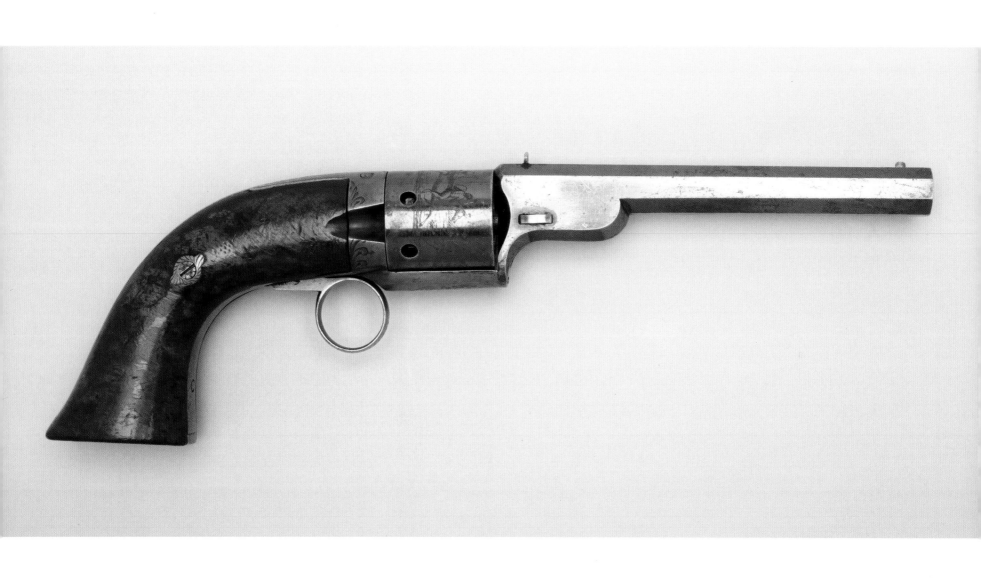

It is unclear if this experimental double-action revolver manufactured in Belgium legally or illegally incorporated many of the features found on the Colt revolver. (87.118.18)

EXPERIMENTAL DOUBLE ACTION BREVETE POCKET MODEL

Licensed Merchandise

Samuel Colt clearly recognized the importance of patent protection. In 1835 and 1836, he first patented his revolver in Europe and the United States. Colt continued to patent various aspects of the revolver around the world as new design techniques and features were developed. On several occasions, Colt took action against those who infringed upon his patent rights. In addition to legal action, Colt knew the best defense against infringement was making sure his revolvers were clearly marked and available in suitable quantities around the world. To meet the international demand for his arms, he opened a factory in London in 1852. Colt also worked with several international manufacturers in Belgium, Austria, and Russia to produce licensed versions of his revolvers.

Belgium seems to have produced the most copies of Colt's revolvers, both licensed and unlicensed. Colt secured patent protection in the country in 1849. His patents covered designs pertaining to the lock frame, the loading lever, and various other parts. Given his patents and the popularity of the revolver in Belgium, Colt granted several manufacturers licensing agreements. The manufacturers were furnished with parts provided by Colt's Hartford armory, and in exchange, Colt charged a fee for every revolver produced. The revolvers were stamped with the marking "Colt / Brevete" to guarantee their legality and quality. (*Brevete* is the French word for patented, and firearms made overseas under Colt's authorization were termed *Brevetes*.) Colt intended for all of the revolvers produced in Belgium to be sold and used within the country.

The Autry Collection contains an interesting revolver manufactured in Belgium with an undetermined relationship to Colt. The revolver does not have a serial number, but it is stamped "J. J. Rissack / Brevete." It is hammerless with a ring-lever trigger. The cylinder is roll engraved with a "Ranger and Indian" scene very similar to the one used on the Walker and Dragoon Models. Colt made a set of drawings circa 1850 that depict many of the features found on this revolver. The drawings could mean that the revolver was designed by Colt and manufactured by Jean-Jacques (J. J.) Rissack at Colt's request. More likely, given the lack of Colt markings, the drawings probably indicate that Colt believed that many of the features found on Rissack's revolver were in violation of his patent rights and Rissack was illegally using them. Colt may have made the drawings in case they were needed in taking legal action against Rissack.

The Rissack revolver is double action, making it different from every other revolver mass-produced by Colt during his lifetime. A single-action revolver requires the user to manually cock the hammer before the trigger can be used to fire the weapon. A double-action revolver, however, can be fired simply by pulling the trigger. A single-action revolver is more accurate and safer than its double-action counterpart. Colt personally denounced the double-action mechanism, but he was not averse to experimenting with it. He personally designed and manufactured at least one double-action revolver that was never entered into mass production. The Rissack revolver, if it was actually designed by Colt, would be a second example. If the Rissack revolver was merely an illegal copy, it proves that the designs and features found on Colt's revolvers were capable of working with a double-action mechanism.

The brass plate on the grip of this Model 1851
Navy was designed for use with a shoulder stock
device patented by Charles L. Holbrook and
Samuel W. Johnson in 1878. (87.118.15)

PRESENTATION MODEL 1851 NAVY WITH JOHNSON-HOLBROOK SHOULDER STOCK DEVICE

An Accurate Model

The Model 1849 Pocket was introduced in 1850, but early Colt collectors inaccurately labeled it. They also misidentified the Model 1851 Navy, as it too was introduced in 1850. The 1851 Navy was the most popular large-caliber percussion revolver produced by Colt's Patent Fire Arms Manufacturing Company. It was manufactured in .36 caliber with a six-shot cylinder and a seven-and-a-half-inch barrel. It weighed two pounds, 10 ounces. The 1851 Navy was a favorite of Samuel Colt, as evidenced by his frequent use of the model for presentation purposes. A rare photograph made in Berlin of Colt is the only known image of the inventor holding a revolver—an 1851 Navy. The model was also a favorite for engraving. A notable example in the Autry Collection is an engraved presentation revolver with a unique shoulder stock device.

Handguns were notoriously inaccurate because an individual's hand often trembled during use. Shoulder or extension stocks were added to handguns so they could be fired more accurately from the shoulder like a rifle. Shoulder stocks were inconvenient, however, because they were large, had to be carried separately, and took time to attach. Samuel W. Johnson and Charles L. Holbrook sought to design a device that solved all these problems. Their solution was a thin shoulder stock with a butt plate that was permanently attached to the revolver and slid into place through a specialized grip. The shoulder stock locked into place when drawn, and it was easily stored under the barrel and frame when not in use. The pair patented their invention in 1878.

Inventors in the 19th century were often ordinary people with no legal or technical expertise. It could be difficult for these individuals to describe their inventions using words or diagrams, so from 1790 to 1880 the United States Patent Office required all patent applicants to submit models. When Johnson and Holbrook submitted their patent application for a shoulder stock device in 1878, they submitted a written description of their invention along with a wooden model that clearly demonstrated how it worked. The model is in the Autry Collection, and the paper tag from the Patent Office is still attached. The invention was given patent number 202,946. The only known handgun with the specialized grip for the shoulder stock device is an engraved presentation Model 1851 Navy, serial number 13718, which is also in the Autry Collection. The specialized grip is inscribed "Pat. April 30th 1878."

Serial number 13718 features rich scroll engraving from the shop of Gustave Young. Manufactured in 1852, it has an inscription on the back strap that reads "Col. Charles L. Holbrook / From the Inventor." "From the Inventor" was one of several ways Colt commonly personalized presentation revolvers. Interestingly, Colt died in 1862, a full 16 years before the shoulder stock device was patented. Although the gap in time might be explained by Johnson and Holbrook waiting many years before patenting their device, it is far more likely that the revolver without the device was presented to Holbrook during Colt's lifetime. When the shoulder stock device was patented in 1878, Johnson and Holbrook probably chose to add the device to the finest revolver that was available to them, the 1851 Navy presented by Colt. Johnson and Holbrook may have hoped the presentation arm would help them sell the shoulder stock device to Colt's, but there is no evidence the device was ever mass-produced by Colt's or any other company.

Opposite:
Charles L. Holbrook and Samuel W. Johnson submitted this wooden patent model in 1878 for their "improvement in extension-stocks for pistols." (87.118.16)

Above:
Sliding through a customized grip, the Johnson-Holbrook shoulder stock device was designed for easy concealment and access. (87.118.16)

The most exclusive 19th-century percussion revolvers feature gold inlay, such as this Model 1851 Navy embellished by master engraver Gustave Young. (2012.2.5; the George Gamble Collection)

MODEL 1851 NAVY WITH GOLD INLAY

All that Glitters

Engraved presentation revolvers are rare, but an even more exclusive group is 19th-century gold-inlaid percussion revolvers. Exhibiting the highest quality and the finest craftsmanship, gold-inlaid revolvers were made almost exclusively for display at fairs and expositions. They were the star attraction at London's Crystal Palace Exhibition in 1851, New York's Exhibition of the Industry of All Nations in 1853, and Paris's Exposition Universelle in 1855. Personally commissioned by Samuel Colt, they were also used for the most important presentations to monarchy, politicians, and key military figures. It is estimated that approximately 25 to 30 gold-inlaid percussion revolvers were produced in the 19th century. A significant amount of these were the work of master engraver Gustave Young.

Born Gustave Jung in Berlin in 1827, Young began apprenticing in engraving and die cutting at the age of eight. Working with German longarms, he mastered the art of engraving prior to immigrating to the United States in 1846. He worked in the city of New York for several years, and in 1852, he moved to Hartford, Connecticut. Young quickly became the leading engraver for Colt's, a position he held until moving to Springfield, Massachusetts, in 1869 to become the chief engraver for Smith & Wesson. While in Hartford, Young also did contract work for other firearm manufacturers, such as Sharps Rifle Company, Winchester Repeating Arms Company, and Smith & Wesson. One of Young's first masterpieces at Colt's was a Model 1851 Navy, serial number 14332, which is now in the Autry Collection.

Clearly prepared as a showpiece, serial number 14332 features finely detailed embellishments on almost every surface of the revolver, including the barrel, frame, loading lever, hammer, and grip straps. Even the screws are embellished. The richly detailed decorative scrollwork is intricately intertwined with images of animals. Wolf heads are engraved on the butt strap, hammer, barrel, and both sides of the frame. The barrel is engraved with several eagle heads, the head of a dog, and serpents. A gargoyle is even engraved on the trigger guard. "Colts / Patent" is hand engraved on the left side of the frame. The brass grip straps are gold plated, and the top flat of the gold-plated back strap is engraved with an American eagle motif and a banner inscribed "E Pluribus Unum." The unique half-moon front site is made of silver-plated steel. The revolver is finished in high-gloss blue, and the grips are select walnut with a high-quality varnish. The most striking aspect of the revolver, however, is the gold inlay.

Crafted in 1852, serial number 14322 is believed to be the first gold-inlaid revolver embellished by Gustave Young. It is also the only known 19th-century percussion revolver featuring a gold-inlaid bust of Samuel Colt. The bust is on the left side of the barrel lug, and Colt is portrayed without a mustache in a style reminiscent of Roman portraiture. The right side of the barrel lug features a gold-inlaid scene of a Native American hunting buffalo on horseback. He is aiming his bow and arrow at a large buffalo to the left, while a smaller buffalo is to the right. The scene may have been taken from a George Catlin painting. The top of the barrel has a gold-inlaid address marking that reads "Address Saml Colt New York City," which is scripted within a gold-inlaid finial design that incorporates two serpents and an arrow. Two gold-inlaid bands are at the muzzle end of the barrel. Given its history, craftsmanship, and iconography, serial number 14322 is one of the most celebrated 1851 Navies ever manufactured.

Opposite:
The Model 1851 Navy features the only gold-inlaid bust of Samuel Colt on a 19th-century percussion revolver. (2012.2.5; the George Gamble Collection)

Above:
The barrel of the Model 1851 Navy has a gold-inlaid address marking accompanied by an elaborate gold-inlaid finial design featuring two intertwined serpents. (2012.2.5; the George Gamble Collection)

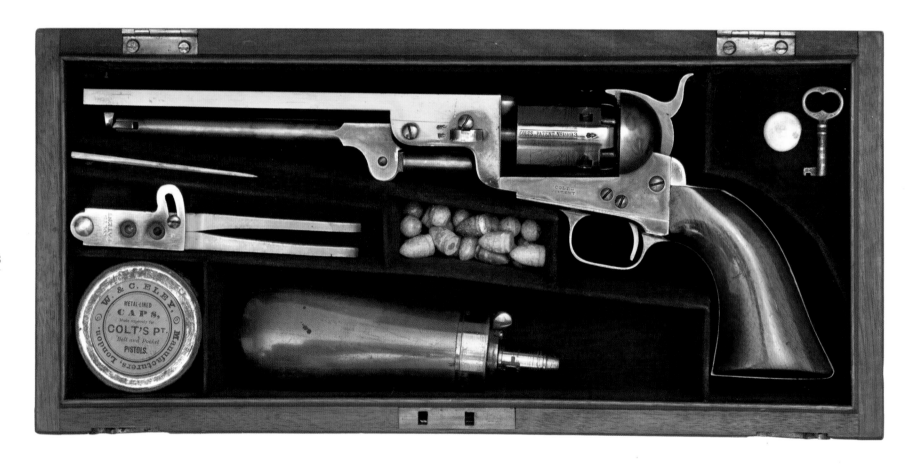

The London Model 1851 Navy, the last model manufactured overseas, was cased in oak or mahogany with a velvet or felt lining unique to the London armory. (87.118.17)

CASED LONDON MODEL 1851 NAVY

Coming Home

Established in 1852, Samuel Colt's London armory manufactured revolvers for several years. Smaller arms were more successful in Great Britain, so the London armory focused almost exclusively on the Model 1849 Pocket and the Model 1851 Navy, although a few hundred Dragoons were also produced. While the majority of the revolvers were manufactured entirely in London, a small portion used Hartford-made parts that were finished in London. As a result, some London arms have a Hartford address and some Hartford arms actually have a London address. An excellent example of a revolver with Hartford parts finished in London is the 1851 Navy, serial number 1993, in the Autry Collection. Manufactured in 1853, the revolver is .36 caliber with a seven-and-a-half-inch octagonal barrel and walnut grips. It features an English cased set with a velvet lining known to collectors as "the English." The bag-type flask was made for Colt's by James Dixon & Sons, a prominent British manufacturer.

The 1851 Navies manufactured in London featured the same roll-engraved cylinder scene as the revolvers manufactured in Hartford. The "Naval Engagement" scene depicted a battle that took place in the Gulf of Mexico on May 16, 1843, between the Republic of Texas and Mexico. Interestingly, the Texas Navy was armed with Colt revolvers during the fight, but they were never close enough to their Mexican adversaries to actually use them. The scene was used on the 1851 Navy, the Model 1860 Army, the Model 1861 Navy, and the Model 1871–72 Open Top Frontier. The scene was the work of professional siderographer Waterman Lilly Ormsby. Siderography is the art of engraving on steel plates, a profession commonly associated with the production of bank notes.

With the Crimean War raging, the British government ordered approximately 23,000 revolvers from the London armory in 1854 and 1855. The revolver was so important to the British military that Colt was called to testify during the war before a Select Committee on Small Arms appointed by the House of Commons. Unfortunately for Colt's company, additional orders from the British government ceased with the end of hostilities in 1856. Significant orders from the civilian market were also limited, due in part to increased pressure from British competitors. As the London armory was beginning to slow down, Colt's Hartford armory was increasing in physical size and productivity. Faced with few options, Colt closed the London armory in 1857. Approximately 53,700 revolvers were manufactured in London from 1853 to 1857. The total included 700 Dragoons, commonly called the Hartford English Dragoon; 11,000 London 1849 Pockets; and 42,000 London 1851 Navies. Ironically, despite the short duration of the London factory, the British government was the largest single buyer of Colt revolvers prior to the outbreak of the American Civil War.

Although the armory closed, Colt's maintained a presence in London for several decades. A shop remained open until 1860 for minor repairs and the purchase of replacement parts. It closed when Colt ordered all parts and finished revolvers returned to America in anticipation of increased orders given the impending hostilities between the American states. A dedicated sales office remained open in London until 1912. As a result, a few revolvers beyond the London 1851 Navy series are known to exist with a London barrel address. These revolvers were manufactured in Hartford, but a London barrel address was used in hopes of making them more appealing to a European market. Despite the closing of the London armory, sales in Europe and Asia continued to be an important aspect of Colt's success.

Samuel Colt presented E. K. Root with a cased Model 1851 Navy for his contributions to the Colt armory and the success of the revolver. (2012.2.6; the George Gamble Collection)

COLT SUPERINTENDENT E. K. ROOT'S CASED PRESENTATION MODEL 1851 NAVY

The American System of Manufacturing

Samuel Colt initially leased several different buildings to manufacture his revolvers when he returned to Hartford in 1847. When his business was firmly established, he decided to build one of the largest armories in the world. In 1851, he began purchasing land in the southeast corner of Hartford along the Connecticut River. The land was prone to flood, so it was unimproved and cheap. Colt eventually acquired 250 acres, and he built a dike nearly two miles long to control the flooding. Construction of the armory commenced in 1854, and it was completed the following year. Colt marked the occasion by reorganizing his business and officially incorporating it as Colt's Patent Fire Arms Manufacturing Company. Unlike the Paterson venture, Colt controlled almost every share. The only exceptions were a few shares that were distributed symbolically to company executives, including E. K. Root.

Root was pivotal in the layout of the armory and the machines that filled it. One of the greatest mechanical engineers of his generation, Root oversaw all aspects of the armory's manufacturing operations, allowing Colt to focus on business and promotion. The armory was one of the most mechanized and efficient factories in the United States because of Root. It was also one of the most beautiful. The four main structures were made of brick and Portland stone, a type of limestone used in the construction of St. Paul's Cathedral and Buckingham Palace. The main factory building was capped with an onion-shaped blue dome supported by columns and adorned with a bronze Rampant Colt sculpture. The armory was a defining landmark in the Hartford skyline.

A notable aspect of armory operations was the use of interchangeable parts. The notion of manufacturing identical or interchangeable parts that could be assembled with little or no fitting grew out of firearm manufacturing. Firearms traditionally were made one at a time by skilled gunsmiths, but in the late 18th century, a French general suggested that muskets could be manufactured faster and cheaper if all of the parts were standardized. American firearm manufacturers such as Colt seized upon the idea, making them key players in what came to be known as the American System of Manufacture. Gauges were an integral part of the process that produced interchangeable parts. Surviving examples of these gauges are of greater rarity than the firearms they served to check for precision machining and manufacture. Two examples from the Colt armory are in the Autry Collection. Like every other aspect of manufacturing at Colt's, the machinery and gauges were designed by E. K. Root.

Root temporarily resigned from Colt's in 1857, and Colt recognized his contributions with a presentation virtually unrivaled in the history of the company. Root was presented with a full line of Colt revolvers. The set included a Third Model Dragoon, a Model 1849 Pocket, a Model 1851 Navy, a Model 1855 Sidehammer Pocket, and a Model 1855 Revolving Rifle. The Dragoon and the 1851 Navy are part of the Autry Collection. The 1851 Navy, serial number 55447, was opulently embellished by Gustave Young and featured detailed scrollwork throughout. An inscription on the case reads "Presented to / E. K. Root / by Col. Saml Colt / Prest. Colts Pt. F. A. Mfg Co. / May 16th 1857." The rosewood case features a glass lid and an exceptionally rare mirrored top. (Root's presentation Dragoon in the Autry Collection also features a mirrored top.) Root's contributions and significance to the company were further recognized when he was named the second president of Colt's when Samuel Colt passed away in 1862. Root served admirably until his own passing in 1865.

11 – P – 14

Above:
E. K. Root was responsible for designing the state-of-the-art machinery and gauges that were used to manufacture the revolver. (85.1.688; acquisition made possible in part by John E. Bianchi Jr.)

Opposite:
Gauges from the Colt armory are important artifacts in the history of the American Industrial Revolution. (85.1.690; acquisition made possible in part by John E. Bianchi Jr.)

Samuel Colt presented a unique Model 1851 Navy to Kansas Territorial Governor Robert J. Walker at a volatile time in American history. (87.56.3)

KANSAS TERRITORIAL GOVERNOR ROBERT J. WALKER'S PRESENTATION MODEL 1851 NAVY

Civil Unrest

Samuel Colt used presentation revolvers as powerful advertising and marketing tools throughout his lifetime. During the brief tenure of the Patent Arms Manufacturing Company, Colt's affinity for giving away revolvers infuriated corporate officers and shareholders. When Colt returned to gunmaking with the introduction of the Walker Model in 1847, he even went so far as to manufacture an additional 100 revolvers for the sole purpose of distributing them to influential individuals who could provide support either directly through sales or indirectly through word of mouth. As the owner and president of Colt's Patent Fire Arms Manufacturing Company, Colt continued to use presentation revolvers as a way to promote himself and his company. A presentation revolver could be a way of saying thank you, or it could be used as an enticement for future assistance. A notable example of both is the Model 1851 Navy presented to Robert J. Walker in 1857.

Politically active his entire life, Walker served in the United States Senate from 1835 to 1845. After helping James K. Polk get elected president in 1844, Walker was appointed Secretary of the Treasury, serving from 1845 to 1849. During that time, Walker defended free trade, fought for an independent treasury, established a network of warehouses to handle imports, and was instrumental in the establishment of the Department of the Interior in 1849. A staunch supporter of American expansionism, Walker was secretary during the Mexican-American War. He played a pivotal role in the financing of the conflict. Walker's duties as secretary also brought him in contact with Samuel Colt. In 1845, prior to Colt's return to gunmaking after the failure of the Patent Arms Mfg. Co., Walker entered into an agreement with Colt for the government's purchase of Colt's waterproof powder cartridges. After leaving the cabinet, Walker practiced law.

James Buchanan was elected president in 1856, and he appointed Walker as territorial governor of Kansas. Walker became governor at a volatile time for the territory and the nation. In the 1850s, the frontier included areas such as the Kansas Territory and border towns in the state of Missouri. The issue of slavery and whether or not it should be allowed in the Kansas Territory was hotly debated, which often led to violence. With so many people losing their lives, prominent newspaper editor Horace Greeley dubbed the area "Bleeding Kansas." As governor, Walker supported the right of the citizens of the territory to choose whether or not slavery should be allowed, a stance that managed to anger both sides. In 1857, at the height of the violence, Colt presented an 1851 Navy, serial number 59492, to Walker. The revolver is now part of the Autry Collection.

The presentation revolver is finely engraved, with coverage on the barrel, loading lever, wedge, frame, hammer, grip straps, and screws. The scrollwork features an eagle's head on the left side of the barrel lug and a gargoyle on the right side of the frame. The engraving appears to be from the shop of Gustave Young. The most intriguing aspect of the revolver is the inscription. Cut on the inside flat of the trigger guard strap, the inscription reads "Col. Colt's Compliments." Both the location and the phrasing are unique. No other presentation revolver from Colt is known to have an inscription in that location, and that exact phrase is not used on any other presentation revolver. Colt likely presented the revolver to Walker in appreciation for his previous support, and given the explosive situation in Kansas, Colt probably hoped for future patronage. Due to the timing of the presentation, the revolver is often referred to as the "Bleeding Kansas Colt."

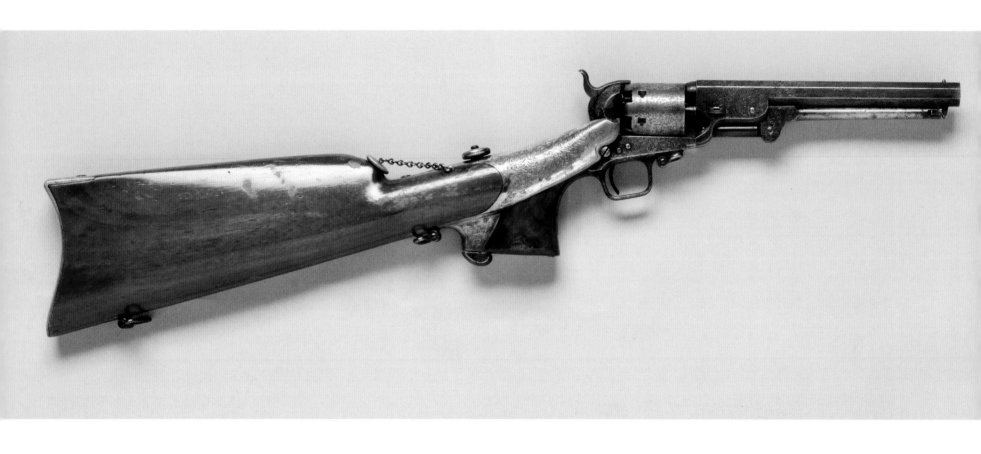

A shoulder stock was designed to improve the accuracy of a revolver, and the engraved stock on this Model 1851 Navy has a built-in canteen. (87.118.41)

MODEL 1851 NAVY WITH CANTEEN SHOULDER STOCK

Taking Stock

Colt's Patent Fire Arms Manufacturing Company introduced attachable shoulder stocks or carbine breeches as a way to improve the accuracy of a revolver. With a stock, a revolver could be fired from the shoulder like a rifle. Samuel Colt credited Jefferson Davis, secretary of war under President Franklin Pierce and later president of the Confederate States of America, with the concept of the attachable shoulder stock. In reality, as Davis himself admitted, the attachable shoulder stock existed in Europe prior to its introduction in America. Colt's produced three different varieties of shoulder stocks, with the variations a result of how the stock attached to the revolver. Shoulder stocks were available for the Third Model Dragoon, the Model 1851 Navy, the Model 1860 Army, and the Model 1861 Navy.

In 1859, Colt personally patented improvements to the shoulder stock, including a distinct variation that included a built-in canteen. Available on all three variations of the shoulder stock, the canteen was accessed by a plug that was secured to the stock by a chain. Granted patent number 22,627, Colt noted that the "nature of my invention consists in converting the butt of the stock into a reservoir having a suitable opening and stopper, and serving, generally, the purposes of a canteen." The canteen could carry water or other liquids. It was added by splitting the stock, inserting the canteen, and gluing the stock back together along the seam. The canteen shoulder stock was one of many designs—including accessories—that Colt patented during his lifetime.

The rarest canteen shoulder stocks are those with engraving. Only about five engraved Model 1851 Navies with matching engraved shoulder stocks are known to exist. The example in the Autry Collection was manufactured in 1857 and both the revolver and stock have the serial number 68220. A dot accompanying the serial number indicated that the revolver and stock were both intended for special finish, handling, and engraving, thus extreme care should be taken at all times. The inclusion of the dot on the butt plate and stock yoke is exceptionally rare. The revolver is .36 caliber with a seven-and-five-eighths-inch barrel. It features floral scroll engraving and border motifs on all of the major parts, including the barrel, loading lever, frame, and grip straps. The hammer, wedge, and screws are also embellished. A unique snake motif appears on the left side of the barrel lug. The back strap and trigger guard strap are made of silver-plated steel. The grips are deluxe select walnut.

The shoulder stock, referred to as a Third Type or Model, is equally impressive. It has engraving on the yoke, stock screws, canteen plug, and butt plate that matches the revolver. The engraving on both the revolver and stock is from the shop of Gustave Young. The stock is made of varnished walnut, and some of the original gold wash is still visible on the engraved yoke. The stock mounts are silver plated, and the deluxe knurling on the bottom of the stock yoke clamp appears to have been done by hand. The stock attaches to the revolver by sliding over the grip and engaging slots cut into the bottom of the recoil shield and the back strap. The stock is secured by tightening a round nut on the top of the yoke to fully engage a clamp onto the butt strap. To help carry the revolver when the stock is attached, sling swivels are located on the trigger guard, the lower tang of the stock, and on the toe of the stock.

Months before the outbreak of the Civil War, Samuel Colt presented Alabama Governor Andrew B. Moore with a Model 1851 Navy in hopes of encouraging future orders. (87.118.104)

ALABAMA GOVERNOR ANDREW B. MOORE'S PRESENTATION MODEL 1851 NAVY

The Southern Cause

The Mexican-American War revived Samuel Colt's fortunes as a gunmaker, but it also renewed the debate over slavery in America. Four general proposals dominated the debate over slavery in the West prior to the American conflict with Mexico. Northern abolitionists pushed for outright exclusion, while Southern slaveholders demanded full recognition of the right to own slaves anywhere in the United States and its territories. Somewhere between these two extremes was the notion of extending the Missouri Compromise Line, an imaginary boundary north of which was free and south of which was slave, and the idea of popular sovereignty, allowing individual state voters the right to choose.

In 1846, as America prepared for war with Mexico, a bill was introduced in Congress calling for a complete ban on slavery in any areas that might be acquired from Mexico either through treaty or conquest. The bill passed the House, but was rejected in the Senate. After the war, the Compromise of 1850, a package of several bills, was passed. It called for California to enter the Union as a free state, with voters in New Mexico and Utah given the right to decide for themselves through elections. The compromise also outlawed slavery in Washington, D.C., and a stronger Fugitive Slave Act was passed. Proponents on both sides of the debate were disappointed with the results, but the compromise managed to diffuse the situation temporarily. A decade later, the Civil War, the bloodiest conflict in American history, ultimately resolved the issue permanently.

Colt's personal views on slavery have been hotly debated. He was a Democrat, but experts differ over what that actually meant. Some claim Colt was a Southern sympathizer who did all he could to support the South and slavery. Others argue that Colt was strongly opposed to slavery and he only supported the Democratic Party because he feared Republican rule would lead to the dissolution of the Union. Regardless of his politics, Colt recognized early on that hostilities between the North and South were likely inevitable. Even if war could be avoided, Colt correctly assumed that both sides would want to stockpile arms as a precaution. Colt knew that either outcome would result in substantial profits for his company. In light of the situation, Colt made sure that his armory was operating at full capacity. He also actively courted sales from the North and the South. To further induce sales from the South, Colt strongly considered building an armory in Virginia or Georgia.

Colt also employed his greatest promotional tool, the gifting of presentation revolvers. In December 1860, Colt presented a Model 1851 Navy, serial number 95844, to Alabama Governor Andrew B. Moore. It is the only known presentation revolver given to a Southern governor by Colt. The revolver is inscribed "Andrew B. Moore, Gov. of Alabama / with Compliments of Col. Colt." Like other Southern governors, Moore was shopping for firearms in preparation for hostilities with the United States government. Moore ultimately placed and received an order for 72 Model 1851 Navies in January 1861. Some of the revolvers Colt sent to the South actually shipped after the fall of Fort Sumter in South Carolina in April 1861. Colt was chastised for these shipments, but he accurately pointed out that they were made legally prior to an official declaration of war that outlawed such activities. Moore's presentation revolver, a unique and important artifact in American history, is now part of the Autry Collection.

The favorite firearm of gunslinger James Butler
"Wild Bill" Hickok was a Model 1851 Navy with
ivory grips. (87.54.1)

GUNSLINGER JAMES BUTLER "WILD BILL" HICKOK'S PRESENTATION MODEL 1851 NAVY

A Combination of Fact and Fiction

James Butler "Wild Bill" Hickok was one of the most iconic figures in the history of the American West. And like the region itself, the story of Hickok's life is a combination of fact and fiction. Countless books and articles have been written about Hickok, with each author claiming to have uncovered the true story. Unfortunately, even the most exhaustive and detailed biographies rely on sources that are clearly embellished, if not downright wrong. Authors also seem to interject their own beliefs and prejudices about Hickok into their work, be it admiration or disdain. Because so much misinformation has been published over the years, it may be impossible to know the exact details of Hickok's life.

Hickok's speed and accuracy with a revolver was unquestionable. Unlike most gunmen, Hickok commonly wore his revolvers in open-top holsters with the butts facing outward. The revolvers were drawn underhand and spun forward in what is commonly referred to as the Plains-draw. The guns could also be drawn across the body. Either way, Hickok was exceptionally fast on the draw and even faster on the trigger. It was reported that he was accurate with his revolvers at distances up to 200 yards, but Hickok's greatest feat of marksmanship was his ability to shoot accurately at close range while under fire. Some estimates have him killing a few dozen men, but recent scholarship has reduced that number to about six or seven. Some were fair fights; others were not.

Hickok earned a reputation across the West as a frontier scout, including time with George Armstrong Custer's Seventh Cavalry, and as a law-enforcement officer in Kansas. He became a national figure when Colonel George Ward Nichols published an article in the February 1867 issue of *Harper's New Monthly Magazine* championing his exploits, many of which were embellished, during the Civil War. Hickok added to his own notoriety through shooting exhibitions and repeated tellings of his many—again highly embellished—accomplishments. He even took to the stage, appearing alongside William F. "Buffalo Bill" Cody in the play *The Scouts of the Plains* in 1873. Hickok's violent death in Deadwood in the Dakota Territory in 1876 cemented his mythic status. Shot in the back of the head while playing poker, the cards he was holding, a pair of black aces and eights, came to be known as the dead man's hand.

It is known through contemporary accounts and period photographs that Hickok often carried a pair of Model 1851 Navies with ivory grips. He probably owned several pairs during his lifetime, and serial number 138813IE in the Autry Collection may have been one of them. The serial number on the revolver's cylinder is actually 138824, but given the fact that it is an exact match, the revolver was likely one of a pair. Manufactured in 1863, the revolver features scroll and border engraving in the style of Gustave Young on the barrel, frame, cylinder, hammer, recoil shield, trigger guard, loading lever, and back strap. The ivory grips have an American eagle motif relief carved on the left side with a banner reading "Liberty." The back strap also features the inscription "J. B. Hickok, 1869." The date has led many experts to conclude that the revolver was presented to Hickok upon his election as sheriff of Ellis County, Kansas, which took place in August of that year. Hickok was originally misspelled on the inscription, and at some point, it was corrected. The change has caused some to question the revolver's authenticity, although it has compelling provenance.

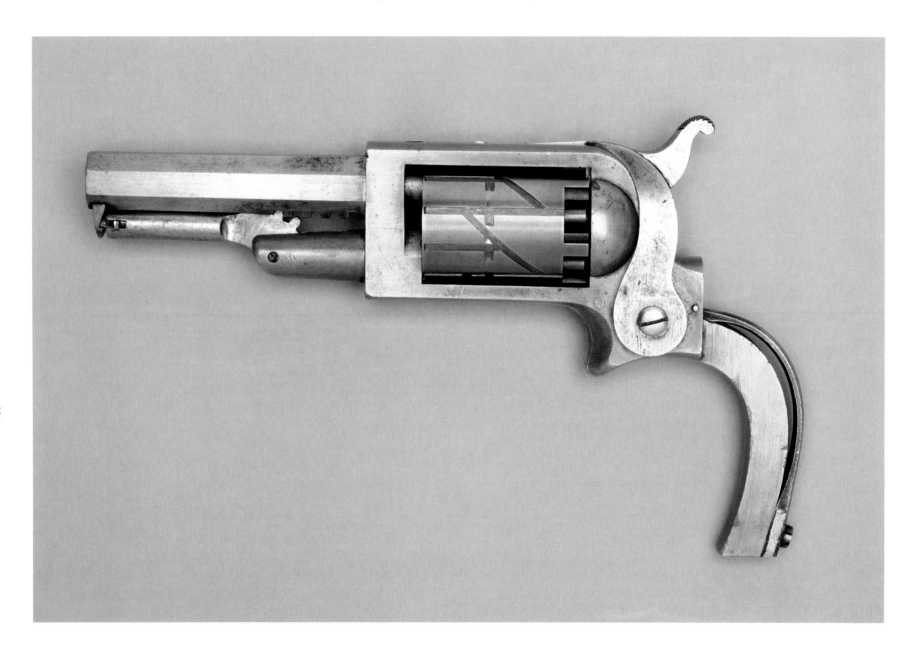

The first Colt revolver mass-produced with a solid-frame design was the Model 1855 Sidehammer Pocket. (87.118.13)

EXPERIMENTAL PROTOTYPE MODEL 1855 SIDEHAMMER POCKET

A Solid Frame

The year 1855 was a pivotal moment in the history of Colt's Patent Fire Arms Manufacturing Company. After several years of planning and construction, the new armory in Hartford along the Connecticut River was finally operational. Colt incorporated his thriving business, and he owned virtually every share. He also introduced a new model that year that was manufactured exclusively at the new armory. Designated the Model 1855 Sidehammer Pocket, the model addressed a serious deficiency in the design of the frame that was used on all Colt's previous revolvers. The new design was crucial in the evolution and long-term success of the revolver, but the Sidehammer actually turned out to be the least successful model introduced by the company during Colt's lifetime.

All of the revolvers manufactured by the Patent Arms Manufacturing Company and Colt's Patent Fire Arms Manufacturing Company prior to 1855 had an open-top frame. Open-top frames were made up of several pieces that were secured together by a steel wedge through a slot in the side of the barrel that engaged the axis on which the cylinder revolved. The open-top frame placed serious stress on the cylinder pin, and it led to loose parts that could cause the gun to misfire. Colt was aware of the design's imperfections, especially when compared to a solid frame. He nevertheless continued to use the open-top design because it allowed for quick disassembly for maintenance and cylinders could be exchanged rather easily for reloading. While the notion of using a solid frame dated all the way back to Colt's first prototypes, a solid-frame model was not mass-produced until the Sidehammer series.

Colt worked with E. K. Root, his superintendent and chief engineer, to perfect a model using a solid frame. Both men were likely inspired by the obvious deficiencies of the open-top frame and the success of solid-frame handguns in Europe. Unveiled in 1855, the Sidehammer had a solid frame that consisted of a single piece, with the cylinder pin or axis removable through the rear of the frame. The hammer was mounted on the right side of the frame, hence the name Sidehammer. The solid frame minimized the number of parts that could come loose, and in that respect, it was more reliable. In reality, the Sidehammer was structurally weak, as evidenced by the fact that it was only produced in a smaller pocket size. The design nevertheless was also used for a complete line of revolving longarms.

The solid-frame construction used on the Sidehammer is clearly evident in an experimental prototype, serial number 6, in the Autry Collection. Manufactured in 1855, the revolver is one of about five prototypes known to exist documenting the development of the Sidehammer series. The frame is made of brass, while the barrel, hammer, and cylinder are made of steel. The steel parts are "in the white" or unfinished. The top of the hammer features a bar that engages the zigzag grooves on the cylinder, causing it to rotate. The prototype is different from the Sidehammers that were mass-produced in several ways. It lacks a front or rear sight, the bottom of the frame is much more rectangular, and the hammer is on the left side. Although Colt's temporarily abandoned the solid frame after the Sidehammer series, it later reemerged and eventually became standard on all Colt revolvers.

Samuel Colt only presented a handful of Model 1855 Sidehammer Pockets with grips made from the famed Charter Oak. (2011.78.1; the George Gamble Collection)

COLT DISTRIBUTOR J. I. SPIES'S CASED PRESENTATION MODEL 1855 SIDEHAMMER POCKET WITH CHARTER OAK GRIPS

A Symbol of Independence

Samuel Colt was willing to use any opportunity to promote his revolvers. A noteworthy example was his exploitation of Connecticut's famed Charter Oak, a large white oak tree that stood in Hartford for several hundred years. The tree's notoriety dates to Connecticut's struggle for freedom from dictatorial British rule. In 1639, the colony of Connecticut adopted a group of laws that established, among other things, that the consent to govern rests with the people. The formal document produced, the Fundamental Orders of 1639, has been championed by some as the first written constitution in the Western world and the beginning of American democracy. The document's primacy led the Connecticut State Assembly to officially declare Connecticut the "Constitution State" in 1959.

In 1662, Charles II granted the colony a new royal charter, which gave it more autonomy and freedom than any of the other American colonies. When James II succeeded Charles II to the British throne, he sought to consolidate his authority over the American colonies in part by demanding the dissolution of Connecticut's independent government. The royal governor to the region arrived in Hartford in October 1687, insisting upon the return of the physical charter housed in the city. According to tradition, a heated debate ensued, and Captain Joseph Wadsworth used the opportunity to hide the charter safely in the hollow of the large white oak tree. Despite questions of the story's validity, the tree was known thereafter as the Charter Oak, a symbol of independence and democracy. The legend of the tree was passed down to generations of Connecticut residents, and during the American Revolution, it became a story of national significance.

A Hartford resident, Colt recognized the significance of the Charter Oak. Viewing it as much more than a notable local landmark, Colt believed that the tree, like his armory, was an important contribution to American exceptionalism and prosperity. In recognition of the tree's significance, Colt named the social and educational center of his industrial empire Charter Oak Hall. The brick structure was 100 feet long and four stories tall. Whereas the main factory building was a testament to manufacturing,

Charter Oak Hall was a symbol of social progress and Colt's benevolence toward his workers. A rare invitation to the inauguration of the hall on May 6, 1856, is part of the Autry Collection. Colt and the other citizens of Hartford were horrified a few months later when the Charter Oak was toppled in a violent storm on August 21, 1856. Relics were sought, and Isaac W. Stuart, the individual upon whose land the tree stood, gave pieces of the Charter Oak to worthy recipients.

Colt used some of the wood that he received to make grips for a small group of special presentation revolvers. These exotic firearms were intended to recognize individuals essential to the success of Colt's company. Known as "the Allies," the group included major American distributors of Colt firearms. All of the presentation revolvers with Charter Oak grips were Model 1855 Sidehammer Pockets, and the back straps testified to their authenticity. Serial number 5886 in the Autry Collection, manufactured in 1856, has an inscription that reads "J. I. Spies from the Inventor / Charter Oak Stock / From I. W. Stuart." The revolver has a rich blue finish and is engraved in a Gustave Young style on the barrel, frame, and hammer. Other Colt-related objects were made from the Charter Oak, including a cane in the Autry Collection with an eagle-head handle inscribed "To Col. I. H. Wright / From the Democrats of Colts Armory / Apr. 2d, 1860 / Charter Oak."

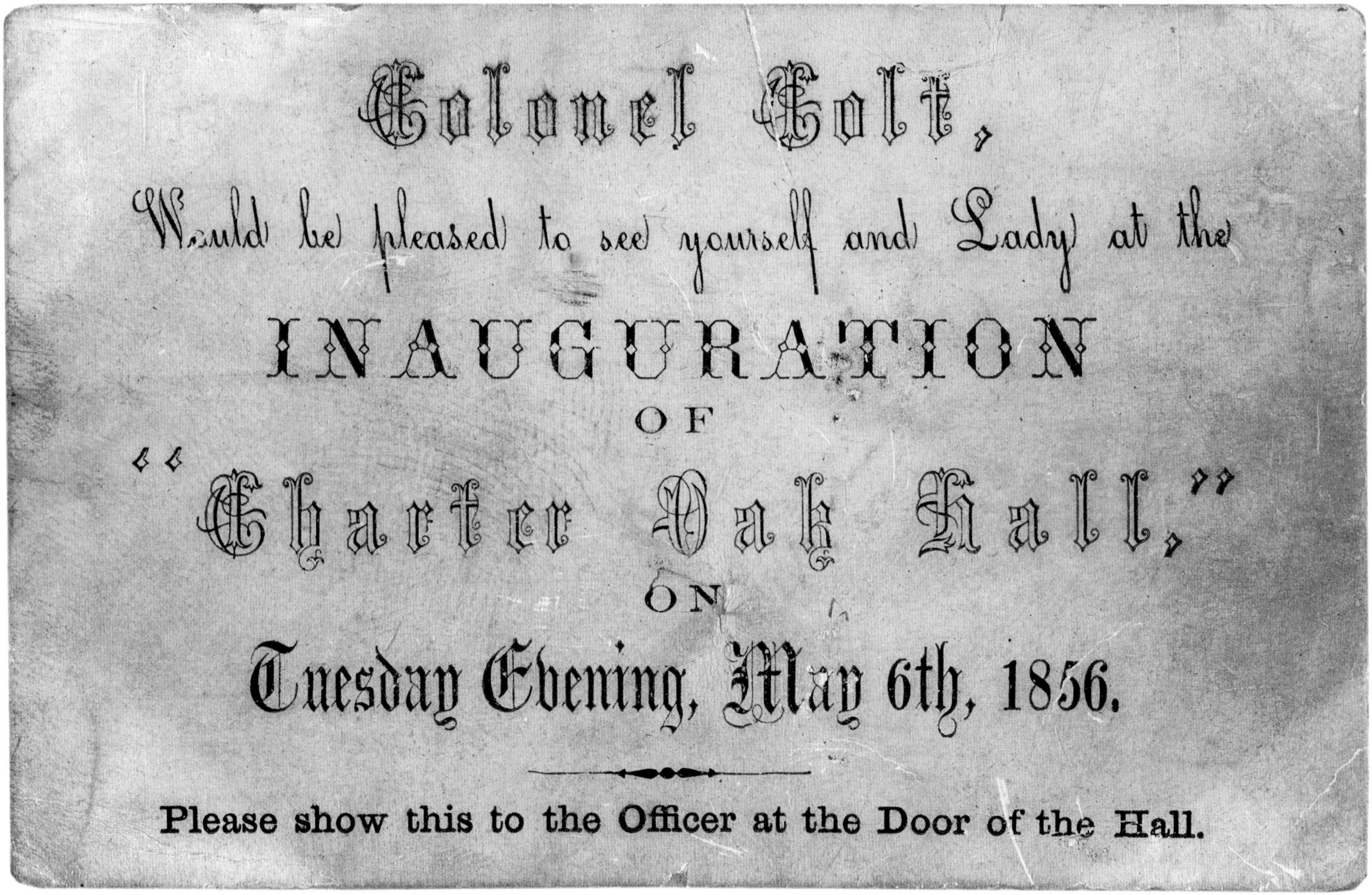

Colonel Colt,

Would be pleased to see yourself and Lady at the

INAUGURATION

OF

"Charter Oak Hall,"

ON

Tuesday Evening, May 6th, 1856.

———

Please show this to the Officer at the Door of the Hall.

Opposite:
Construction on Colt's Charter Oak Hall, named in honor of Connecticut's famed tree, was completed in 1856, and surviving invitations to its inauguration are exceptionally rare. (2011.78.25; the George Gamble Collection)

Right:
Democrats employed at Colt's armory presented this cane made from relics of the Charter Oak in April 1860 to Colonel Isaac Hull Wright, a prominent military officer and politician. (2011.78.19; the George Gamble Collection)

Cutaways were produced only for a few models, and the most extensive cutaway percussion revolver is this Model 1855 Sidehammer Pocket. (87.118.20)

CUTAWAY MODEL 1855 SIDEHAMMER POCKET

Mechanics and Special Features

The most noticeable difference between the Model 1855 Sidehammer Pocket and the previous revolvers produced by Colt's Patent Fire Arms Manufacturing Company was the solid frame. On close inspection, a significant amount of other differences were evident. The Sidehammer was the first Colt revolver to employ a creeping loading lever that worked on a ratchet, as opposed to being hinged to the frame. The Sidehammer was the first and only revolver manufactured at the Hartford armory that did not have a trigger guard. The working parts of the Sidehammer's lock operated in the opposite direction than previous Colt revolvers. The model was unique in the fact that it was offered in two calibers, .265 (commonly known as .28) and .31. The Sidehammer was also the first and only design that was adapted for use on handguns and longarms.

The cutaway Sidehammer in the Autry Collection, serial number 6475, clearly reveals many of these differences. Serial number 6475 is actually the most extensive cutaway percussion revolver ever produced by Colt's. Manufactured in 1856, it is superbly machined to reveal the inner workings of the barrel, rammer, barrel lug, frame, cylinder, and grips. The chambers in the cylinder received special attention. One chamber is slightly machined, another is machined approximately in half, and two other chambers are cut into entirely. Serial number 6475 is the only cutaway known to have a cartridge in the chamber. The frame was never finished or left "in the white." A dot accompanying the serial number on the butt indicated that the revolver received special treatment throughout its manufacture. Like other cutaway arms, serial number 6475 was used to demonstrate mechanics and special features, especially relevant on this revolutionary model.

Countless variations existed within the Sidehammer series, with seven distinct models identified. Noticeable differences included the shape of the frame and where the barrel entered the frame. Round and octagonal barrels were available with lengths ranging from three and a half inches to four and a half inches. Cylinders were either round or fluted. Round cylinders featured either the "Stagecoach Holdup" scene or a scene depicting a fight between a settler and a Native American. The .265-caliber Sidehammer was manufactured from 1855 to 1861, while the .31 caliber was produced from 1860 to 1870. Both were numbered in their own serial number range with approximately 28,000 manufactured in .265 caliber and 14,000 in .31 caliber. Complaints about the model's small caliber and problems with the cylinder pin led to slow sales.

The Sidehammer series has been called several different names. When introduced in 1855, Samuel Colt referred to it as the "New Model" or the "New Model Pocket Pistol." Collectors refer to it as the "Sidehammer," the "Model 1855," or even the "Root Model." The term "Root Model" was used because a key American patent relating to the Sidehammer series, number 13,999, was granted to E. K. Root in 1855. This was one of the most significant American patents associated with Colt's that incorporated a solid frame, and it is stamped on the barrel of some of the Sidehammer series. Nevertheless, it is important to note that Colt personally designed solid-frame revolvers prior to 1855. The revolvers were not mass-produced, but Colt was issued a few patents related to the solid-frame design prior to Root. Colt was also responsible for many of the subsequent American patents related to the Sidehammer series. As a result, it is somewhat inaccurate to refer to the Sidehammer as the "Root Model," as Colt was intricately involved in its design.

With the advent of the Sidehammer series, Samuel Colt sought to introduce a variety of revolving longarms, including the Model 1855 Half Stock Revolving Sporting Rifle. (87.118.131)

MODEL 1855 HALF STOCK REVOLVING SPORTING RIFLE

A Complete Line

Samuel Colt was one of the most successful firearm manufacturers in history by 1855. His company dominated the handgun market, and it was home to the largest private armory in the United States. Colt was also one of the richest and most famous men in America, and his name was known around the world. For Colt, however, there was still more to accomplish. From his first attempt at mass production, he sought to introduce a complete line of firearms. This included handguns, rifles, carbines, muskets, and shotguns. The Patent Arms Manufacturing Company produced a full line, but the longarms were never successful, despite Colt's repeated attempts to promote them. With the success of his second company, Colt sought to reintroduce revolving longarms.

Experimental prototypes were produced using various designs, but Colt finally embarked on the mass production of revolving longarms with the solid-frame design of the Model 1855 Sidehammer. The revolving longarms featured the side-mounted hammer, the creeping loading lever, and the removable cylinder pin found on the Sidehammer revolving handguns. Introduced circa 1856, Sidehammer revolving longarms were manufactured in rifle, carbine, musket, and shotgun variations. The revolving rifle was subdivided further into distinct models. Major differences existed among the various revolving longarms, including different calibers, barrel lengths, and shot capacities. From circa 1856 to 1864, approximately 18,300 revolving longarms were manufactured.

The revolving longarm that saw the most use in the American West was probably the Model 1855 Half Stock Revolving Sporting Rifle, arguably the most advanced of all of Colt's revolving longarm line. It was one of many tools used by mountain men, trappers, and hunters on the frontier. The rifle was also carried by some of the United States Cavalry stationed in the region. Approximately 1,500 Half Stock rifles were manufactured. The example in the Autry Collection, serial number 1340, is one of the most deluxe and exotic Colt longarms ever made. Manufactured circa 1863, it features double-set triggers for target shooting. The custom trigger guard

is larger than average, as is the 31¼-inch barrel. The special-order, select walnut stocks have a checkered wrist. The hammer is offset to allow for the tubular scope sight that is attached with special mounts on the front and rear of the barrel. The scope, which was used for sighting and not magnification, features rare Colt markings. Instead of the standard gutta-percha ramrod, serial number 1340 includes a hickory ramrod and a set of extension rods inside the butt stock. The more standard features include its .36 caliber and six-shot cylinder.

Several factors led to slow sales for Colt's revolving longarms, including gas leakages, multiple discharges, and mechanical failures. Significant competition also emerged from breech-loading repeating longarms made by other companies that employed the new metallic cartridge. Despite Colt's best efforts, revolving longarms once again proved to be a failure. Production on revolving longarms officially ended when the Colt armory was ravaged by fire in February 1864. The Sidehammers were the last revolving longarms manufactured by the company. (Several models of multishot cartridge longarms were introduced after Samuel Colt's death, but they were not revolvers.) The entire Sidehammer series, including handguns and longarms, represented one of the biggest failures for Colt since the closing of the Paterson armory.

Samuel Colt presented a pair of inscribed
Model 1860 Armies cased with an attachable
shoulder stock to his friend and supporter
Colonel Charles Augustus May. (2012.2.7;
the George Gamble Collection)

COLONEL CHARLES A. MAY'S CASED PRESENTATION MODEL 1860 ARMY PAIR WITH SHOULDER STOCK

From Colonel Colt

Colonel Charles Augustus May was one of Samuel Colt's closest friends and biggest supporters. Born into an affluent family, May joined the United States Army in 1836 and was assigned to the Second Regiment of Dragoons. He first made a name for himself when he aided in the capture of King Philip, one of the Seminole's key chieftains, while fighting in Florida during the Second Seminole War. His efforts earned him a promotion to captain. May was introduced to Colt during the war when the struggling gunmaker personally traveled to Florida to promote his revolvers. May had the opportunity to use Colt's revolving rifle in service, and he found it rather effective.

May became a national hero with his exploits in the Mexican-American War. On May 9, 1846, American troops under the command of Brigadier General Zachary Taylor faced fierce opposition from Mexican forces at the Battle of Resaca de la Palma. May and his Second Regiment of Dragoons were ordered to take a key Mexican artillery battery that was halting the American advance. May reportedly shouted, "Remember your regiment and follow your orders," as he led his men into action. Exactly what happened next is hotly debated. According to official government reports, May and his men "gallantly and effectually executed" their orders and took the battery. Critics, however, contend that May's charge was ineffective and poorly led. They argue that the battery was not actually taken and may have even been abandoned by the time May and his men arrived.

The aftermath of the charge is also a source of controversy. Upon making it to the battery, May and the Dragoons continued to charge until they ran into heavy fire. The regiment was scattered and forced to retreat. Somewhere in the confusion, Mexican Brigadier General Rómulo Díaz de la Vega, a prominent military figure, was captured. May personally took credit for capturing the general, and his exploits earned him national fame. At least nine different prints were commissioned showing May in action during the war. One of the more popular prints by Nathaniel Currier of Currier & Ives showed May apprehending General Vega on horseback while in full gallop. Critics are quick to point out that General Vega was likely captured by the regimental bugler, and May took credit hoping the deed would garner him fame, thus overshadowing his failed leadership. Regardless of what actually happened, May continued to distinguish himself during the rest of the Mexican-American War, rising to the rank of brevet colonel.

After the war, May continued to serve in various Army posts, including on the American frontier and in the Ordnance Department. Throughout his service, he was a user and champion of the Colt revolver. He was even asked to testify on the company's behalf when Colt sued the Massachusetts Arms Company for patent infringement in 1851. At the Ordnance Department, May was instrumental in the Army's adoption of the shoulder-stocked Model 1860 Army. In appreciation for his friendship and support, Colt presented May with several revolvers, including a pair of 1860 Armies cased with an attachable shoulder stock. Manufactured in 1861, the cased set is now part of the Autry Collection. The revolvers, consecutive serial numbers 2259 and 2260, and the shoulder stock are inscribed "To / Col. C. A. May U. S. A. / from Col. Colt." Elizabeth Colt, Samuel's wife, also recognized May's friendship with her husband. When Colt passed away in 1862, Elizabeth asked May to be a pallbearer at the funeral.

Actor William S. Hart's Model 1860 Army
is emblematic of his simplistic style and the
authenticity he brought to the Western genre.
(97.2.1; donated in memory of Charles K. French
by his granddaughter, Edna T. Hunt)

ACTOR WILLIAM S. HART'S MODEL 1860 ARMY

The Reel West

William Surrey Hart was one of the first cowboy stars of the silver screen. His silent films offered drama, lessons in morality, and a nostalgic vision of the American frontier. His style and dedication to the Western genre had a tremendous impact on all future screen cowboys. Hart was a Shakespearean stage actor who made the transition to the motion picture industry late in his career. As a producer, screenwriter, director, and actor, he tried to make his Western movies as authentic as possible. The settings, stories, costumes, stages, and props were all carefully researched. Bringing artistic credibility to the genre, Hart proved that Westerns could be critically and financially successful.

Hart made his professional acting debut in his 20s on stage with *Romeo and Juliet,* and he spent the next two decades perfecting his craft. His first critical acclaim came in 1899 with his role as Messala in the original theatrical company of *Ben Hur.* Hart also appeared on stage in several Westerns, including *The Squaw Man* and *The Virginian.* Like most serious actors, Hart had little respect for the burgeoning motion picture industry. He was especially disheartened by the way the West was portrayed on film. Hart had spent some time in the region as a boy, and his understanding of the West differed dramatically from what was shown on-screen. Hart nevertheless saw as many Western films as he could. He learned the standard plot points, settings, characters, and costumes. Hart knew he could make better, and, in his mind more accurate, Western films if given the opportunity.

While on tour in Los Angeles with the production of *The Trail of the Lonesome Pine,* Hart took the opportunity to contact the New York Motion Picture Company to express his interest in acting in Western films. He learned that his old friend and roommate Thomas H. Ince was manager of the studio. Ince tried to warn Hart that Westerns were cheap and their popularity had passed, but Hart was insistent upon making Western films. Ince finally relented, and Hart was given his first Western role in 1914. He made several Western shorts before making his debut in feature films later that year. He quickly took on greater responsibility, including writing and directing. Hart's Westerns were unique. Focusing on melodrama and character development, he initiated what would later come to be known as adult Westerns. His films captivated audiences, and he became one of the biggest stars in the motion picture industry.

Hart's popularity began to fade in the early 1920s. While his age and decreased vitality certainly played a role—he was well into his 50s at this time—the real culprit was fellow actor Tom Mix. Mix was making films prior to Hart's arrival in Hollywood, but it wasn't until the 1920s that Mix's brand of action and flash came to dominate the Western genre. Audiences viewed Hart's films as slow, drab, and overtly nostalgic when compared to the spectacle Mix brought to the screen. The contrast between the two was also seen in their appearance. While Mix was opulently attired and his guns were heavily engraved, Hart wore simple clothing and carried guns that showed plenty of use. His Model 1860 Army in the Autry Collection, serial number 12959, is the perfect example. Manufactured in 1861, the revolver had no original finish left and was in relatively poor condition by the time Hart acquired it. Recognizing that his time had passed, Hart retired from the motion picture industry after making the silent classic *Tumbleweeds* in 1925. He spent his final years at his ranch in Santa Clarita, California.

Samuel Colt's greatest contribution to the Civil War was the Model 1860 Army, a revolver primarily issued to officers and the cavalry. (87.118.23)

ENGRAVED MODEL 1860 ARMY

E Pluribus Unum

Samuel Colt anticipated hostilities between the North and South, and he legally provided firearms to both sides prior to the outbreak of the American Civil War. To meet the ever-increasing demand, Colt's armory was operating at full capacity in 1860 and 1861, with 1,500 men working day and night in two 10-hour shifts. Colt and the company were making record profits as a result. Sales to the South were outlawed when hostilities officially began, but Colt's continued to do record business as the company focused exclusively on supplying the Union war effort. Demand was such that Colt added a new factory to his Hartford armory complex in November 1861. One of the most important revolvers being produced at this time was the Model 1860 Army.

The 1860 Army was the first Colt revolver to be made with a new material known as silver steel. Initially used in European gunmaking, silver steel, or Silver Spring steel, was lighter and stronger than the previous steel used by Colt's for firearm production. The new material allowed Colt's to manufacture a medium-frame revolver chambered in the powerful .44 caliber. In comparison to the large .44-caliber Dragoon, the 1860 Army had superior ballistics, a lighter weight, and improved balance. The new model also featured the more efficient loading lever initially introduced on the Model 1855 Sidehammer Pocket. The 1860 Army commonly came with a seven-and-a-half- or eight-inch round barrel and a rebated cylinder large enough to accommodate the .44-caliber bullet. More than 200,000 were manufactured from 1860 to 1873. The United States government purchased more than 130,000 for use during the Civil War.

Countless firearms by a multitude of manufacturers were used by both sides during the war. The guns used by the Union, however, were a clear indication of the North's technological and manufacturing superiority. Whereas the South only had two small armories in Richmond, Virginia, and Fayetteville, North Carolina, the North had several of the largest and most efficient armories in the world, including Colt's. The war was fought primarily by troops armed with rifles or muskets, but handguns were issued to officers and the cavalry. Individual troops also purchased their own revolvers. Colt's major contribution to the Union war effort was the 1860 Army, the handgun that saw the most use during the war. Because the majority of the revolvers manufactured were purchased by the government, 1860 Armies are often found in very poor condition.

A notable exception is serial number 183225E in the Autry Collection. The letter E accompanying the serial number indicates that the revolver was intended for engraving, thus special handling and care was necessary throughout its manufacture. The engraving was executed in an extremely rare and unusual style. Only a handful of similar examples are known to exist. The heavy leaf scroll pattern dates to circa 1870, and it represents a brief window between the periods of master engravers Gustave Young and Cuno A. Helfricht. The name of the revolver's engraver is currently unknown. Interestingly, serial number 183225E was manufactured in 1869, but it did not ship from the factory until 1877. With the conclusion of the Civil War and the introduction of the metallic cartridge, sales of percussion revolvers plummeted in the late 1860s and early 1870s. As a result, even beautifully engraved revolvers like serial number 183225E were difficult to sell. The revolver ultimately was shipped to B. Kittredge & Co. in Cincinnati, Ohio, one of Colt's largest sellers in the Midwest. Many of the guns shipped to Kittredge were taken farther west, but the pristine condition of 183225E clearly indicates that it never saw rugged use on the frontier.

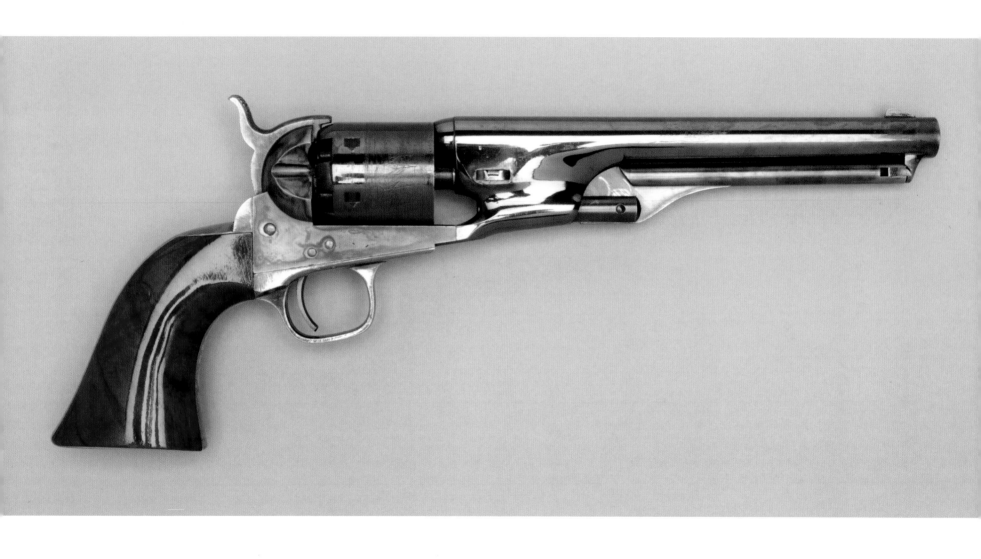

Samuel Colt presented revolvers to important individuals associated with the Union war effort, including a Model 1861 Navy to Edward S. Sanford of the Military Telegraph Corps. (87.118.24)

MILITARY TELEGRAPH CORPS SUPERVISOR EDWARD S. SANFORD'S PRESENTATION MODEL 1861 NAVY

Staying Connected

The American Civil War took place at a time when technology was rapidly changing all aspects of life in America. Using its superiority in population, wealth, and manufacturing, the North was better equipped to capitalize on these changes. A notable example was the electric telegraph. In 1836, Samuel Morse developed a method that used electricity and wires to send messages over long distances. Morse's electric telegraph initially sent a coded message that was interpreted visually, but telegraph operators soon learned how to interpret the code audibly. Morse's electric telegraph and the mechanics that allowed it to work had applications beyond the field of communications. After the closing of the Patent Arms Manufacturing Company, Samuel Colt failed to sell the government on a technique that detonated underwater explosives using Morse's technology. Colt was also unsuccessful in his attempt to establish a telegraph communications company.

Where Colt failed, others prospered, and by the outbreak of the Civil War, three major telegraph companies controlled lines that connected most of the United States and its territories. The companies were headquartered in the North, where the majority of the lines were located. When war broke out in 1861, President Abraham Lincoln quickly recognized the importance of the telegraph, and he ordered the seizure of all commercial lines for military purposes. The United States Military Telegraph Corps was established for the purpose of maintaining communication between the federal government in various locations in Washington, D.C., and the Union armies spread across the continent. Because lines did not exist in all the necessary locations, the specially designated Telegraph Construction Corps was charged with constructing telegraph lines to the battlefields as they emerged.

One of the most important individuals associated with the Military Telegraph Corps was Edward S. Sanford. Born in 1816, Sanford was named general agent of the express firm Adams & Company in 1846. When Adams and several of its competitors merged in 1854 to form the Adams Express Company, Sanford was named a company director. Adams Express had many important clients, and it served for many years as Colt's regular

shipper of firearm orders. Sanford was also a director of the American Telegraph Company, and in 1860, he was named the company's president. When war broke out between the North and South in 1861, Secretary of War Edwin M. Stanton offered Sanford the position of supervisor of the Military Telegraph Corps. Sanford initially declined, but he ultimately accepted when pressured by President Lincoln. Sanford and others in the Military Telegraph Corps were instrumental in helping coordinate the war effort.

In November 1861, Sanford received a presentation Model 1861 Navy, serial number 1806, from Colt. Now part of the Autry Collection, the revolver is inscribed "E. S. Sanford / with compliments of Col. Colt." Given his positions within the Military Telegraph Corps and the Adams Express Company, Sanford was a worthy recipient of a presentation revolver. Other notable individuals associated with the war effort were also presented revolvers in November 1861. The list included Generals George McClellan, William Tecumseh Sherman, and Irvin McDowell. Sanford served as supervisor of the Military Telegraph Corps at the rank of colonel until the end of hostilities. After the war, Sanford was elected vice president of the Adams Express Company, a position he held until his death in 1882.

Germans have a long association with the American West, and this Model 1861 Navy features an intriguing German inscription on the back strap. (2012.2.8; the George Gamble Collection)

CASED MODEL 1861 NAVY

A Treasure from Silver Lake

The Model 1861 Navy is considered by many to be the most beautifully executed Colt percussion revolver in terms of both design and aesthetics. The 1861 Navy was similar to the Model 1851 Navy, with the exception of the round barrel and the creeping loading lever. The 1861 Navy was chambered in .36 caliber and weighed two pounds, 10 ounces. Standard models featured a blued finish with walnut grips. Approximately 39,000 were manufactured from 1861 to 1873. Production numbers would have been higher, but several factors led to decreased sales, including an armory fire in 1864, the surplus of weapons following the Civil War, and the introduction of the metallic cartridge in the 1860s. Interestingly, the most lasting feature of the 1861 Navy was the grip frame, which was incorporated into the design of Colt's most famous and successful revolver, the Single Action Army.

A remarkable example of the 1861 Navy is serial number 21838 in the Autry Collection. The revolver was originally shipped to Schuyler, Hartley & Graham, one of the largest retailers of Colt firearms in the 19th century, where it was subsequently embellished and engraved. The revolver is primarily silver plated with gold plating on the cylinder, loading lever, and hammer. Almost every part of the revolver was engraved by Louis D. Nimschke, one of the premier firearm engravers in the second half of the 19th century. The checkered ivory grips are hand carved and feature an American eagle with a shield on the left side. The wood and leather case is silver mounted and contour lined with silk and velvet. The back strap features a German inscription written in an uncommon dialect that reads "Aloys Seinem Joseph" (most likely a dedication from Aloys to his friend or son Joseph). The revolver's inscription highlights an interesting connection between Germans and the American West.

Individuals from German-speaking regions made up a significant portion of European immigrants to the American West in the 19th century. At the same time, German American painters such as Albert Bierstadt and Karl Ferdinand Wimar were some of the chief chroniclers of the majestic beauty and native inhabitants of the region. Germans back in Europe were captivated by these works of art, and they vigorously consumed reports of life on the frontier, both real and imagined. Following in the tradition of James Fenimore Cooper's "Leatherstocking" series, German author Karl

May thrilled generations of Germans with his novels set in the American West. *The Treasure of Silver Lake* and other novels by May were in stark contrast to American stories of the West, as German authors often portrayed Indians as noble heroes fighting the imperialist and corrupt Americans. Western movies have been popular in Germany for decades, and Wild West clubs, where individuals dress up to play cowboys and Indians, still exist.

A notable story of a person of German descent in North America that may relate to serial number 21838 in the Autry Collection actually took place in Mexico. In 1864, Habsburg nobleman Ferdinand Maximilian Joseph became Maximilian I, the only monarch of the Second Mexican Empire. Members of the Mexican aristocracy, with the support of key European nations, persuaded Maximilian to take the position of emperor of Mexico, hoping it would solidify their dominance of the country. Maximilian supported some liberal policies, such as land reform, extended voting rights, and absolution of debt, but republicans, many of whom were peasants, strongly disagreed with any sort of foreign rule. Maximilian's short reign was plagued with upheaval and violence. He was finally overrun by his enemies in 1867 and executed. Given the fact that serial number 21838 was manufactured in 1864, discovered in Mexico, and featured a German inscription written in a style and with names common to the House of Habsburg, many experts have speculated that it once belonged to an aide to Maximilian I.

Banker William H. Cox was presented a magnificent Model 1861 Navy in appreciation for his work on behalf of the company. (87.118.25)

BANKER WILLIAM H. COX'S CASED PRESENTATION MODEL 1861 NAVY

Compliments of the Company

The success of Colt's Patent Fire Arms Manufacturing Company was due in large part to Samuel Colt, but countless others—from factory workers to outside executives—played a crucial role in the development of the firm. William H. Cox, the individual responsible for the company's account at Mechanics National Bank of New York, was one of these contributors. Cox helped in the rebuilding of the Colt armory in Hartford after it was ravaged by a fire in 1864. Prior to the fire, Colt's was in the midst of record production and profits as a result of the Union's insatiable demand for firearms during the Civil War. The Model 1860 Army was the most popular handgun among Union soldiers, and it was far superior to any revolver manufactured in the South. Recognizing Colt's contributions to the Union war effort, it is believed that Southern saboteurs set fire to the armory on February 5, 1864.

The damage was catastrophic. The office and one half of the armory were completely destroyed. The machinery, drawings, and models were gone, as were the documents and ledgers describing production and distribution of firearms from 1847 through 1860. Approximately 900 workers were immediately out of work, but amazingly only one person was killed. Damages were estimated at $782,000 (the equivalent of $11 million today). Unfortunately for the company, Colt did not believe in insurance, due in part to his thinking that his armory and works were fireproof. Luckily, some insurance was purchased in the 1860s, and the company was able to recoup some of its losses. Company executives immediately set about rebuilding the armory, and New York banker William H. Cox was instrumental in securing the necessary financing.

In appreciation for his work, Cox was presented with a cased Model 1861 Navy, serial number 23371IP. The revolver was manufactured in 1864. Embellished by Gustave Young, it is scroll engraved, with a sailor firing a Colt revolver on the right side of the barrel lug and a bare-breasted maiden on the left side. No other Colt percussion firearm from the 19th century is known to have a nude female figure. The grips are made of ivory with a rare checkered panel on each side, and an inscription on the back strap reads "To Wm H. Cox, Esq. / With compliments of Colt's P.F.A.M.Co." The walnut case, attributed to Hartford cabinetmaker William Milton, is lined with purple velvet and features rare silk hinge covers. Cox's cased presentation revolver, now part of the Autry Collection, is one of the finest examples of its type. It also represents one of the most important and crucial periods in the history of Colt's.

Tokens of appreciation given on behalf of the company and its employees were presented at other key moments, and they were not limited to firearms. Two notable examples are part of the Autry Collection. During the difficult transition from the percussion system to the metallic cartridge, company foreman James D. Smith was presented a deluxe set of drafting tools. Inscribed "James D. Smith / From the workmen under / his charge at Colts Armory / Hartford June 2nd 1863," the set was housed in a multitiered rosewood box lined with maroon velvet. Decades later, as World War I was raging, Colt President Charles Leonard Frost Robinson passed away unexpectedly in 1916. Having served as president since 1911, Robinson steered the company as it successfully met the Allied demand for armaments at the outset of the war. In appreciation of his efforts, the company presented his family a folio, bound in full Morocco leather with vellum paper, featuring hand-drawn vignettes about Robinson and the company. Both the Smith and Robinson presentation items are one of a kind, and like Cox's 1861 Navy, they are important parts of Colt's corporate history.

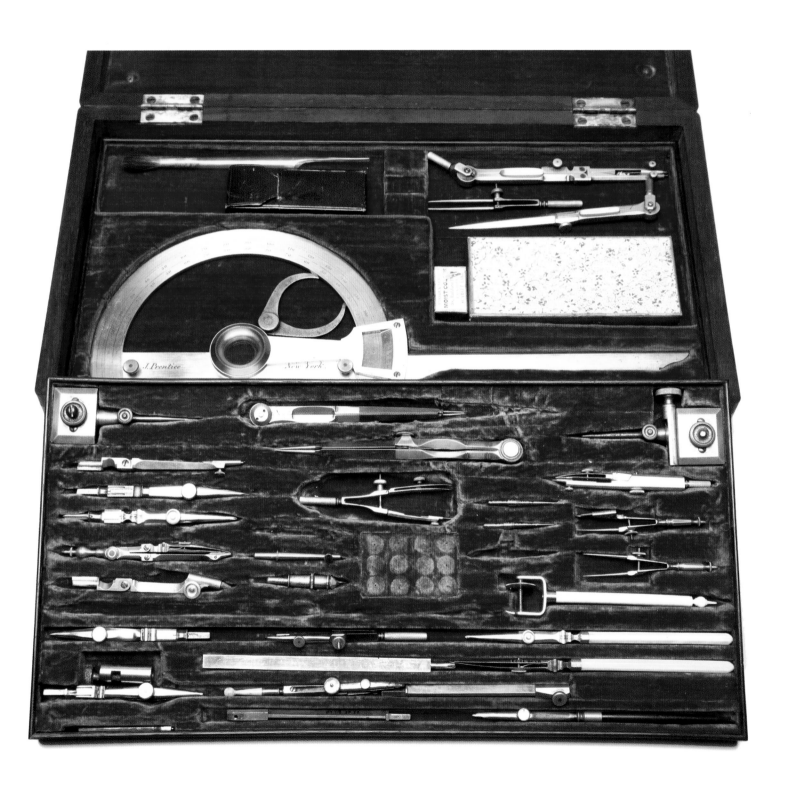

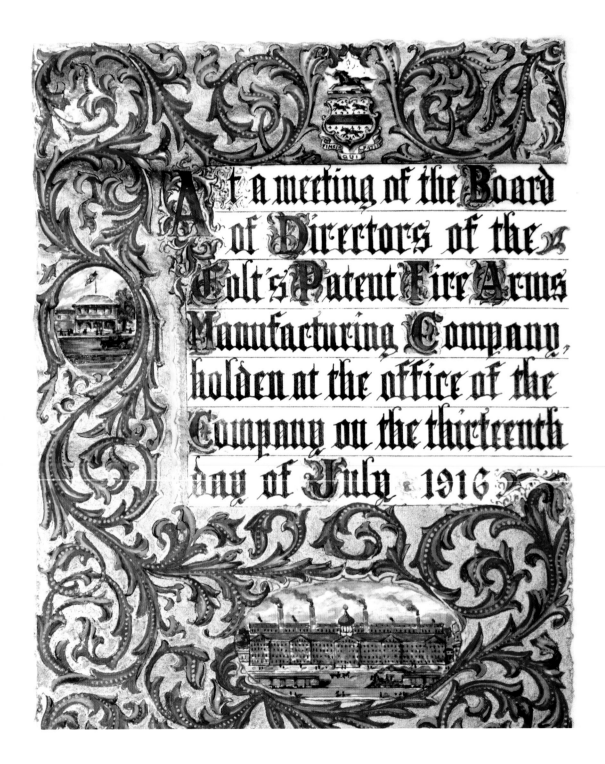

At a meeting of the Board of Directors of the Colt's Patent Fire Arms Manufacturing Company, holden at the office of the Company on the thirteenth day of July 1916

Opposite:
Presentation items were not limited to firearms, as company foreman James D. Smith was presented a multitiered set of drafting tools in 1863. (87.118.30)

Right:
A folio featuring pages hand illuminated in full color was presented in 1916 to the family of Colt President Charles Leonard Frost Robinson. (87.118.166)

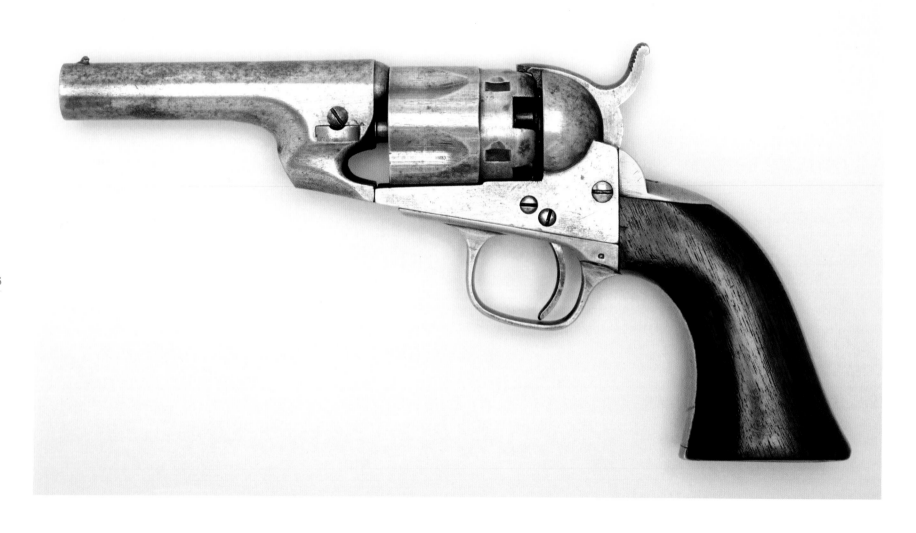

The rare "Trapper's" Model 1862 Police was introduced at a good time in the professional and personal life of Samuel Colt. (87.118.27)

PROTOTYPE "TRAPPER'S" MODEL 1862 POLICE

A Life of Luxury

Throughout his entire adult life, Samuel Colt dedicated all of his time and energy to his revolvers. He spent a few years after the failure of the Patent Arms Manufacturing Company exploring other business opportunities, but he never lost sight of his greatest invention. By the 1850s, the success of Colt's Patent Fire Arms Manufacturing Company allowed Colt to spend some time focusing on his personal life. In 1856, Colt married Elizabeth Hart Jarvis. Twelve years younger than Colt, Elizabeth—the daughter of an Episcopal minister and a prominent socialite—was raised in affluence in Rhode Island. She attended school in Hartford in the 1840s, but it has been speculated that she first met Colt in Newport, Rhode Island, a prominent resort community, sometime in the late 1840s or early 1850s. The couple married in June 1856, and they spent several months honeymooning in Europe.

A few months after their return to Hartford, the newlywed couple moved into a monarchical estate adjacent to Colt's armory. The brownstone building was three stories tall with almost two dozen rooms. Construction on the estate, known as Armsmear, began in the summer of 1855 and was completed in June 1857. Colt played a key role in the design of the mansion, finding inspiration in his many overseas trips. The estate was filled with the finest of luxuries. Many of the items found in Armsmear were decorated with the crest from the Colt coat of arms. The defining feature of the crest was the Rampant Colt, a symbol that dated back to Colt's English ancestry and later became the trademark of Colt's company. A tureen with hand-painted Rampant Colt crests in the Autry Collection was crafted for Colt circa 1855. One of the finest pieces of Colt china known to exist, it was typical of the adornments found in Armsmear. In 1858, the couple welcomed Caldwell Hart Colt, their only child to live to adulthood.

With his personal life in order, Samuel Colt entered the 1860s full of energy. The looming threat of unrest in the United States between the North and South was a tremendous boom for business, and Colt's was operating at full capacity. Despite the flurry of activity, the company managed to introduce several new models, including the Model 1862 Police. The rarest variation of the 1862 Police was known as the "Trapper's" Model. Fewer than 50 were manufactured in 1861, and only about a half dozen specimens are known to still exist. The defining features of the model are a three-and-a-half-inch barrel made without a loading lever and an opening in the barrel lug for loading. A separate brass ramrod was the standard accessory. The "Trapper's" Model in the Autry Collection is the factory prototype. It is without a serial number, but a "0" is stamped on the cylinder face between two of the chambers. This is usually interpreted as a prototype mark. The revolver was made without finish, and the original tool marks are still present.

Like his father, Caldwell Hart Colt also lived a life of luxury. Just three years old when his father passed away in 1862, Caldwell was highly educated and extremely wealthy. Caldwell's social status was evidenced by a beautifully engraved and embossed sterling-silver pitcher presented to him at a lavish 21st birthday party. Part of the Autry Collection, the pitcher was a gift from his aunt and uncle and is inscribed "Caldwell Hart Colt / 1858 November 24th, 1879 / C.N.B. & H.H.B." Elizabeth ultimately wanted Caldwell to take an active role in the company his father founded, but instead he chose to lead the life of a playboy and sportsman. Caldwell's notable contribution to the company was the Double Barrel Rifle, a model with a limited production run of about 40. Caldwell was the impetus for and maybe even the designer of the rare model. He ultimately died at a young age in 1894. The exact cause of his death is shrouded in mystery, with reports ranging from suicide and murder to tonsillitis and drowning.

Opposite:
Adorned with several hand-painted Rampant Colt crests, Samuel Colt's tureen was emblematic of the lifestyle his wealth afforded him. (87.118.156)

Right:
Despite contributing almost nothing to his father's company, Caldwell Hart Colt also lived a life of affluence, as evidenced by the sterling-silver pitcher given to him on his 21st birthday. (2010.57.2; donated by Petra and Greg Martin)

Captain H. A. Brigham of the Ordnance Department was presented with a Model 1862 Police with a rare case designed to look like a book. (87.118.28)

CAPTAIN H. A. BRIGHAM'S CASED PRESENTATION MODEL 1862 POLICE WITH BOOK CASING

Essential Reading

The Model 1862 Police and the Model 1862 Pocket Navy were both introduced in 1861. Collectors initially thought the 1862 Pocket Navy was introduced in 1852, and for many years, it was referred to as such. Ironically, while the name collectors commonly use has changed, it is still wrong. The name used for the 1862 Police obviously is also wrong. Both models were .36 caliber, five-shot, and came in various barrel lengths. The major differences between the two models were the cylinder (the Police was fluted while the Pocket Navy was round), the barrel (the Police was round and the Pocket Navy was octagonal), and the loading lever (a creeping loading lever was used on the Police with a hinged loading lever on the Pocket Navy). The two models shared a serial number range, with approximately 28,000 Police and 19,000 Pocket Navies manufactured.

A few 1862 Police revolvers were housed in cases designed to look like books. The book cases had leather covers and were made by actual bookbinders. They had clever titles such as *Law for Self Defense, Common Law of Texas,* and *Colt's Pocket Companion.* Book casings have only been identified with a few models, including the Model 1855 Sidehammer Pocket and the 1862 Police. One example is also known to date from the Paterson period. Along with the revolver, the portioned interior commonly included a powder flask, bullet mold, a can of percussion caps, and bullets. Book cases were never marketed and were used only for special occasions. As a result, they are exceptionally rare and highly collectible.

The 1862 Police with a book casing in the Autry Collection is serial number 26378. It is one of the finest examples in existence. Manufactured in 1864, the revolver was presented to Captain H. A. Brigham, a master storekeeper of the Ordnance Department during the Civil War. An inscription on the revolver's back strap, executed by Gustave Young, reads "H. A. Brigham / U.S.A." The revolver is blued with a silver-plated brass back strap and varnished mahogany grips. Chambered in .36 caliber, it has a three-and-a-half-inch barrel and a five-shot cylinder. The casing is made of red Morocco leather, and the partitioned interior is lined in maroon velvet. The front and back are embossed in gold leaf with patriotic designs, including a bust of George Washington. The spine includes the title, *Colt on the Constitution: Higher Law & Irrepressible Conflict,* along with "Dedicated by the Author to" and the date "Jany. 1st 1861."

The book cased set has an interesting history or provenance. It was acquired by Albert Foster Jr. in 1929. Foster was the sales manager at Colt's New York office for more than 40 years, and he was also a pioneer collector of Colt firearms. The set was later acquired by William M. Locke, another key collector in the 20th century. The set won the prestigious top prize for antique arms at the 1960 National Rifle Association annual show. It was featured in the 1962 exhibition and accompanying publication "Samuel Colt Presents: A Loan Exhibition of Presentation Colt Firearms" at the Wadsworth Atheneum Museum of Art in Hartford, Connecticut. The exhibition brought together some of the finest Colt revolvers known to the collecting community at that time, and the set was featured prominently. Colt Chairman George Strichman later acquired the set for the company's corporate collection, and it became part of the Autry Collection in 1987.

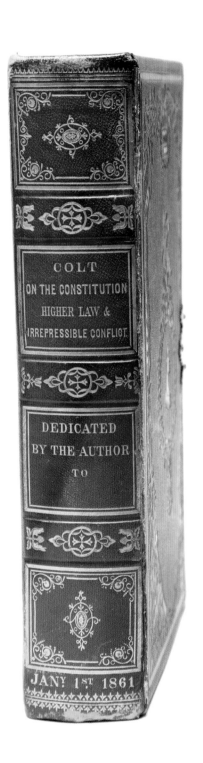

COLT
ON THE CONSTITUTION
HIGHER LAW &
IRREPRESSIBLE CONFLICT.

DEDICATED
BY THE AUTHOR
TO

JANY 1ST 1861

Left:
All of the book casings featured witty titles that provided subtle clues to their actual contents. (87.118.28.2)

Opposite:
Reserved for special presentations, book casings were never advertised, nor were they offered to the general public. (87.118.28.2)

The Model 1862 Police was one of the last models introduced during Samuel Colt's lifetime. (2012.2.9; the George Gamble Collection)

CASED MODEL 1862 POLICE

End of an Era

Samuel Colt was a tireless worker. Even as his business thrived, Colt pushed himself to the limit. Exhaustion and a severe case of rheumatic fever took its toll, and beginning in 1860, Colt's health began to decline. During the Civil War, when the demand for firearms was at an all-time high, Colt seemed to be working day and night. The strain ultimately proved to be too much, and on January 10, 1862, Colt passed away. A service bell, a Christmas gift inscribed with flowers and Colt's name, was at his bedside at the time of his death. This sobering piece of Colt memorabilia is now part of the Autry Collection. More than 600,000 Colt revolvers were made during the inventor's lifetime, and another 400,000 specimens from models he created continued to be made following his untimely death.

The last models introduced during Colt's lifetime were the Model 1862 Police and the Model 1862 Pocket Navy. One of the finest 1862 Police ever produced was serial number 37951E in the Autry Collection. Manufactured in 1868, it features a high-polish blue finish and vibrant case-hardened colors. The barrel, frame, hammer, and grip straps are engraved in the late vine style, with attribution to engraver Conrad F. Ulrich. "Colts / Patent" is engraved on the left side of the frame, and a wolf-head motif is engraved on each side of the hammer. The Mexican coat of arms, an eagle perched atop a cactus with a snake in its mouth, is relief carved onto the left side of the ivory grips. The case is varnished mahogany lined with burgundy velvet. It includes a powder flask, bullet mold, a tin of percussion caps, a multipurpose tool, two packets of cartridges, and a key.

Elizabeth Hart Jarvis Colt, Samuel's widow, assumed the bulk of Colt's $15 million estate upon his passing. She also gained control of Colt's Patent Fire Arms Manufacturing Company and quickly named E. K. Root the second president in the company's history. When the Colt armory was devastated by a fire in 1864, she ordered it rebuilt at any cost. She continued to oversee the company during key moments in its history, from the introduction of the Single Action Army to the establishment of a relationship with designer John Moses Browning. She financed the first biography of her husband, titled *Armsmear*, and distributed it beginning in 1866 at no cost. A deluxe edition in the Autry Collection is inscribed "Mrs. Rogers / With the sincere regard of / Elizabeth H. Colt / Armsmear / April 25th 1879." After 40 years of steady leadership, Elizabeth Colt ultimately sold the company to a group of outside investors in 1901. Samuel Colt's technical genius and promotional savvy were irreplaceable, but Elizabeth Colt proved to be a worthy successor to her husband.

During her lifetime, Elizabeth was also a prominent philanthropist and community leader. She was actively involved in several charitable and cultural organizations in Hartford and Connecticut. She helped organize the state's first suffragette convention in 1869. She built several monuments, including the Church of the Good Shepherd, a place of worship intended for all of Colt's employees from upper management to factory workmen, and the Caldwell Colt Memorial House, the parish house of the Church of the Good Shepherd. Elizabeth's enduring commitment to the cultural, spiritual, and social life of Hartford and greater Connecticut led others to dub her "the first lady of Hartford." When she passed away in 1905, she bequeathed her family's world-class collection of art and artifacts to the Wadsworth Atheneum Museum of Art and the family's monarchical estate was given to the city of Hartford.

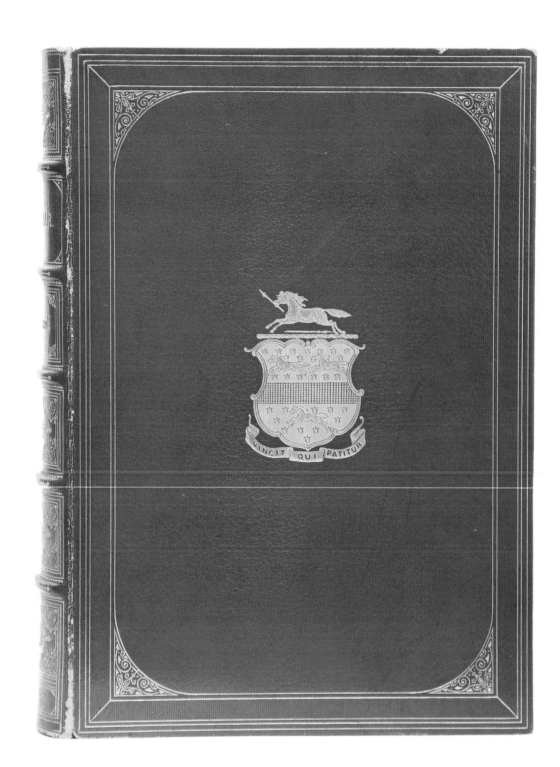

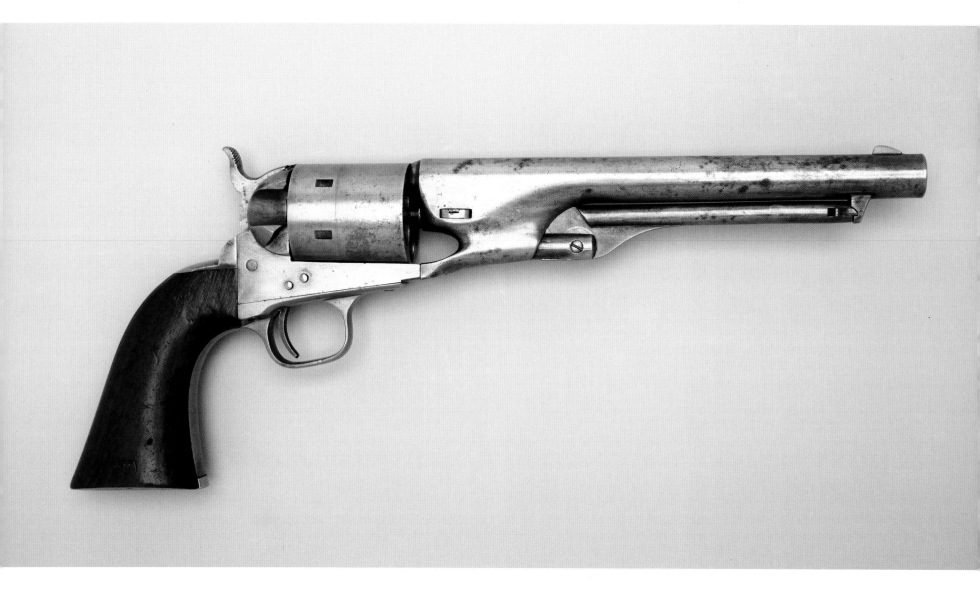

In an attempt to understand Smith & Wesson's key patent related to the metallic cartridge, Colt's manufactured this experimental Model 1860 Army with a breech-loading, bored-through cylinder. (87.118.35)

EXPERIMENTAL CONVERSION OF THE MODEL 1860 ARMY

The Self-Contained Metallic Cartridge

The next landmark invention in the history of firearms after Samuel Colt's mechanically rotating cylinder was the self-contained metallic cartridge. Unlike percussion firearms that required the user to individually load the primer (a percussion cap), powder charge, and bullets, the metallic cartridge contained all of these elements in a single unit. The metallic cartridge first gained popularity in Europe during the 1840s. Once it appeared in America, it was quickly recognized as a vast improvement over the percussion system. Colt, however, initially failed to grasp the importance and revolutionary implications of the metallic cartridge. As a result, Colt's Patent Fire Arms Manufacturing Company found itself in a difficult situation.

Various forms of metallic cartridges were produced in the 1850s and 1860s, but the most important component for their use with a revolver was a cylinder bored through from end to end that could be loaded at the breech. It is believed that Roland White was an employee at Colt's when he came up with the crucial design. White presented his findings to Colt, but the inventor and company president reacted negatively. So when White patented his design in 1855, he sold the rights to Smith & Wesson, one of Colt's leading competitors. The patent rights effectively gave Smith & Wesson a monopoly on breech-loaded cylinders bored through end-to-end until 1869. Whereas Colt's once controlled a key patent that gave it dominance in the field of handgun manufacturing, the company now was forced to find ways to legally circumvent a patent controlled by someone else.

Colt's entertained the notion of licensing the patent rights from White and Smith & Wesson, but the proposed figure of more than a million dollars was deemed too high. The company thus focused its efforts on finding a way to employ the metallic cartridge without using a bored-through cylinder that was loaded at the breech. However, in order to understand exactly how White's patent worked prior to its expiration in 1869, Colt's experimented with but did not mass-produce a few revolvers with cylinders bored through from end to end. A unique experimental revolver in the Autry Collection, constructed circa 1868–1869, is a notable example. Built on a Model 1860 Army frame, the experiment represented an attempt to alter a percussion revolver to accept the metallic cartridge using old parts, as evidenced by various serial numbers found on the revolver. A special hammer with firing pin was added, and the recoil shield was machined to allow loading of the cylinder from the breech while the revolver was still assembled.

The experimental Model 1860 Army was a successful conversion, but similar examples could not legally be manufactured for sale. Various legal conversions were mass-produced in the 1860s and 1870s, but it was clear to executives and designers at Colt's that their conversions were inferior to the Smith & Wesson revolvers that employed cylinders bored through from end to end that were loaded from the breech. Until Smith & Wesson's patent expired, Colt's was at a severe disadvantage. As a result, the failure to recognize the revolutionary implications of Roland White's breech-loading, bored-through cylinder marked the single greatest failure of Colt's remarkable career. Samuel Colt's passing, however, meant that others would be left to guide the company through one of its most difficult periods of the 19th century.

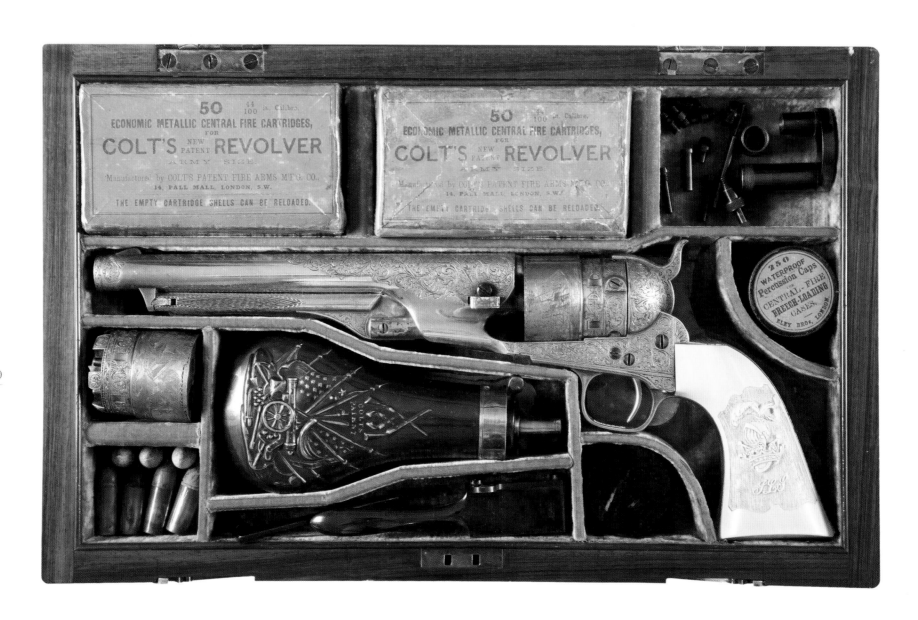

F. Alexander Thuer developed the conversion system that was used on this opulent presentation Model 1860 Army. (2012.2.10; the George Gamble Collection)

PUERTO RICAN GOVERNOR JOSÉ LAUREANO SANZ'S CASED PRESENTATION THUER CONVERSION OF THE MODEL 1860 ARMY

A Not-So-Quick Fix

F. Alexander Thuer designed the first conversion system that was mass-produced on a Colt revolver. The conversion enabled percussion revolvers to fire metallic cartridges. An employee of Colt's since 1849, Thuer was one of many engineers at the company searching for a way to legally circumvent the key patent Smith & Wesson controlled relating to a breech-loading cylinder bored through from end to end. Thuer's novel idea was to load the cartridge through the front instead of the back of the cylinder. As a result, the cylinder did not need to be bored through completely. A standard percussion cylinder could be used by machining off the back end, where the percussion caps were loaded onto the nipples. A conversion plate, a specially designed section with its own firing pin, replaced the part that was removed. Conversion plates allowed for the use of metallic cartridges without infringing upon Smith & Wesson's patent, so they became standard on almost all Colt conversions, although their design and function changed over time.

The Thuer conversion was available on several models, including the Model 1849 Pocket, Model 1851 Navy, Model 1860 Army, Model 1861 Navy, and Model 1862 Police and Pocket Navy. Although the system was fairly simple and could be employed on basically any Colt revolver, it had several significant issues, the most noticeable of which was the procedure for ejecting spent casings, which remained in the cylinder after a bullet was fired. To remove the spent casings, the user had to turn the conversion ring and cock and release the hammer. As the hammer fell, it engaged a bar device that moved forward, ejecting the casing. This time-consuming step had to be repeated for each chamber.

Thuer designed the tapered, rimless centerfire cartridges that were used with his conversion system. Although the casings were difficult to extract, they were reusable. By combining the used casings with fresh primer, black powder, and a new bullet, users could make their own metallic cartridges. Thuer also patented a loading apparatus to aid in the process. An additional selling point for the Thuer conversion system was the fact that it could alternate from the percussion system to metallic cartridge ammunition simply by switching the cylinder. Unfortunately for Colt's, the Thuer system was not popular with the military or civilians. The system was inefficient, especially when compared to Smith & Wesson's metallic cartridge revolvers. Sales were slow, and fewer than 5,000 Thuer conversions were mass-produced.

One of the most spectacular Thuer conversion revolvers is the cased Model 1860 Army, serial number 185326 I.E., in the Autry Collection. The set was presented to Don José Laureano Sanz, the Marquis de San Juan and Governor General of Puerto Rico, circa 1869. It supposedly was a gift from the people of Puerto Rico. The revolver is plated entirely in silver, with the exception of the cylinder, conversion plate, hammer, and rammer plunger, which are plated in gold. A leaf-and-vine pattern is finely engraved over most of the revolver, although it is unclear if it is the work of master engraver Gustave Young or Cuno A. Helfricht. The one-piece, relief-carved ivory grips feature the governor's family crest on one side and his initials on the other. Inscribed "JLS," the Brazilian rosewood case features all of the equipment necessary for operation, including a gold-plated percussion cylinder and two boxes of Thuer cartridges. All of the tools are finished with a high-gloss blue, a treatment reserved for only the finest cased sets.

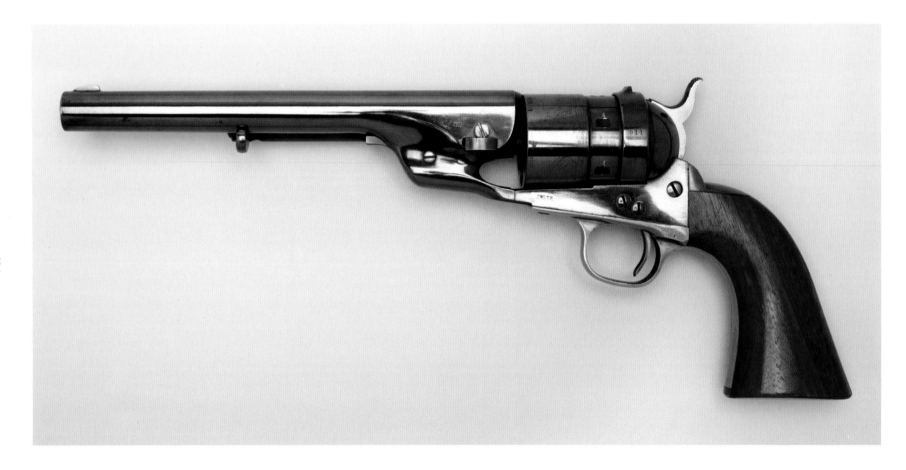

The United States military ordered a special group of Model 1860 Armies that were converted to the metallic cartridge under a system designed by Charles B. Richards. (87.118.36)

RICHARDS CONVERSION OF THE MODEL 1860 ARMY

Military Orders

C harles B. Richards was a prominent engineer and the assistant factory superintendent at Colt's. Richards spent a few years at the company in the 1850s, before leaving to make significant contributions to the evolution of the steam engine. In 1861, he returned to Colt's and guided the company through the hurried pace of the Civil War, the downturn following the war, and the transition to the metallic cartridge. Richards is probably best remembered at Colt's for his contributions to the design of the famed Single Action Army. After leaving Colt's again in 1880, Richards helped found the Society of Mechanical Engineers, and he taught mechanical engineering at Yale University for 25 years.

In the early 1870s, Richards played a prominent role in the design of two methods that converted Colt percussion revolvers to the metallic cartridge system. His initial design for the conversion of the Model 1860 Army produced the first large-frame Colt revolvers capable of firing a breech-loaded metallic cartridge. The Richards conversion employed a breech plate with a rebounding firing pin. The face of the recoil shield was milled down to accommodate the breech plate, and the hammer was ground flat so it could properly strike it. The barrel was milled on the right side to add an ejector rod and casing. Unlike the Thuer conversion system, revolvers employing the Richards conversion could no longer use the percussion system due to all of the alterations. Approximately 9,000 Model 1860 Army revolvers were converted using the Richards conversion.

The military was eager to obtain Colt revolvers capable of firing the metallic cartridge, and the Richards conversion was used on a special group of 1,200 revolvers returned to the company by the government for alteration. Completed circa 1877–1878, the entire run was supervised by the Springfield armory, the United States government's primary center for the manufacture of firearms for almost 200 years. The revolvers featured two serial numbers; one represented the original percussion series and a

new number was added to specify the government conversion. Most of these revolvers saw extensive use on the American frontier and are thus difficult to find in fine condition. The example in the Autry Collection, with serial numbers 311 and 109642, is the only one of the group known to be in original, unfired condition. The revolver's pristine state proves that the government conversions featured a special full blue finish, new grips, and a slightly shortened barrel.

Richards also contributed to the design of a second method that converted percussion revolvers to the metallic cartridge. In this instance, Richards's design elements were combined with contributions from William Mason, the superintendent at Colt's. The resulting Richards–Mason conversion was based on three United States patents: number 117,461 issued to Richards; number 119,048 issued to Richards; and number 128,644 issued to Mason. Although the Richards–Mason conversion improved upon Richards's earlier design, only around 2,100 Model 1860 Armies were converted under the system. This was due in large part to timing. When the Richards–Mason conversions reached the market in the 1870s, a new model designed by the two men had already been introduced. The new model was the Single Action Army.

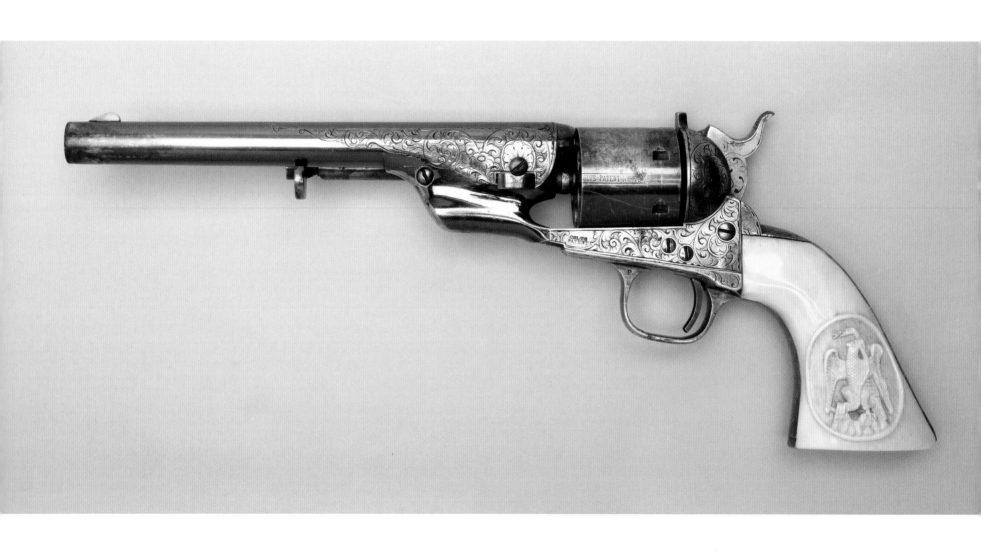

A skilled gunsmith with no association with Colt's deftly altered this Model 1861 Navy so it could accommodate the metallic cartridge. (87.118.39)

FIELD CONVERSION OF THE MODEL 1861 NAVY

Outside the Factory

Colt's Patent Fire Arms Manufacturing Company was in a difficult situation as the firearms industry transitioned from the percussion system to the metallic cartridge. First and foremost, the company had to find a way to manufacture firearms capable of using the metallic cartridge without infringing upon a patent controlled by its chief rival, Smith & Wesson. Engineers at Colt's experimented with various systems that did not employ a breech-loading cylinder bored through from end to end. The company also increased production of single-shot firearms, such as rifles and deringers, which did not need a cylinder to operate. Colt's other major problem was finding a way to use up a stockpile of increasingly obsolete percussion parts and revolvers. The company searched tirelessly for solutions.

Conversion systems were championed by executives at Colt's because they seemed to solve several problems. Conversions allowed for the legal use of the metallic cartridge, and they used up obsolete parts that management was determined to exhaust. Conversions were so popular with company executives that they were sold in the United States and around the world even after Smith & Wesson's key patent expired. At the same time, Colt's also continued to sell standard percussion revolvers. This was especially true in the American West, where it was initially difficult to obtain metallic cartridges. When the production and availability of metallic cartridges increased, due in large part to the sale of repeating rifles, the demand for percussion revolvers decreased dramatically. A sizable number of Colt percussion revolvers were actually sent back to the company for conversion, and in some instances, the revolvers were converted in the field by capable gunsmiths.

Arguably the finest field conversion known is the Model 1861 Navy, serial number 13129E, in the Autry Collection. Ingeniously altered by an unknown gunsmith circa 1872–1878, the changes effectively converted the percussion revolver to the metallic cartridge system. The cylinder was machined at the breech, removing the nipples of the percussion ignition system. A thin loading gate was added to the face of the recoil shield, along with a rear sight. A pointed firing pin was fitted onto the face of the hammer. The

loading lever was removed and replaced with a steel plug. An ejector rod and housing were also added along the bottom right side of the barrel. The final product seemed to work perfectly. Besides the conversion itself, the most striking aspect of the revolver is its appearance and condition. Executed in the style of Gustave Young, the revolver features engraving on the barrel, frame, wedge, back strap, and trigger guard strap. The one-piece ivory grips feature the Mexican coat of arms on the left side.

The Mexican coat of arms is a common engraving found on the grips of firearms, especially those made of ivory. The image depicts an eagle perched atop a cactus devouring a snake. The scene was taken from an important episode in the history of the Aztec people. According to legend, an ancient prophesy stated that the Aztec would be given a sign from the god Huitzilopochtli letting them know where to build the capital of their empire. The sign would come in the physical form of an eagle eating a snake while sitting on a cactus. The prophecy came true when the eagle was witnessed in the middle of the marshy Lake Texcoco. The Aztec people drained the lake and established the capital city of Tenochtitlan, the site of present-day Mexico City. The scene with minor differences was recorded in the *Codex Mendoza*, a pictorial history written by Aztec scribes around 1542, some two decades after the Spanish conquest of Mexico.

Captain Cyrus McKneeley Scott of the Kansas Cavalry Patrol carried this Model 1862 Police and Pocket Navy conversion with "Tiffany" grips on the American frontier. (2004.71.1; donated by Petra and Greg Martin)

CAPTAIN CYRUS MCKNEELEY SCOTT'S PRESENTATION MODEL 1862 POLICE AND POCKET NAVY CONVERSION WITH "TIFFANY" GRIPS

Luxury and Sophistication

Synonymous with luxury and sophistication, Tiffany & Co. began selling high-quality jewelry in the middle of the 19th century. The company also produced exotic military items, primarily for rich or famous officers, throughout its history. In the 1860s and 1870s, Colt revolvers with opulent, cast-metal grips appeared on the market. The grips were traditionally bronze and plated in gold or silver. They came in three distinct styles: "Missionary and Child" (or "Eagle and Justice"), "Civil War Battle Scene," and the "Mexican Eagle" or "American Eagle." All the designs were exceptionally rare. When early 20th-century firearm collectors began standardizing names, they naturally assumed that these aesthetically and artistically beautiful grips were made by Tiffany, so they called them "Tiffany" grips.

Modern scholarship, however, seems to indicate that the majority of the grips were actually crafted by Schuyler, Hartley & Graham, one of the largest suppliers of military and sporting goods in the 19th century. An 1864 catalog for the company featured several revolvers with elaborate cast metal grips, including the "Civil War Battle Scene" and "American Eagle" designs. Records also indicate that an employee of the Ames Manufacturing Company, the makers of some of the finest swords in 19th-century America, was responsible for the "Missionary and Child" motif. While some cast-metal grips may have been produced by Tiffany & Co., it is clear that collectors were wrong and Tiffany does not deserve all of the credit. Nevertheless, for the sake of continuity, the term "Tiffany" grips continues to be used.

The "American Eagle" design featured on the Model 1862 Police and Pocket Navy conversion in the Autry Collection, serial number 23773E, is silver plated. The revolver is engraved on the barrel, ejector rod housing, cylinder, frame, hammer, and trigger guard. The engraving on the frame is so profuse that the left side is without the customary "Colts / Patent" marking. The engraved cylinder is also rare. The punched-dot background scrollwork and the wavy line motif on the barrel and frame clearly indicate the work of Louis D. Nimschke. The original gold- and silver-plated finish is evident in some areas. The oval escutcheon plate of the grip is inscribed "C. M. Scott," and the revolver's inscription provides insight into its condition.

Captain Cyrus McKneeley Scott was a member of the Kansas Cavalry Patrol. He was responsible for scouting the movement of Native Americans from South Dakota to Texas. He also served as the first editor of the *Arkansas City (Kansas) Traveler*, a newspaper established in 1870. Scott unsuccessfully ran for one of Kansas's United States Senate seats, and he later toured Europe with Pawnee Bill's Wild West show. The revolver, manufactured circa 1873–1880, was presented to Scott around 1880 for distinguished service and bravery while serving in the Kansas Cavalry Patrol. A contemporary photograph shows Scott with the revolver, making serial number 23773E a rare example of a revolver with "Tiffany" grips that has a documented history to its original owner. Serial number 23773E is also unique in the fact that, unlike most beautifully engraved revolvers with "Tiffany" grips, it actually saw use on the American frontier.

Left:
The "American Eagle" motif found on Captain Scott's revolver is one of the rarest of all the "Tiffany" grips. (2004.71.1; donated by Petra and Greg Martin)

Opposite:
Many of the decorative elements found on "Tiffany" grips were designed for aesthetic and not practical purposes. (2004.71.1; donated by Petra and Greg Martin)

The Model 1871–72 Open Top Frontier was designed specifically for the metallic cartridge, and this example features deluxe "Tiffany" grips. (87.118.40)

MODEL 1871–72 OPEN TOP FRONTIER WITH "TIFFANY" GRIPS

A Bored-Through Cylinder

Roland White's patent for bored-through cylinders loaded from the breech was vital to the manufacture of revolvers capable of firing the metallic cartridge. With control of White's patent, Smith & Wesson dominated the field of metallic cartridge revolvers in the 1850s and 1860s. White sought to extend his patent rights in 1868, following the precedent Samuel Colt established years earlier when he successfully lobbied for an extension of his patent rights related to his revolving mechanism. White's request, however, was denied. As a result, Colt's and other manufacturers were finally able to produce revolvers with breech-loading bored-through cylinders capable of firing metallic cartridges. Nevertheless, after the expiration of White's patent, Colt's initially focused on converting old percussion revolvers rather than introducing new models in an attempt to use up increasingly obsolete parts.

One of the first Colt revolvers designed specifically for the metallic cartridge was the Model 1871–72 Open Top Frontier. The model was chambered in .44 rimfire caliber, the most abundant metallic cartridge then in use. The Open Top Frontier bridged the gap between the three-piece construction found on most Colt percussion revolvers (except for the 1855 Sidehammer series) and the solid frame of the Single Action Army. Based on the Model 1860 Army frame, the Open Top Frontier was designed by Charles B. Richards and William Mason. It included many of the design elements incorporated into the Richards–Mason conversion system. Because the model featured an open-top frame, it suffered from the same problems that plagued Colt's earlier percussion models, including significant stress on the cylinder pin and loose parts that caused the gun to misfire. The model was also overshadowed by continued development and improved features related to the metallic cartridge. As a result, only 7,000 were manufactured, primarily in 1871 and 1872.

A superb example of the Open Top Frontier is serial number 4974 in the Autry Collection. The revolver features engraving by Louis D. Nimschke. Based out of New York, Nimschke engraved revolvers made by various manufacturers primarily for the company Schuyler, Hartley & Graham. Serial number 4974 features engraving on the silver-plated barrel and frame. The gold-plated ejector rod housing is also engraved. The revolver's gold-plated cylinder features the roll-engraved naval battle scene found on previous percussion models such as the Model 1851 Navy, the Model 1860 Army, and the Model 1861 Navy. The Open Top Frontier was the last 19th-century Colt revolver to feature a roll-engraved cylinder scene.

Serial number 4974 also features silver-plated "Tiffany" grips with the "Civil War Battle Scene" design. The left side has an image of a cavalry officer leading a charge, and the right side shows the officer wounded and being attended to by his fellow troops. The back of the grip shows the shield of the United States. Other decorative elements are present, such as an axe and spears, along with an escutcheon that is standard on almost all "Tiffany" grips. The escutcheon is not inscribed. An American eagle graces the butt cap. All other areas of the grips are covered in a low-relief, intertwined ribbon design. The details and craftsmanship found on all "Tiffany" grips are truly amazing.

The "M" clearly marked on the left side of the grip strap indicates that this revolver is the model gun for the New Line .38 Caliber. (87.118.67)

MODEL GUN FOR THE
NEW LINE .38 CALIBER

A Quality-Control Device

Along with the Model 1871–72 Open Top Frontier, Colt's manufactured several pocket models designed specifically for the metallic cartridge shortly after the expiration of Roland White's patent rights. The Cloverleaf House Model, introduced in 1871, was the first. Chambered in .41 short and long rimfire, it had a standard three-inch barrel and weighed 14½ ounces. It featured a solid-frame construction similar to the Model 1855 Sidehammer Pocket. The solid-frame construction would soon become standard on all Colt models. The Open Top Pocket Model was introduced the same year as the Cloverleaf House, but it had an open-top, three-piece frame similar to Colt's standard percussion models. The Open Top Pocket was chambered in .22 short and long rimfire. It came in barrel lengths of two and three-eighths inches and two and seven-eighths inches and weighed as little as eight and three-quarter ounces. The Open Top was rather antiquated in design, and it was quickly replaced by the New Line series.

Manufactured from 1873 to 1884, the New Line series was a completely comprehensive line of pocket revolvers. The majority of the series was based on patent number 155,095 issued to William Mason on September 15, 1874. The patent application was rare in that the drawings depicted were almost identical to the standard production model. The revolvers were available in .22, .30, .32, .38, and .41 rimfire along with .32, .38, and .41 centerfire. Barrel lengths ranged from two and one-quarter inches to 10 inches. The frame came in five different sizes, and the grips came in three different sizes. Countless other variations existed. Several changes to the series were implemented in 1876, such as the location of the cylinder stops and the barrel markings, so individual revolvers are generally grouped according to the date of manufacture.

The New Line .38 Caliber was introduced in 1874 with production ceasing in 1880. Approximately 12,516 were produced. The revolver came in .38 short and long rimfire and .38 short and long centerfire. It was manufactured with either a two-and-one-quarter-inch or a four-inch barrel. The two-and-one-quarter-inch variation weighed 13½ ounces. The rarest New Line .38 is the model gun in the Autry Collection. Model guns form an exclusive subset of Colt firearms. They were made primarily from circa 1848 to circa 1920, but not all models had a corresponding model or master gun. Model guns were used frequently in the factory, often on the production line for various manufacturing and quality-control purposes. They were primarily stamped "M" prior to circa 1872 and either "M" or "MODEL" thereafter. In a few rare instances, "O" was also used. Model guns were sometimes repurposed and rebuilt into other arms, or they were scrapped entirely. As a result, only about 20 model guns are known to still exist.

The model gun for the New Line .38 has no grips, so the "M" marked on the left side of the grip strap is clearly visible. Manufactured circa 1874, the revolver is .38 rimfire with a barrel length of two and one-quarter inches. It is unfinished or "in the white." The model gun has several rare features, including short cylinder flutes, a stubby knurled cylinder pin, cylinder stops located on the cylinder periphery, and a German silver front sight. The model gun is also cut away on the left and right sides of the frame. This example is the only known model gun for the entire New Line series, and it is the only known New Line cutaway. The revolver's near mint condition increases its significance. The model gun was maintained by the Colt engineering department for reference until the 1920s, when it was given to one of the engineers upon his retirement. It was in the collection of prominent collector Robert Q. Sutherland for many years before it made its way into the Colt Industries corporate collection.

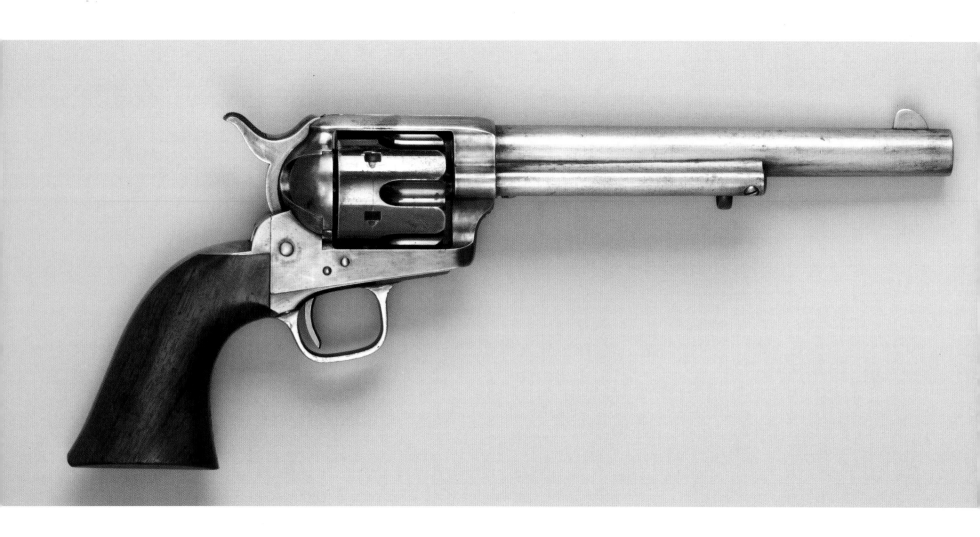

Serial number S1 was the first specimen ever produced of the Single Action Army, the most celebrated revolver in history and a symbol of the American West. (90.183.2)

THE FIRST SINGLE ACTION ARMY MODEL

The Handgun that Won the West

olt's Single Action Army Model is the most successful and recognizable revolver of all time. It has been in constant use for more than 130 years, and it remains one of the most popular firearms with collectors. Although it has been employed around the world, it was especially popular in the American West in the last few decades of the 19th century. Relied upon by people on both sides of the law, the Single Action Army was indispensable on the American frontier. It was used by pioneers, peace officers, gunslingers, outlaws, cowboys, and the military. More than any other handgun, it played a crucial role in the history and settlement of the region. Not surprisingly, it is commonly called "the handgun that won the West."

The use of the Single Action Army by Western entertainers solidified its status as a veritable symbol of the region. From 19th-century Wild West shows to contemporary Western movies and television series, the Single Action Army is the firearm most commonly used by Western entertainers. The revolver was so ubiquitous in popular culture that a television Western series, aptly titled *Colt .45*, was even named after it. A script from the series, which ran from 1957 to 1960, is part of the Autry Collection. A single-action revolver requires the user to manually cock the hammer before the trigger can be used to fire it, so Western entertainers often "fan" the hammer with their free hand to fire rapidly. This practice is extremely inaccurate and was used only by the best marksmen on the American frontier. Regardless of how it is used, the Single Action Army has been and will continue to be a staple of Western entertainment.

Colt's promoted the connection between the Single Action Army and the West in a variety of ways. A notable example is the advertising poster distributed by the company in 1926 featuring artwork by Frank Schoonover. The image, based on a real person, features a lone sheriff carrying a Single Action Army while riding a horse in the desert. Commonly called "Tex and His Horse, Patches," the advertisement was discontinued in 1934. A rare Spanish language version of the poster is part of the Autry Collection.

The first Single Action Army ever produced was serial number S1, now in the Autry Collection. It was manufactured in 1872 as a sample of the company's new large-caliber revolver that they planned to unveil the following year. It was taken to England for promotional purposes by General William B. Franklin, Colt's vice president and general agent, in June 1872. Serial number S1 was returned to the Hartford armory in 1875. At least two other samples were produced. One was given to the United States Ordnance Department for testing in November 1872 and another was likely retained by the Hartford armory as a model. Exactly what happened to these revolvers is unclear, as serial number S1 is the only sample known to still exist.

Serial number S1 has many unique and rare features. It is the only Single Action Army known to exist that was originally manufactured in .44 S & W American caliber. No other frame is known to have the flattened frontal configuration. The size and shape of the markings found on the revolver are also unique. These features indicate that the revolver was produced prior to the design being finalized for mass production. Other rare features include a German silver blade front sight, a pinched frame forming the rear sight, a thick trigger guard, a bulbous loading gate, and a back strap notched for a shoulder stock. As the first Single Action Army ever produced, serial number S1 is an amazing piece of American history.

FINAL

COLT .45

"Dead Aim"

August 4, 1958

Opposite:
The Western television series *Colt .45* both capitalized on and helped increase the popularity of the Single Action Army. (IT99-112-254; courtesy of Mr. and Mrs. Gene Autry)

Right:
An image of a cowboy carrying a Single Action Army in the American West is one of the most famous advertisements ever distributed by Colt's. (2012.2.41; the George Gamble Collection)

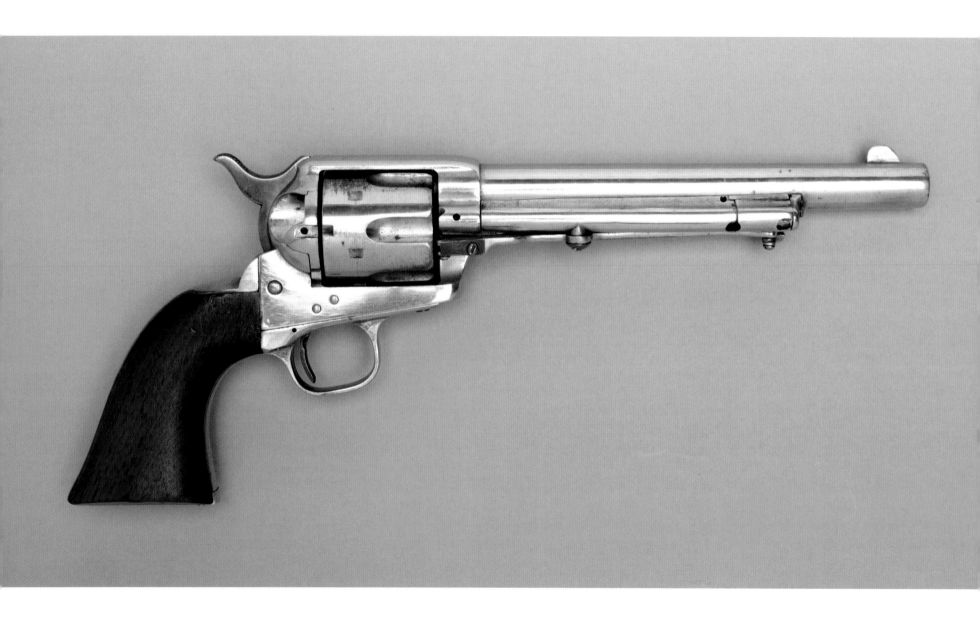

The experimental cartridge extraction system resting along the bottom of the barrel was designed to address the biggest critique of the Single Action Army. (87.118.43)

EXPERIMENTAL SINGLE ACTION ARMY MODEL

A Cartridge Extraction System

The success of the Single Action Army is a result of its superior design and craftsmanship. Since its introduction, it has been hailed as one of the finest firearms ever manufactured. Three distinct production runs beginning in 1873 have produced more than 450,000 revolvers for the civilian and military markets. With so many revolvers manufactured, it is not surprising that considerable variations and special features exist within the model. For example, the Single Action Army was manufactured in 30 different calibers and barrel lengths ranging from two to 16 inches. The overall appearance of the model, however, has remained relatively constant since the first prototypes or samples were produced in 1872.

The adoption of the Single Action Army by the United States military was instrumental to the success of the model. An early sample was sent to the Ordnance Department in 1872 and testing continued into 1873. The military ultimately approved and adopted the model, declaring it superior to the competition in almost every regard. The Single Action Army remained the dominant sidearm of the military for the rest of the 19th century. The first government contract was placed on July 23, 1873, with the last order being delivered in April 1891. Approximately 37,000 revolvers were purchased by the government. Military arms included inspectors' marks on the grips and various metal parts, with a "U.S." stamping on the left side of the frame.

The only critique of the Single Action Army was its relatively slow cartridge extraction process. In an attempt to resolve this issue, especially with the military, Colt's manufactured a revolver in 1874 with an experimental cartridge extraction system. Now part of the Autry Collection, the revolver is serial number 13947. A unique ejector assembly system is attached to the cylinder and rests along the bottom of the barrel. When the ejector is pulled, it automatically rotates the cylinder and plunges a rod through the chamber, extracting the spent cartridge through an opening in the loading gate. Records indicate that the cartridge extraction system was proposed to the Ordnance Department in 1875, but it was never sent for final testing. Apparently, the system was not fully perfected and further experiments never took place. Serial number 13947 is so unique it was the only example to have an entire chapter devoted exclusively to it in the groundbreaking publication *A Study of the Colt Single Action Army Revolver* (1976) by Ron Graham, John A. Kopec, and C. Kenneth Moore.

The provenance of serial number 13947 is rather interesting. No shipping records for the revolver exist, indicating that it may have never left the factory. The revolver, however, appears to be a cavalry-inspected model, as the customary "U.S." is stamped on the left side of the frame, so it may have been with the military for a short time. It was featured in the Colt corporate collection for many years. Singer Mel Tormé, the "Velvet Fog," acquired it directly from Colt's in 1951. Tormé was an avid collector of single-action Colts, and serial number 13947 was arguably the featured specimen in his collection. He reluctantly sold the revolver and many others in 1978 to cover the costs of a divorce settlement. The revolver made its way into the Colt Industries corporate collection, and it became part of the Autry Collection when the museum acquired Colt's collection in 1987. Given its history and provenance, serial number 13947 is a unique specimen in the storied production of the Single Action Army.

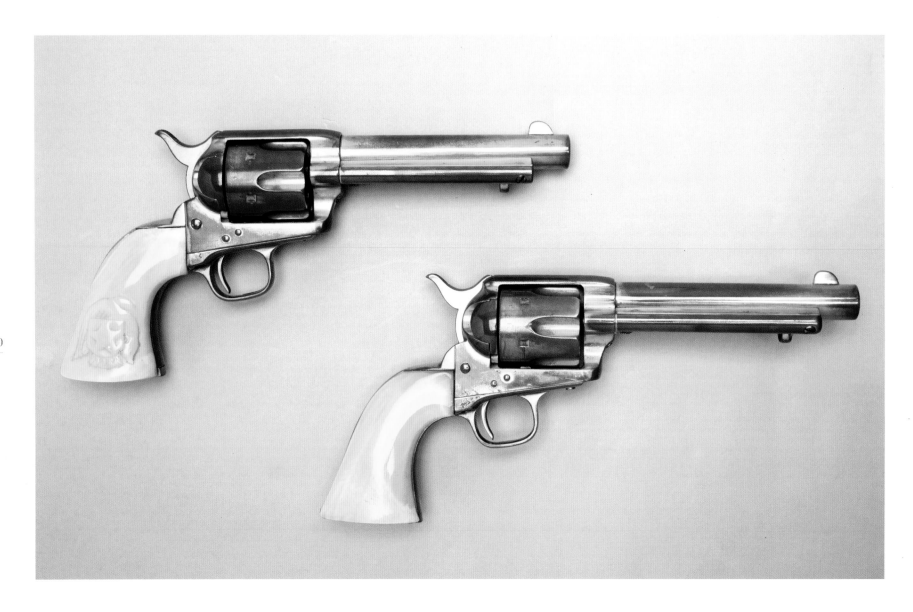

Pawnee Bill had an affinity for matched revolvers, and he used this pair of Single Action Armies while performing in a Wild West show. (2001.74.1-.2; donated by Petra and Greg Martin)

WILD WEST SHOWMAN PAWNEE BILL'S SINGLE ACTION ARMY MODEL PAIR

The Other Bill

Gordon William Lillie was one of the great contributors to the Wild West show, but he is often overshadowed by his more famous contemporary, William F. "Buffalo Bill" Cody. Born in Bloomington, Illinois, in 1860, Lillie grew up fascinated with the American West and the colorful characters that defined it. One of his most vivid recollections as a child was seeing Buffalo Bill, James Butler "Wild Bill" Hickok, and John Baker "Texas Jack" Omohundro in Bloomington while they were promoting their stage play *The Scouts of the Plains* as it toured the country. While still in his teens, Lillie made his way into Indian Territory, finding work as a trapper and cowboy. Introduced to the Pawnee tribe, he spent his free time learning their customs and language. In 1879, Lillie became a teacher for the Pawnee while serving as an interpreter and secretary to a federal Indian agent. It was during this time that the tribe gave him the nickname "Pawnee Bill."

In 1883, Pawnee Bill became acquainted with an associate of Buffalo Bill's, who was attempting to secure several Pawnee for service in Buffalo Bill's newly established Wild West show. The associate was captivated by Pawnee Bill's appearance and ability to communicate with Native Americans, so he recommended him to his employer. Buffalo Bill was also impressed, so he hired him to take part in the show and act as an interpreter. Pawnee Bill worked for Buffalo Bill for two years, one season with the main show and another with a smaller traveling show. Both shows took Pawnee Bill across the country, where he and his fellow performers dazzled audiences. While traveling with the show in Philadelphia, Pawnee Bill met a young Quaker girl named May Manning. After two years of courtship, the couple was married.

Manning and her family convinced Pawnee Bill to start his own Wild West show. With financial backing in place, "Pawnee Bill's Wild West" began touring the country in 1888. The show was a financial disappointment. The following year, Pawnee Bill led a group of settlers into present-day Oklahoma when the territory was opened up to white settlement. His exploits led to national attention, and Pawnee Bill used the opportunity to revive his Wild West show. Organized under several different names, Pawnee Bill's shows often featured Manning as the "Champion Girl Horseback Shot of the West." The shows traveled across America and Europe, operating with varying degrees of success. In 1908, Pawnee Bill acquired a controlling interest in Buffalo Bill's struggling show and the two were merged as "Buffalo Bill's Wild West and Pawnee Bill's Great Far East." The show operated for several seasons. Pawnee Bill spent his later years preserving the history of the American West through various business ventures, including ranching and filmmaking.

As a showman and entertainer, Pawnee Bill had an affinity for matched revolvers. Factory records indicate that Colt's presented a pair to him in 1902 and another in 1906. The only pair known to still exist is in the Autry Collection, and it predates the two factory presentations by many years. The revolvers feature rare consecutive serial numbers, 14844 and 14845, both manufactured in 1874. Although one of the revolvers was originally shipped to New York, the pair was purchased by Pawnee Bill in England while he was on tour. They were used frequently, but their fine condition reveals they were properly cared for. Both revolvers have a gold finish with relief-carved bone grips. One side of each grip is embellished with an eagle wrapping its wings around a heraldic shield decorated with a single star. The embellishments are on opposite sides of each revolver so both are visible when worn as a pair. The revolvers also feature an inscription written in script on the back strap that reads "Major Gordon W. Lillie."

Internal mechanisms and the rifling of the barrel are evident in this rare demonstrator, assembler, and cutaway Single Action Army. (87.118.42)

CUTAWAY SINGLE ACTION ARMY MODEL

A Skeletonized Army Regulation Pistol

The Single Action Army was initially called the "New Model Army Metallic Cartridge Revolving Pistol" by the company. Countless other nicknames have been used over time, including "Peacemaker," "Equalizer," "Thumb Buster," "Plow Handle," "Hog Leg," and the "Colt .45." Designed by William Mason and Charles B. Richards, the most noticeable difference between the model and the vast majority of percussion models that preceded it was the solid frame. Another noticeable difference was the addition of an ejector rod and ejector rod housing along the bottom right side of the barrel. This replaced the loading lever, which was no longer necessary with the use of the metallic cartridge. Significant but less noticeable changes also included the way the cylinder was attached to the frame, how the hand turned the cylinder, and the shape of the hammer. Two of the gauges used in the manufacture of the parts that composed the first Single Action Armies are now part of the Autry Collection.

Colt's produced a cutaway or skeletal arm of the Single Action Army early in its production run in an attempt to entice government orders. In 1875, General William B. Franklin, Colt's vice president and general agent, wrote to the Ordnance Department informing it of his desire to donate a "skeletonized Army Regulation pistol" for deposit in the museum at the Springfield armory, America's first and last national armory. The Ordnance Department confirmed the acceptance of the revolver and thanked Franklin for the donation. The cutaway appears to have made a dramatic impression given the number of Single Action Armies the government ultimately contracted. It is believed that the cutaway revolver was eventually returned to Colt's sometime after the model was no longer being used by the military. The revolver was later featured in the Colt Arms Collection at the Connecticut State Library and then in the Colt Industries corporate collection. The cutaway revolver was serial number 15407, and it is now part of the Autry Collection.

One of the rarest cutaways, serial number 15407 was also a demonstrator and assembler model. Manufactured in 1875, the revolver is exceptionally crafted and in excellent condition. The frame and loading gate are case hardened, and the revolver has a high-gloss blue finish. The grips are one-piece, varnished walnut. The barrel is seven and a half inches and the caliber is .45 Colt. The revolver is devoid of patent markings, probably due to the fact that the markings would have been made partially illegible during the cutaway process. The revolver is cut away extensively on the frame, barrel, and cylinder to reveal the mechanics of this truly revolutionary model. In fact, out of a production run of more than 450,000, serial number 15407 is the only example that is cut away to show the operation of the internal mechanisms of the Single Action Army.

The left side of the frame is cut away in two spots forward of the cylinder, in nine places on the recoil shield, and to the left of the trigger screw. This clearly reveals the locking mechanism, while the left side of the barrel is cut away near the muzzle to reveal the rifling. The left side of the grip is cut away in two places. The right side of the frame is cut away forward of the cylinder and five times to the right of the hammer screw, including over the loading gate spring. The cylinder is cut away completely through one of the chambers. Additional cuts include the trigger guard strap twice by the guard bow and once on the right side of the strap and at the muzzle end of the ejector rod housing. All the cuts on serial number 15407 clearly expose the features and craftsmanship of Colt's greatest model.

Gauges like this were used to check the cylinder
of the Single Action Army during its initial
production. (85.1.687; acquisition made possible
in part by John E. Bianchi Jr.)

The hammer-trigger gauge used in the production
of the Single Action Army was originally given
to the United States Army for instructional
purposes. (85.1.689; acquisition made possible in
part by John E. Bianchi Jr.)

The defining feature of the famed "Buntline
Special" Single Action Army is the extra-long
barrel, in this instance 16 inches. (87.118.93.1)

"BUNTLINE SPECIAL" SINGLE ACTION ARMY MODEL

The Life and Legend

The "Buntline Special" is the most celebrated variation of the Single Action Army. Approximately 30 of the revolvers were produced in 1876. The defining feature of the revolver is an exceptionally long barrel that ranges from 10 to 16 inches. Serial number 28802 in the Autry Collection has a 16-inch barrel. The revolver gets its name from dime novel author Ned Buntline. In the book *Wyatt Earp: Frontier Marshal*, published in 1931, author Stuart N. Lake claimed that Buntline presented five of the revolvers to several prominent Dodge City lawmen, including Wyatt Earp. Earp subsequently was portrayed on film and television carrying the revolver. The accuracy of the story is hotly debated by experts on both sides. Although the true story of the "Buntline Special" may never be known, a clearer understanding of how it got its name is possible.

Born Edward Zane Carroll Judson in the early 1820s, Ned Buntline lived a life that was stranger and more fascinating than any of the characters he wrote about in his dime novels. He served two stints in the military, one honorably and one dishonorably. He was arrested on several occasions, having killed at least one man and having shot another. He was run out of several towns and almost lynched. In 1849, he was an active participant in the deadly Astor Place Riot in the city of New York that pitted nativists against immigrants. Throughout all of his newsworthy exploits, Buntline found time to work as a writer and publisher. Today, he is remembered primarily for his highly fictionalized Western stories, a few of which centered on the life of William F. "Buffalo Bill" Cody. In 1872, Buntline wrote a Western play called *The Scouts of the Prairie*, which introduced Buffalo Bill to show business and served as an early variation of the Wild West show.

In 1931, several decades after Buntline's death, a biography written by Stuart Lake about a little-known lawman named Wyatt Earp was published. Titled *Wyatt Earp: Frontier Marshal*, the book portrayed Earp as the embodiment of law and order on the American frontier. It was extremely popular with the public, and it catapulted the recently deceased Earp to everlasting fame. According to Lake, Buntline traveled to Dodge City, Kansas, sometime around 1876 to pay tribute to Earp and several other notable lawmen that had been the inspiration for some of his Western stories. The other lawmen included Bat Masterson, Charles Bassett, Neal Brown, and Bill Tilghman. Buntline supposedly presented all of the men with custom-made Single Action Armies that featured extra-long barrels. While some of the men ultimately cut the barrel down because it was unwieldy, Lake wrote that the long-barreled Colt quickly became Earp's favorite weapon. The association with Earp made the revolver famous, and it soon became known as the "Buntline Special."

Several motion pictures about Earp were released in the 20th century, many of which credit Lake's biography as their source, and almost all of them show Earp using the weapon. On the television series *The Life and Legend of Wyatt Earp* (1955–1961), starring Hugh O'Brian in the title role, the "Buntline Special" was practically its own character. Despite Lake's claim and its subsequent acceptance by the general public, many historians and authors question the validity of Earp's or Buntline's association with the revolver. Critics point to few contemporary references to the revolver, including none by Buntline or Earp. Critics also attack the specifics of the supposed presentation, including Buntline's motives and relationship with Earp, pointing out that many of the recipients were not lawmen or even in Dodge City at the time. Finally, critics note that Colt factory records do not corroborate Lake's story. Supporters of the story have an answer for every accusation, and their assertions are often as compelling. Controversy aside, the name "Buntline Special" continues to be used, and the revolver remains an indelible part of Western history.

In pristine condition, serial number 28819 reveals
how the "Buntline Special" originally looked when
it left the factory in 1876. (86.2.2.1a)

"BUNTLINE SPECIAL" SINGLE ACTION ARMY MODEL

The Complete Package

While the association between Ned Buntline, Wyatt Earp, and the "Buntline Special" is unclear, Colt's did manufacture several Single Action Armies with exceptionally long barrels in 1876. The revolvers are all found in the serial number range between 28800 and 28830. While as many as 31 may have been manufactured, factory records only provide information on about half of them. In the range, 11 revolvers are listed with 16-inch barrels, one is listed with a 12-inch barrel, and three are listed with 10-inch barrels. While the factory records are unclear on the rest of the serial number range, expert analysis has led to the confirmation of 22 "Buntline Specials." They are serial numbers 28800, 28802, 28803, 28805, 28806, 28807, 28808, 28809, 28810, 28811, 28812, 28813, 28815, 28816, 28818, 28819, 28822, 28823, 28824, 28825, 28826, and 28830. Of these, approximately 12 are known to still exist in their original condition.

The "Buntline Special" has a unique frame to accommodate its long barrel, and in fact, it is the combination of the frame and long barrel that makes the revolver unique. Several Single Action Armies have barrels ranging from eight inches to 10½ inches, but they have normal frames so they are not considered "Buntline Specials." The frame of a true "Buntline Special" has a flat top strap above the cylinder with a folding recessed sight. When the sight is laying flat in the top strap groove, a small notch is available for aiming at objects that are in close range. The sight flips up for long-distance aiming using an adjustable bar with an aperture. "Buntline Specials" also have rifled front sights that differ from the standard model, although the exact design of the front sight on the "Buntline Special" fluctuates on individual examples.

Another unique design feature of the "Buntline Special" is the extended trigger screw designed to accommodate a skeletonized shoulder stock. An example of the stock can be found in the Autry Collection. Made of nickel-plated brass, the stock attached to the revolver using the extended trigger screws with a clamp that fit onto the bottom of the grip. The stock was secured by tightening a knurled nut near the back of the grip. The design

of the "Buntline Special," with its extended barrel and shoulder stock, was intended to turn a handgun into a rifle. Unfortunately, the "Buntline Special" did not perform as anticipated. This is evidenced by the limited number manufactured, and the fact that several surviving examples have barrels that were purposely shortened at some point.

The "Buntline Special" was originally introduced at the Philadelphia Centennial Exhibition in 1876. Like the rest of the revolvers on display at the exhibition, the "Buntline Specials" were of the highest quality and condition. However, those that exist today are often in very poor condition. A notable exception is serial number 28819 in the Autry Collection. It is in virtually mint condition. The revolver retains its deep-blue finish and the brilliant, case-hardened colors are clearly evident. The revolver's original nickel-plated stock is also in near mint condition. Even more impressive, serial number 28819 is the only "Buntline Special" accompanied by an original, custom-made holster. The hand-tooled holster is designed to carry the gun on the inside and the stock on the outside. Given its condition and accessories, serial number 28819 is the finest "Buntline Special" known to exist.

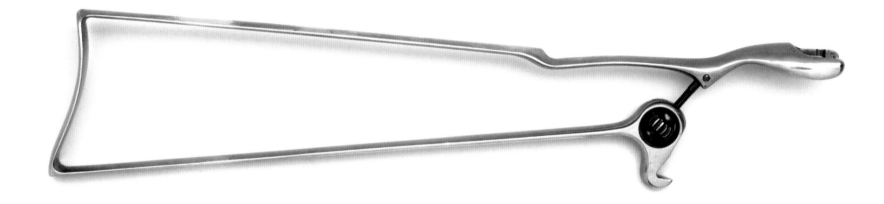

All "Buntline Specials" originally came with
a skeletonized nickel-plated shoulder stock.
(86.2.2.1b)

Serial number 28819 is the only "Buntline Special" that is accompanied by an original custom-made holster. (86.2.2.2)

Mexican silversmiths elaborately customized the
Single Action Army carried by trick roper and
Wild West show performer Vicente Oropeza.
(2012.2.15; the George Gamble Collection)

TRICK ROPER VICENTE OROPEZA'S SINGLE ACTION ARMY MODEL

Charro Mexicano

Wild West shows were extremely popular and an indelible part of American culture from 1883 to around the outbreak of World War I. Millions of Americans witnessed the spectacle, with countless shows achieving varying degrees of success. Some of the more successful shows, such as those organized by William F. "Buffalo Bill" Cody and Gordon "Pawnee Bill" Lillie, even toured Europe. Wild West shows featured a variety of acts that showcased the supposed adventure, excitement, danger, and glory of life on the American frontier. Performers at various times included sharpshooter Annie Oakley, future actor Tom Mix, pioneer African American cowboy Bill Picket, Native American Chief Sitting Bull, and Buck Taylor, "King of the Cowboys." Another popular performer who is all but forgotten today was Vicente Oropeza, the man who popularized trick roping in the United States.

Billed as the "Premier 'Charro Mexicano' of the World," Vicente Oropeza, of Puebla, Mexico, was Buffalo Bill's chief of vaqueros and a gifted performer. Oropeza joined Buffalo Bill's Wild West show in 1893, and his trick roping wowed audiences for more than a decade. Oropeza's lasso seemed to be a living creature. He spun it horizontally, vertically, in figure eights, around his body, and over his head. He jumped in and out of it. He even used a lasso to spell his own name. He also performed intricate tricks catching horses and riders. Many of his routines were the basis for events performed at modern-day rodeos. In 1900, Oropeza won the first World Champion of Trick and Fancy Roping competition in New York. His performances and accolades garnered him legions of fans across North America.

One of the most striking aspects of Oropeza was his appearance. He wore the finest of vaquero clothing, including an embroidered jacket, buckskin trousers, and an elaborately decorated sombrero. He also carried a beautifully engraved Single Action Army, serial number 35521, which is now part of the Autry Collection. The revolver originally was shipped to Omaha, Nebraska, in 1877, with a nickel-plated finish. Sometime around 1881 it was customized by Mexican silversmiths who added silver plating and sterling-silver grips. The final product features a detailed scroll pattern relief engraved on most of the revolver's surfaces. A similar motif is relief

engraved on the grips. A rope border is located along the butt and a ribbed design is used along the trigger guard and the bottom of the frame. Inscribed on the right panel of the sterling-silver butt is "Para el mejor Charro / Don / Vicente Oropeza" (translated "For the best Charro / Don / Vicente Oropeza") and inscribed on the left is "De sus amigos / Los Charros / Mexico 1881" ("Your Friends / Los Charros / Mexico 1881").

Will Rogers was one of Oropeza's biggest fans. A 13-year-old Rogers saw Oropeza perform in Chicago in 1893 as part of Buffalo Bill's Wild West show. Like countless other spectators, Rogers was captivated by the Mexican trick roper, and he began practicing the moment he returned home. Crafting his skills over several years, Rogers performed at circuses, on the vaudeville circuit, and in motion pictures. Rogers eventually became the most popular and famous trick roper in American history. Rogers's magnetism and presence allowed him to parlay his success as a trick roper into movie stardom. Rogers also found success as a writer and radio personality. He came to be known as America's humorist-philosopher, a commentator on the reality and often absurd nature of life in early 20th-century America. While many individuals had a profound impact on Rogers's life, it was an early opportunity to see Vicente Oropeza that started him on a path to fame.

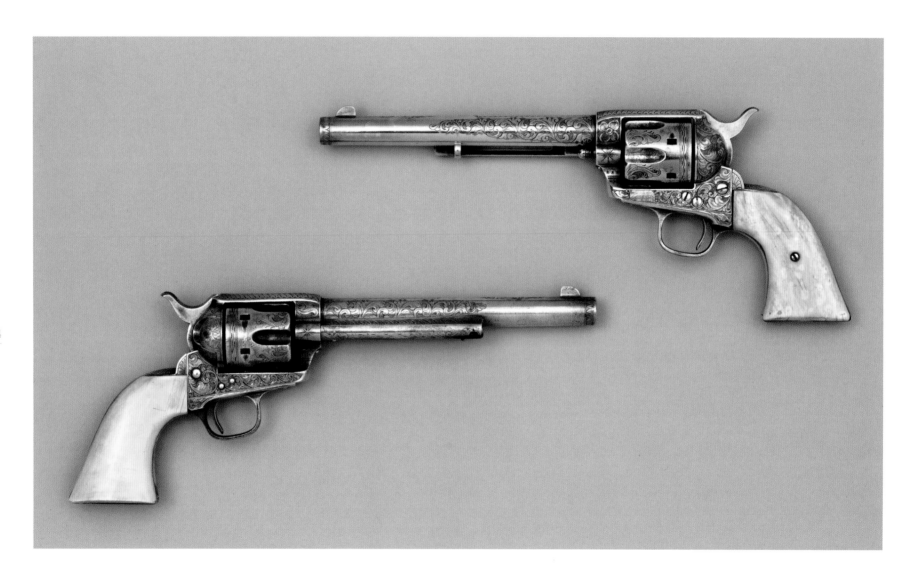

A pair of vintage Single Action Armies was refurbished for use by Paul Newman in the film *Buffalo Bill and the Indians, or Sitting Bull's History Lesson.* (85.1.1337-.1338; acquisition made possible in part by John E. Bianchi Jr.)

ACTOR PAUL NEWMAN'S
SINGLE ACTION ARMY MODEL PAIR

The Star

Director Robert Altman was a Hollywood legend. A true auteur, Altman used a naturalistic but highly stylized perspective to deconstruct some of the industry's most beloved genres and the conventions that held them together. He deftly skewered long-standing traditions, assumptions, and values. While he could be extremely difficult to work with, he was beloved by actors for his creativity and the performances he was able to cultivate. He brought out the best in every actor on a film, from Hollywood's biggest stars to background performers. Encouraging spontaneity and improvisation, his films featured overlapping dialogue and unexpected quirks. In a Hollywood career that lasted almost 50 years, he saw many ups and downs. One film that was highly criticized at the time of its release but reevaluated in later years was *Buffalo Bill and the Indians, or Sitting Bull's History Lesson* (1976), starring Paul Newman.

Newman was one of the 20th century's greatest movie stars. Playing a variety of flawed heroes and charming antiheroes, he was the embodiment of the likable rebel. His magnetism and appeal were complimented by his good looks and vibrant personality. Even as he aged and took on more weathered characters, he remained a movie star with a commanding presence. By 1976, he was one of Hollywood's biggest stars and a seasoned veteran of Westerns, having appeared in *The Left Handed Gun* (1958), *Hud* (1963), *Hombre* (1967), *Butch Cassidy and the Sundance Kid* (1969), and *The Life and Times of Judge Roy Bean* (1972). The film *Buffalo Bill and the Indians* was supposed to reteam him with George Roy Hill, his director on the hugely successful *Butch Cassidy and the Sundance Kid*, but Hill dropped out before the project began. Newman stayed on board and eventually found himself teamed with one of Hollywood's great mavericks.

Buffalo Bill and the Indians was loosely based on the play *Indians* (1968) by Arthur Kopi. Whereas Kopi's play was a dark political comedy that focused on the mistreatment and injustices visited upon Native Americans, Altman's film broadened the perspective to focus on American history, Western mythology, and the notion of hero worship. Besides Newman as William F. "Buffalo Bill" Cody (the star), it featured Joel Grey as Nat Salisbury (the producer), Harvey Keitel as Ed Goodman (the relative),

Geraldine Chaplin as Annie Oakley (the sure shot), Burt Lancaster as Ned Buntline (the legend maker), and Fred N. Larsen as Buck Taylor (the king of the cowboys). The film was set in Wyoming, but it was shot primarily on location in Alberta, Canada. It was released in June 1976.

Careful attention went into making sure every set and prop looked authentic. For example, a pair of vintage Single Action Armies used by Newman, serial numbers 57956 and 58725, was refurbished to look more like the fancy guns Buffalo Bill often carried. The revolvers, now part of the Autry Collection, were given ivory grips and were silver plated with an engraved floral design. But while the film looked like a traditional Western, it was clear that Newman's Buffalo Bill as envisioned by Altman was not the hero that had been portrayed valiantly in dime novels, Wild West shows, and other movies. Newman's Buffalo Bill was a man who had bought into his own mythology and capitalized on it at the expense of historical reality and the perception of Native Americans. Newman's Buffalo Bill was content until Sitting Bull joined his show and demanded changes that forced the star to confront his sense of history and audience expectations. The film's initial reviews were negative and box office performance was poor. However, as the years passed and other films took on the notion of mythmaking in the American West, *Buffalo Bill and the Indians* gained a new audience and its critical reception improved dramatically.

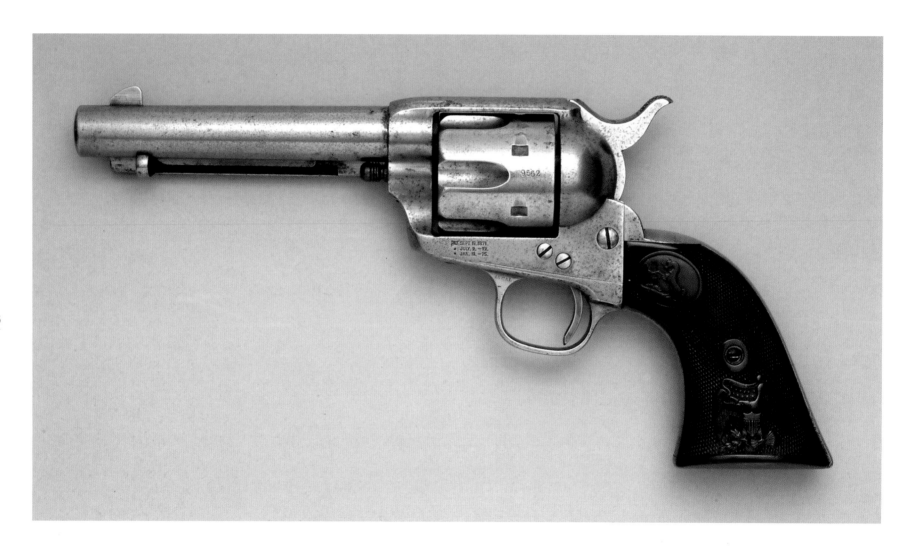

Wyatt Earp's Single Action Army was a prized possession of Captain Fred Dodge, a Wells Fargo agent and friend of the lawman. (85.1.1628; acquisition made possible in part by John E. Bianchi Jr.)

LAWMAN WYATT EARP'S SINGLE ACTION ARMY MODEL

Frontier Marshal

The name Wyatt Earp is synonymous with justice on the American frontier. Earp was a peace officer in various Western towns, but he also found himself on the opposite side of the law on many occasions. Not surprisingly, Earp owned many firearms during his lifetime, including Single Action Army serial number 69562, which is now in the Autry Collection. Earp gave the revolver, manufactured in 1881, to his friend Captain Fred Dodge, another colorful figure in the history of the American West who spent time as a special agent for Wells, Fargo & Co. Earp is best remembered for his participation in the so-called Gunfight at the O.K. Corral, an altercation that has come to symbolize the struggle between legal authority and banditry on the American frontier. Although Earp's reputation was tarnished during his lifetime, accounts of his Western exploits after his death revitalized his image. Today, he is remembered as an icon of the American West.

Born in 1848, Earp's first foray into law enforcement was as a constable in Lamar Township in Barton County, Missouri, in 1869. Earp was constable for about 15 months, and during that time, he performed a variety of routine law-enforcement tasks. He left Lamar in 1871 under a cloud of suspicion prior to the fulfillment of his term. Earp was accused, but never convicted, of embezzling funds and defrauding his creditors. A few months later, he was indicted for stealing horses in Indian Territory. Earp failed to appear in court, and a warrant was issued for his arrest. When he was never located, he was branded a fugitive from federal justice. Earp later served as a policeman in Wichita, Kansas, for one year from 1875 into 1876. He was fired after getting into a fistfight with one of the candidates running for city marshal. He then moved to Dodge City, where he served on and off as an assistant marshal from 1876 to 1879. Earp's time in Dodge City supposedly garnered him fame across the West as a feared lawman. In reality, Earp was a rather common assistant marshal.

Earp arrived in Tombstone late in 1879. He was involved in various business activities in the community, and in 1880, he was appointed deputy sheriff of Pima County, which included jurisdiction over Tombstone. Earp and his brothers, Virgil—the region's deputy United States marshal—and Morgan, along with Earp's friend John "Doc" Holliday, soon found themselves at odds with a group of rustlers and ruffians known as the Cowboys. The animosity was a result of political, social, and emotional differences. On October 26, 1881, the two sides faced off around 3:00 p.m. at a narrow lot between Harwood House and Fly's Boarding House and Photography Studio about six doors down from the O.K. Corral on Fremont Street. Approximately 34 bullets were exchanged over the course of 30 seconds. In the end, Earp emerged unscathed, Holliday was bruised, and Virgil and Morgan Earp were wounded. The Cowboys—Billy Clanton, Tom McLaury, and Frank McLaury—were killed.

Murder charges were filed against the Earps and Holliday, but after a monthlong hearing, it was determined that there was not enough evidence to indict the men. Earp left Tombstone, and he spent his final years roaming the West and Alaska. He even spent time in Los Angeles serving as a consultant for Western movies. Late in life, Earp unsuccessfully tried to sell his story to the film studios, and a book about his life written by his friend and secretary John Flood was never published. Finally, two years after his passing in 1931, author Stuart Lake published a popular biography of Earp titled *Wyatt Earp: Frontier Marshal*. The book glossed over Earp's unsavory past and instead portrayed the lawman as a hero of unquestionable courage, morality, and character. The gunfight in Tombstone, portrayed as a battle of good versus evil, was his shining moment. The book was the basis for many of the more than 50 films and television episodes that have turned Earp into an American institution.

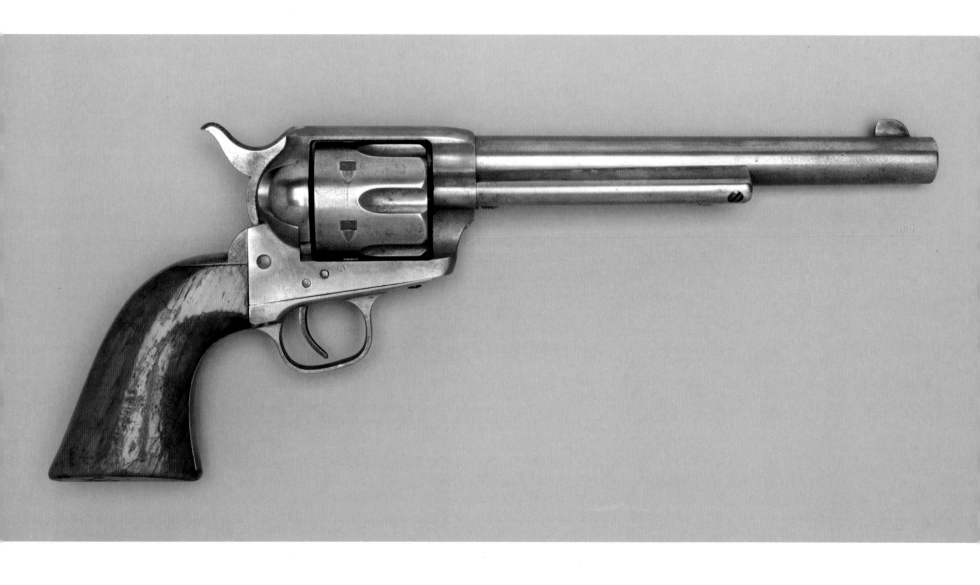

John Clum carried a Single Action Army for protection in the aftermath of the Gunfight at the O.K. Corral. (85.1.639; acquisition made possible in part by John E. Bianchi Jr.)

TOMBSTONE MAYOR JOHN CLUM'S SINGLE ACTION ARMY MODEL

The Site of the Gunfight

J ohn Philip Clum played a pivotal role in two of the biggest events in the history of the Arizona Territory: the Apache Wars and the so-called Gunfight at the O.K. Corral. These events had lasting implications for Western and American history. In 1874, the Office of Indian Affairs, now the Bureau of Indian Affairs, appointed Clum the Indian agent for the San Carlos Apache Reservation in the Arizona Territory. Only 22 years old, Clum had no formal experience in such matters, but he had sufficient connections to land the position. Recognizing that the Apache had been treated horribly by former Indian agents and the United States Army, Clum hired Apache police officers and appointed Indian judges. While Clum was proud of his system of "Indian self-rule," the Apache actually had no say in the laws that governed their lives. Clum was also quick to make distinctions between "good" and "bad" Indians. Despite its limitations, Clum's system was better and far more effective than previous attempts aimed at regulating the reservation.

In 1876, officials at the Office of Indian Affairs closed the Chiricahua Apache Reservation in the southeastern part of the territory and ordered Clum to move the inhabitants to San Carlos. Official government policy sought to turn all Native Americans into farmers, but this was contrary to the Chiricahua way of life. A group of Chiricahua, led by the mighty Geronimo, fled during the relocation. The activities of Geronimo and his band of Chiricahua threatened the government's hegemony in the region, so Clum was ordered to capture him. In April 1877, Clum and about 100 Apache policemen arrested Geronimo and a number of his followers near the Ojo Caliente Reservation in the New Mexico Territory. It was the first and only time Geronimo was captured without a shot being fired by either side.

Clum left the Office of Indian Affairs, and in 1880, he moved to the newly established mining town of Tombstone. With some prior experience in publishing, Clum established *The Tombstone Epitaph* that same year. Still in existence to this day, the *Epitaph* is the oldest continually published newspaper in Arizona. Clum was also involved in various aspects of the town's social and cultural life. He was elected mayor in 1881, and when the town was officially incorporated as a city a short time later, Clum became the city of Tombstone's first mayor. He was serving in that capacity when

the Gunfight at the O.K. Corral took place on October 26, 1881. Clum was a friend and prominent supporter of the Earp faction. His support, especially in the hearing that followed the gunfight, angered those who sided with the Cowboys. A stagecoach carrying Clum was riddled with bullets, and he was threatened on several other occasions. In response, Clum carried a Single Action Army for protection. Clum's revolver, serial number 72157, which was manufactured in 1881, is now part of the Autry Collection.

The controversy surrounding the gunfight and Clum's unwavering support of the Earp faction tarnished his reputation. His tenure as mayor ended in 1882, and he sold his interest in the *Epitaph* that same year. After spending a few years in various local positions, he finally left the Arizona Territory for good around 1886. His final years were just as adventurous as his early ones. He established a real estate firm in Southern California, promoted the citrus industry for the San Bernardino County Board of Trade, worked as the assistant editor for the San Francisco *Examiner*, and served as an inspector for the United States Postal Service. He was also an active participant in the Alaskan gold rush, one of America's last great frontiers. By the time Clum died in 1932, he could honestly say he had seen the West at its wildest.

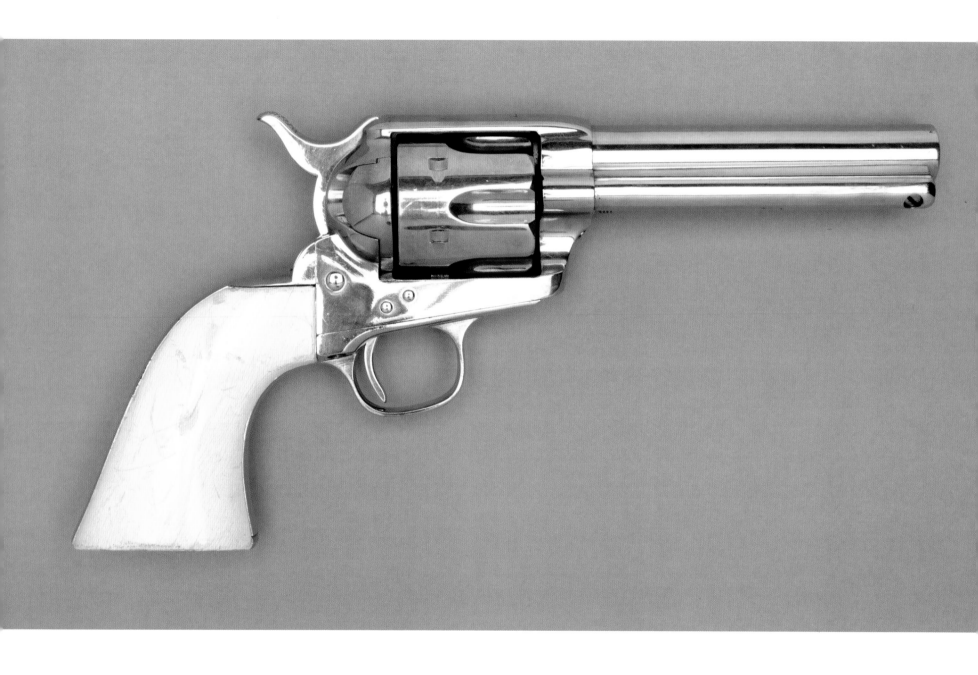

Clayton Moore used this nickel-plated Single Action Army with ivory grips on-screen as the Lone Ranger. (88.381.5; acquisition made possible in part by Jim Hoiby)

ACTOR CLAYTON MOORE'S SINGLE ACTION ARMY MODEL

Who Was that Masked Man?

Clayton Moore had a long and distinguished career as an actor, but he will always be associated with one iconic role. Moore played the Lone Ranger on television from 1949 to 1951 and from 1954 to 1957. He also played the character in two feature films, and he donned the mask for more than 40 years of personal appearances. Moore's Lone Ranger and his Native American sidekick Tonto roamed the West, righting wrongs and helping the less fortunate. Throughout his adventures, the Lone Ranger always carried nickel-plated Single Action Armies with cream-colored grips, such as serial number 81584 in the Autry Collection. The revolver was manufactured in 1882. The Lone Ranger only used his guns and trademark silver bullets as a last resort to disarm his opponents as painlessly as possible. He never shot to kill.

Born in Chicago in 1914, Jack Carlton Moore began performing at an early age. He grew up as a passionate fan of Westerns, and he recalled in later years that he always wanted to be a policeman or a cowboy. He performed in his youth as a trapeze artist, and he also spent time as a model. He moved to Hollywood in the late 1930s and initially found work as a stuntman and bit player. At the suggestion of a producer, he adopted the stage name "Clayton" Moore. He was cast in several Westerns in the 1940s, including the lead role of Jesse James in two serials produced by Republic Pictures. He even donned the mask of Zorro in the 1949 serial *Ghost of Zorro*. A fan of Moore's Zorro was broadcasting executive and producer George Washington Trendle.

Trendle began his association with the entertainment industry as a lawyer in Detroit, Michigan, specializing in movie contracts and leases. He owned an interest in various entertainment enterprises, including the radio station WXYZ. Westerns were not a part of early radio programming, but when Trendle sought to create a new program for his station, he believed a Western could be successful. With the help of scriptwriter Fran Striker and WXYZ staff director Jim Jewell, Trendle created the Lone Ranger, a western hero combining the traits of Robin Hood and Zorro. Marketed specifically to children, the Lone Ranger was designed to teach patriotism,

tolerance, fairness, sympathy, and compassion. The radio program became an instant success, spawning licensed merchandise, novels, comic strips, comic books, and motion pictures. In 1949, the character was adapted for television.

Moore was hired to play the Lone Ranger, with Jay Silverheels, a Mohawk Indian from Ontario, Canada, cast as his trusted sidekick, Tonto. With General Mills sponsoring the show, it debuted on ABC in September 1949. Within a year, the show averaged five million viewers, making it the top-rated Western on television. The show ran until 1957, and for many years it was a fixture in the Nielson Top 10. Moore played the title character in more than 160 episodes. When he left the show for one season over a contract dispute, it was clear that audiences had trouble identifying with anyone else in the role. After the television show was cancelled, Moore played the Lone Ranger in two feature films. Moore spent the rest of his life traveling the country as the Lone Ranger. In 1979, the company that owned the Lone Ranger acquired an injunction barring Moore from wearing the character's signature black mask. Even without the mask, audiences still identified Moore with the character and the company eventually relented. Although other actors have played the role, Clayton Moore will always be the Lone Ranger.

Theodore Roosevelt's Single Action Army
was used at a pivotal time in the life of one
of America's greatest politicians. (85.5.6;
acquisition made possible in part by Paul S. and
June A. Ebensteiner)

PRESIDENT THEODORE ROOSEVELT'S SINGLE ACTION ARMY MODEL

The Most Expensive Style

Theodore Roosevelt was the most accomplished and versatile individual to ever hold the office of president of the United States. An important chapter in his early life was the time he spent in the American West. Roosevelt first entered the region seeking adventure in 1883. He was attracted to the romantic notion of life on a cattle ranch and the virtues that came from surviving in the open country. He established the Maltese Cross Ranch, sometimes called the Chimney Butte Ranch, near Medora in the Dakota Territory (in a region now part of North Dakota) before returning to his home in New York. On February 14, 1884, unthinkable tragedy struck when Roosevelt's mother and wife died of separate causes within hours of each other in the same house. Despondent and heartbroken, Roosevelt sought solace on the frontier.

He returned to the Dakota Territory, spending the next few years living the life of a cowboy and frontiersman. He increased his interest in the cattle industry and purchased a second ranch, the Elkhorn, in 1884. Not content to simply oversee his cattle operation, he performed all the arduous tasks necessary for the upkeep of his herd. He became proficient in riding and roping, and he hunted almost daily. Roosevelt also found time to write, ultimately publishing three books about his time in the West. An exceptionally cold winter in 1886–1887 decimated his cattle, and he headed back east permanently thereafter. Roosevelt eventually became a national figure and many of the issues he championed as president, including the virtue of leading a strenuous life and the importance of conservation, were solidified during his tenure in the West.

Throughout his Western adventures, Roosevelt was the fanciest cowboy on the frontier. He brought with him, in his own words, "equipments finished in the most expensive style." He was always impeccably dressed in custom-made shirts, trousers, boots, and chaps. Buckskin was a favorite material. All of his equipment and gear was of the highest quality and opulently embellished. Roosevelt's firearms were particularly striking. His custom-order Winchester rifles and carbines were specially engraved and had deluxe features. Roosevelt also carried two Single Action Armies. One in particular, serial number 92248, he described as his "best Western revolver."

Roosevelt carried the revolver in a hand-tooled leather holster that he often attached to a Winchester cartridge belt. The revolver, holster, and cartridge belt can be seen in many pictures from the period, and all three are now part of the Autry Collection.

The revolver originally was shipped to Hartley and Graham in New York and was custom engraved by Louis D. Nimschke according to Roosevelt's personal instructions. The revolver was plated completely in silver with the exception of the cylinder, hammer, and ejector rod housing, which were plated in gold. Over the course of its rugged use, almost all of the plating was worn off. The elaborate scroll engraving includes a TR monogram relief engraved on the left side of the recoil shield. The TR monogram is also relief engraved on the right side of the one-piece ivory grips. The left side of the grips features a relief-engraved buffalo head, a reminder of Roosevelt's first Western big-game trophy. Roosevelt cherished the revolver for the rest of his life as a memento of a pivotal moment in his development as a citizen and statesman. Given the revolver's appearance, pedigree, and condition (in this instance the fact that it was used only adds to its significance), it can be argued quite convincingly that serial number 92248 is the most important and historic Single Action Army ever made. It is certainly the cornerstone of the Autry Collection.

184

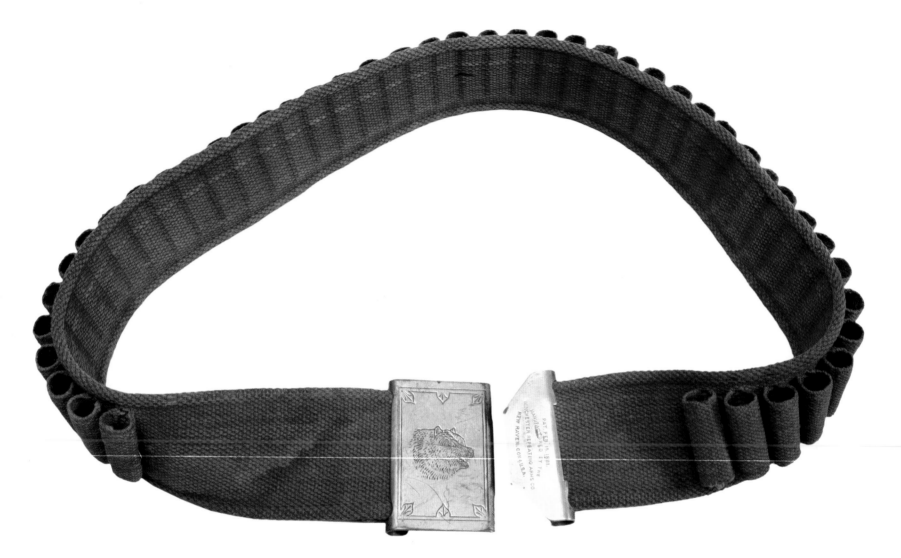

Opposite:
Roosevelt carried his favorite Single Action Army in this hand-tooled leather holster lined with chamois. (85.5.5; acquisition made possible in part by Paul S. and June A. Ebensteiner)

Above:
The holster often was attached to this Winchester cartridge belt alongside ammunition for all of Roosevelt's Western firearms. (2001.87.1)

M. HARTLEY CO.
313 and 315 Broadway, New York, N. Y.

Research indicates that William F. "Buffalo Bill"
Cody presented this Single Action Army to
Dr. George Powell, nicknamed "Night Hawk."
(2012.2.12; the George Gamble Collection)

NIGHT HAWK'S CASED PRESENTATION SINGLE ACTION ARMY MODEL

History Detectives

The ability to trace the provenance or history of an object is one of the most important aspects of firearm or any other type of collecting. A certifiable history is equally important for a museum and a private collector. A variety of records can be used to document an artifact's history. For Colt revolvers, a factory letter is the best place to start. Anyone can contact Colt's with a model and serial number, and for a nominal cost, the company will provide you with the shipping record of the revolver. The factory record will indicate such information as the caliber, barrel length, finish, type of stock, who it was originally shipped to, the date of the shipment, and the number of guns in the shipment. Sometimes not all of the information is listed in the corporate records, and on a few occasions, absolutely no information exists. This is due in part to key documents having been destroyed in the fire that ravaged the Colt's armory in 1864.

A factory letter is a good starting point, but it only describes what a revolver looked like and where it was first located when it left the factory. It does not give any information on who ultimately purchased the revolver, where it was used, or how it might have been altered outside the factory. Other documents, such as court transcripts, newspapers, and photographs, can provide this type of information. Family records or a notarized letter from someone who is familiar with the firearm, oftentimes a former owner or a relative of a former owner, can provide additional information. While notarized letters and family documents are valid forms of provenance, they have to be carefully scrutinized. Records can be altered or even faked, especially when the financial stakes are extremely high. Family members are not always so unscrupulous. Sometimes things simply get mislabeled, someone remembers something inaccurately, or misinformation is inadvertently passed down through generations.

Single Action Army serial number 127109 in the Autry Collection is a notable example of a revolver whose history was determined by careful analysis of existing records. Factory records indicate the revolver was shipped to the Western Arms & Cartridge Company in Salt Lake City, Utah, with nickel plating, factory engraving, and a Mexican eagle carved on the right side of the pearl grips. The rare felt-lined oak case was supplied by M. Hartley Co. of New York. At some point, the left side of the pearl grips was inscribed "Night Hawk / 1876." (The inscription was touched up with ink to make it stand out more, but the ink has faded over time.) According to an affidavit signed by the sister of the longtime owner, the revolver was given to Dr. George Powell, nicknamed "Night Hawk," in February 1876 by George Armstrong Custer. Unfortunately, undisputable facts contradict this claim. Custer was still alive in February of 1876—the Battle of Little Bighorn did not take place until June of that year—but the revolver left the factory in 1888 so a presentation in 1876 could not have happened.

Additional research conducted on the revolver determined that Powell's sister, who was quite old when she signed the affidavit, had actually confused Custer with William F. "Buffalo Bill" Cody. Records clearly indicate that Buffalo Bill was a friend of Powell and his brothers, all of whom had colorful nicknames. A cabinet card of Buffalo Bill and the Powell brothers exists, and it appears to have been taken in the early to mid-1880s. While more information is known about the other brothers than George, records indicate he was a general practitioner in La Crosse, Georgia. He claimed to have seen service in the West with the Army, and it was during this time that Native Americans gave him the nickname "Night Hawk." George was known to have an extensive collection of firearms, several of which were presentations from Buffalo Bill. It appears that serial number 127109 was one of those guns. However, the significance of the date 1876 inscribed on the revolver's grip remains a mystery.

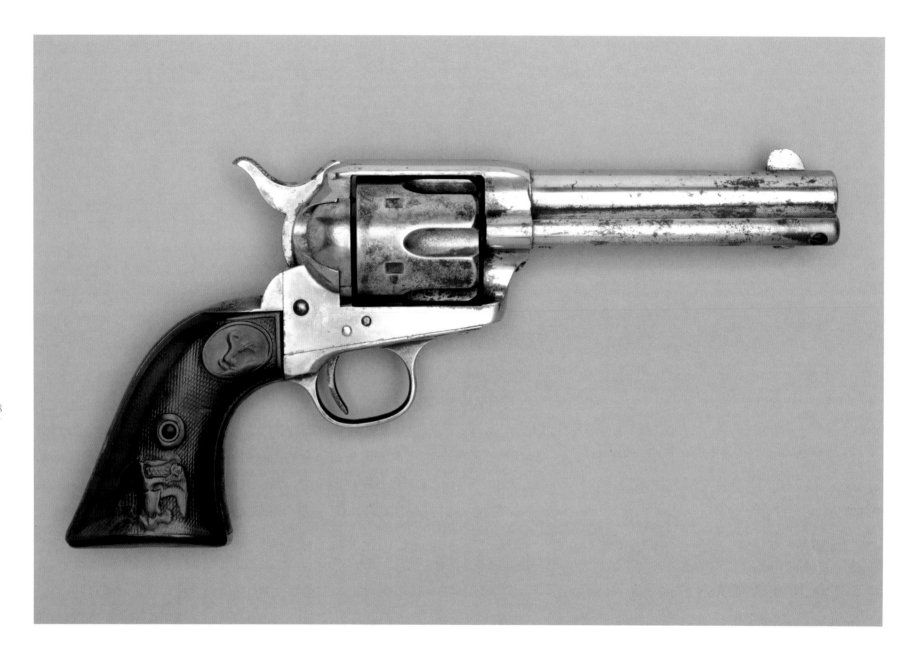

Harvey "Kid Curry" Logan, a member of the infamous Wild Bunch, reportedly owned this Single Action Army. (85.1.492; acquisition made possible in part by John E. Bianchi Jr.)

OUTLAW KID CURRY'S
SINGLE ACTION ARMY MODEL

The Wildest of the Bunch

arvey "Kid Curry" Logan was a notorious outlaw and gunman. Some say he was one of the deadliest outlaws to ever roam the American frontier. He is probably best known for being a member of the Wild Bunch gang alongside Butch Cassidy and the Sundance Kid. Kid Curry was wanted on warrants for 15 murders during his lifetime, and he was doggedly pursued by the Pinkerton Detective Agency. William Pinkerton, head of the agency, said Kid Curry was "the only criminal I know of who does not have one single good point." While Butch Cassidy and the Sundance Kid have been immortalized on film and television, the wildest member of the Wild Bunch was Kid Curry.

The earliest years of Kid Curry's life are unclear. One of four brothers, he was born in Kentucky or Iowa sometime around 1867. His parents passed away when he was young, so he and his brothers went to live with relatives in Missouri. He spent time working as a cowboy in Texas, and some say it was there he first met "Flat Nose" George Curry. According to the traditional narrative, George became a mentor to the young cowboy, and in deference to his idol, Harvey Logan changed his last name to Curry. While this story is often repeated, it is highly speculative and exactly why Logan changed his name is unclear. Kid Curry's life as an outlaw began with the murder of Powell "Pike" Landusky in 1894. Landusky accused Kid Curry and his brother, Lonny, of rustling or stealing cattle, but the real source of friction was the fact that Lonny appears to have been sleeping with Landusky's daughter. Kid Curry ultimately confronted Landusky, and when Landusky pulled a gun, Kid Curry shot and killed him. He fled and assumed a life of crime.

Kid Curry became proficient at robbing banks, trains, and post offices. He rode with Tom "Black Jack" Ketchum before he decided to start his own gang. After robbing a bank in Belle Fourche, South Dakota, in 1897, he was tracked down and arrested. He managed to break out of prison and fled to Montana and Wyoming. Around this time, he met up with Robert LeRoy Parker, better known as "Butch Cassidy." Kid Curry and Butch Cassidy were the de facto leaders of the Wild Bunch, a group that also included at times Harry A. Longabaugh, the "Sundance Kid"; Ben Kilpatrick, the "Tall Texan";

Will "News" Carver; and "Flat Nose" George Curry. The Wild Bunch was one of the most successful criminal operations in the West. Despite being some of the most wanted men in America, they pulled off countless jobs without being caught. The main difference between the members of the gang was their demeanor. While Butch Cassidy and the Sundance Kid were known to be gentlemanly robbers, Kid Curry was a ruthless killer. When he was confronted or cornered, Kid Curry was not afraid to kill anyone who stood in his way.

Kid Curry carried many guns during his criminal escapades, but he especially liked Colt revolvers. At some point in his notorious career, he reportedly owned Single Action Army serial number 127662, which is now in the Autry Collection. Manufactured in 1888, it has been speculated that he took the gun from a traveling firearm salesman during a train robbery. Kid Curry's preference for Colt revolvers was revealed at one of his trials for robbing a train owned by the Great Northern Railway. According to court transcripts, Kid Curry put a Colt to the head of one of the railroad employees and demanded that he open the safe. All of the money was taken, and when the bandits went to leave, the employee asked the famous Kid Curry for a memento to remember the event. Kid Curry laughed, emptied the revolver's chambers, and threw him the gun. After robbing yet another train in 1904, Kid Curry was wounded in a confrontation with a posse. To avoid capture, he took his own life with a Single Action Army.

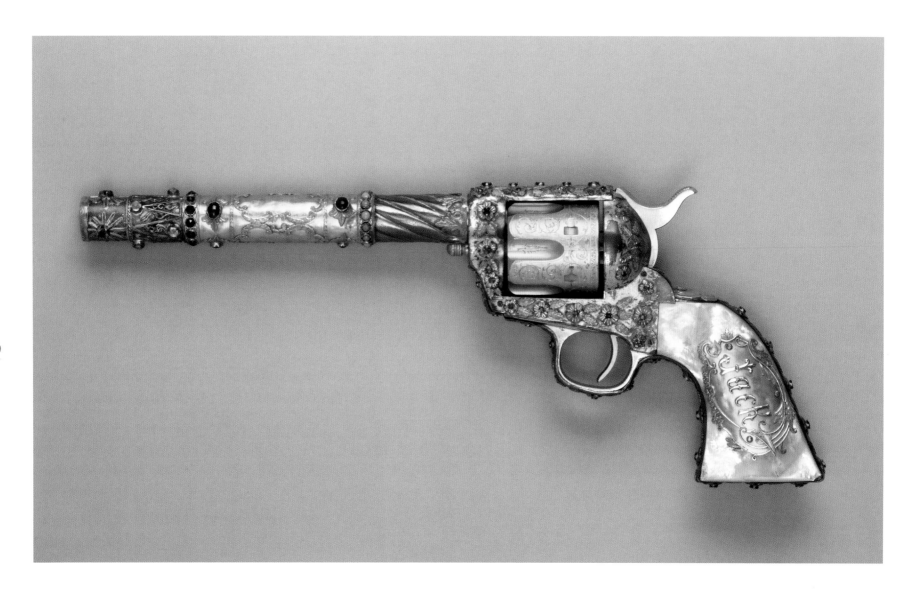

Jack Sinclair fired blanks from his bejeweled
Single Action Army as he directed the Dodge City
Cowboy Band. (86.23.3)

DODGE CITY COWBOY BAND DIRECTOR JACK SINCLAIR'S PRESENTATION SINGLE ACTION ARMY MODEL

Western Swing

Dodge City, Kansas, often called the wickedest city in the West, was the bustling center of the cattle trade in the 1880s. The industry employed various characters, including a few cowboys who enjoyed playing music in their free time. About a dozen of these musical cowboys decided to form a group called the Dodge City Cowboy Band sometime around 1881 to furnish music for local stockmen's conventions. Instead of trying to appeal to an Eastern audience, the cowboys chose to wear the flashiest and most outlandish Western clothing they could find. The group quickly gained a local following. In 1884, the band accompanied the Kansas delegation to the prestigious National Stock Growers Convention in St. Louis, Missouri. The band was the star attraction at the convention, and soon thereafter, they performed in various cities across the Midwest.

The band's prominence increased with the addition of Jack Sinclair. A native of Canada, Sinclair moved to Kansas in the 1870s, and he got a job working as a cowboy. He found the work tedious, but he enjoyed entertaining his fellow cowboys in the evening with his clarinet. Sometime around 1884 or 1885—accounts differ—Sinclair tried out for the band and was accepted. He soon found out, however, that life as a first clarinetist was about as romantic as life as a cowboy, so he quit. Sinclair nevertheless thought the band had potential. He convinced a wealthy cattle baron to purchase the band and appoint him the new director. Under his leadership, better equipment and costumes were acquired, including broad-rimmed cowboy hats, brightly colored neckerchiefs, wooly chaps, spurs, and gunbelts with revolvers. More importantly, the quality of the music improved dramatically.

Jack Sinclair's Dodge City Cowboy Band toured all around the country, and its popularity skyrocketed. It played at the inauguration of President Benjamin Harrison in 1889 and at the Democratic National Convention in Denver in 1908. When Dodge City ceased to be the center of the cattle industry, Sinclair moved the band to Pueblo, Colorado. The band was a Western institution by the time Sinclair retired as director in the 1910s. The popularity of the band was evident in the elaborate gifts that were presented to Sinclair. His diamond- and jewel-studded baton, a gift from the citizens of Pueblo, was inscribed "Leader, the Original Cowboy Band, Dodge City, Kans." and "Presented to Jack Sinclair by His Friends, Pueblo, Colo." An equally elaborate pair of matching gold- and silver-plated bejeweled spurs was presented on a different occasion by members of the Elks Convention in Pueblo.

The most interesting object presented to Sinclair was an amazing, one-of-a-kind Single Action Army that matched the spurs and baton. All three of the presentation items are part of the Autry Collection, and they appear to have been decorated by the Cornwell Jewelry Company in Pueblo. The revolver, serial number 138054, was manufactured in 1891. It was presented to Sinclair by the Knights Templar conclave in 1892. It is sheathed in silver and gold plates that are engraved and mounted with a variety of precious and semiprecious stones. The left side of the pearl grips features a gold plate inscribed "Jack," while the right side features a relief-carved steer head. Sinclair actually used the revolver as a baton to lead the Dodge City Cowboy Band, and he fired blanks from it to punctuate the band's performance. Sinclair also joked that he would use the revolver "to shoot the first man who played a false note." Jack Sinclair's "baton" is one of the best known and most visually stunning revolvers in the Autry Collection.

Opposite:
Although Jack Sinclair often used his Single Action Army as a baton, he also carried a real baton that was as impressive as the revolver. (86.23.4)

Above:
The Cornwell Jewelry Company of Pueblo, Colorado, likely decorated Sinclair's matching spurs, baton, and Single Action Army. (92.83.4; donated in memory of Robert Kendall Ellithorpe)

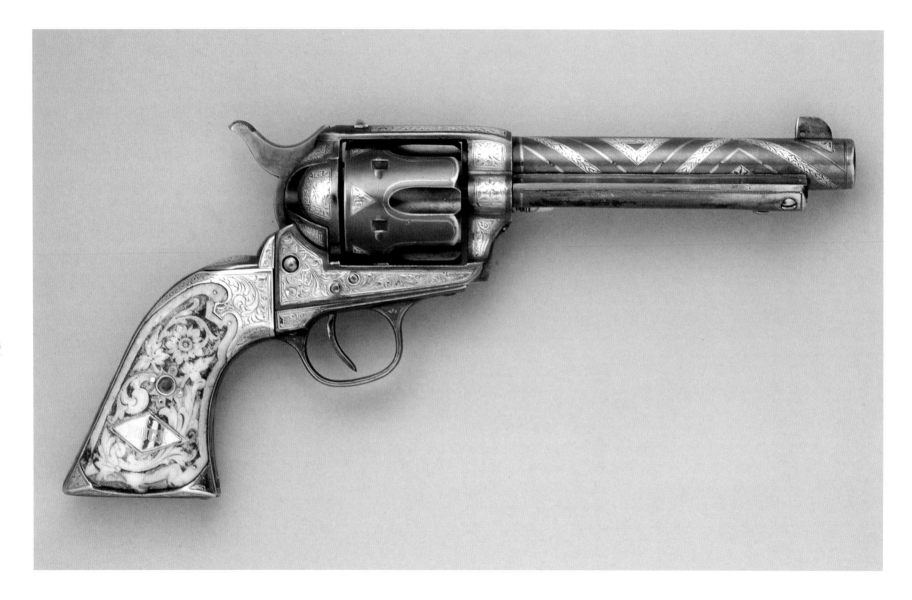

Buck Jones's Single Action Army was personally engraved by Edward H. Bohlin, "saddlemaker to the stars." (90.211.1.1)

ACTOR BUCK JONES'S
SINGLE ACTION ARMY MODEL

Celebrity Clientele

Buck Jones was a popular Western star in the late silent and early sound eras. At one point, he was the most popular screen cowboy. His career was unique in that he seamlessly combined some of the most striking aspects of the foremost movie cowboys in the first half of the 20th century. His simplistic style and rugged demeanor was reminiscent of William S. Hart, the first cowboy superstar. The action and showmanship in his films was on par with Tom Mix, Hart's antithesis and the most popular cowboy of his generation. Finally, whereas most Westerns of the period had a sidekick that was responsible for generating laughs, Jones was like Hoot Gibson and willingly allowed himself to be at the center of most comedic situations.

Jones was born Charles Frederick Gebhart in 1891. As with actors of his generation, the studios embellished Jones's early life so the facts are not always clear. His studio biography stated that he grew up on a large ranch in the Oklahoma Territory, and ranch hands gave him the nickname "Buckaroo," later shortened to "Buck," when he learned how to ride. Scholars report that he was actually a child of divorce who grew up in Indianapolis, Indiana, with his mother and stepfather. Records clearly indicate that he joined the United States Army in 1907 at the age of 16. Assigned to Troop G of the Sixth Cavalry Regiment, Jones was stationed in the Philippines and saw action during the Moro Rebellion. After two separate stints in the military, Jones finally left the Army in 1913.

Jones's time in the cavalry taught him how to ride, and he found work as a cowboy with the Miller Brothers 101 Ranch, a working cattle operation in Oklahoma and a nationally touring Wild West show. Jones became one of the show's star performers, and after a brief stint performing with the Ringling Brothers Circus, Jones made his way to Hollywood, where he initially found work as a stuntman and bit player. His first starring role occurred in 1920, and with a new stage name, he went on to make more than 60 silent films for the Fox Film Corporation. The studio started the Buck Jones Rangers, a youth club that had some five million members at its peak. Jones unsuccessfully attempted to establish his own production company,

and he also ran a Wild West show that failed. Jones finally returned to the studio system and revived his career by starring in popular sound films for Columbia and Universal. The *Motion Picture Herald* named him the most popular cowboy film star in 1936, and he was in the Top 10 for many years. Jones's career was cut short when he died tragically in 1942, along with almost 500 other people, due to injuries sustained in Boston's Cocoanut Grove nightclub fire.

Jones was not the flashiest screen cowboy, but he was always impeccably attired. A lot of his gear, from his saddle to his gunbelt, was designed by Edward H. Bohlin, "saddlemaker to the stars." One of Bohlin's finest creations for Jones was a Single Action Army, serial number 139166, that he engraved personally for the Western star. Manufactured in 1891, the revolver was a Christmas gift from Buck's wife Dell, a gifted equestrian and stuntwoman. Focusing primarily on gun grips, the Bohlin shop rarely decorated firearms, and those engraved by Bohlin himself are exceptionally rare. Jones's revolver features silver inlay executed in floral and geometric designs. The grips are silver with carved panels of ivory incised with a floral pattern enameled in green and red. Gold panels on the right and left sides are engraved "Buck" and "Dell," respectively. The Single Action Army, now part of the Autry Collection, was truly worthy of an actor of Jones's stature.

The Dalton Gang ordered 10 Single Action Armies,
including this one carried by Emmett Dalton,
prior to their failed robbery attempt in Coffeyville,
Kansas. (85.1.505; acquisition made possible in part
by John E. Bianchi Jr.)

OUTLAW EMMETT DALTON'S
SINGLE ACTION ARMY MODEL

A Place in History

The Dalton Gang's failed attempt to rob two banks in Coffeyville, Kansas, at the same time in broad daylight on October 5, 1892, was pivotal moment in the history of the American West. Although the criminality that took place on the American frontier has been exaggerated in popular culture, the failed raid on Coffeyville is often heralded as the end of the lawlessness that defined the Old West. The Daltons were a notorious gang of outlaws that specialized in bank and train robberies. The gang consisted of brothers Bob, Gratton or "Grat," and Emmett Dalton. The raid on Coffeyville was an attempt to secure the Daltons' place in history by outdoing anything ever attempted by the infamous Jesse James and the James-Younger Gang. The rivalry was due in part to the fact that the Daltons were actually related to the Younger brothers.

Raised in Coffeyville, Kansas, several members of the Daltons began their careers as lawmen. Oldest brother Frank served admirably as a deputy United States marshal, and in 1887, he was tragically killed in the line of duty. Grat and Bob followed in Frank's footsteps and became lawmen. Youngest brother Emmett often accompanied them in posses, but he never officially became a peace officer. Emmett spent most of his youth working as a cowboy. Many lawmen of the period found themselves on the other side of the law at some point, and Grat and Bob were no exception. Bob was charged with selling alcohol in the Osage Nation in 1890, and Grat was arrested for stealing horses. Discredited as lawmen, the two jumped bail. They ultimately teamed up with Emmett and several other acquaintances to form a gang. (Bill Dalton also joined the gang for a brief time before leaving his brothers to become one of the leaders of the Doolin-Dalton gang.)

The Dalton Gang quickly gained a reputation by robbing banks and trains across the West. The brothers, along with Dick Broadwell and Bill Power, ultimately decided to commit one great robbery that would garner them significant money and lasting fame. The plan was to return home to Coffeyville, Kansas, and rob both of the city's banks at the same time in broad daylight. Nothing quite so ambitious had ever been attempted. Wanting to commit the crime in style, the gang ordered 10 engraved

Single Action Armies directly from Colt's. The revolvers had blue, case-hardened finishes and deluxe pearl grips. The engraving was the work of Cuno A. Helfricht. The revolvers were shipped on August 18, 1892, to Simmons Hardware Company in St. Louis, Missouri, to the attention of A. E. Williams. It is believed that Williams was either an acquaintance of the brothers or an alias of Bob.

With each outlaw carrying a pair of revolvers, the gang set out to rob the C. M. Condon & Company Bank and the First National Bank in Coffeyville. Despite wearing rudimentary disguises, the brothers were recognized as they entered town. When the outlaws entered the banks and pulled their guns, the townspeople were prepared. The ensuing shootout left Grat, Bob, Dick Broadwell, and Bill Power dead. Emmett was shot around 20 times, but he managed to survive. Upon his arrest, Emmett gave his revolvers to his court-appointed attorney, J. R. Fritch. The exchange was reported in a local newspaper. One of those revolvers was serial number 147305 in the Autry Collection. Sentenced to life in prison for his part in the failed robbery, Emmett was pardoned in 1907. He later became an actor in Hollywood and wrote a book about the exploits of the Dalton Gang. The Daltons proved to be one of the last great outlaw gangs to roam the American West. Not surprisingly, the gang and the attempted robbery at Coffeyville have become part of Western folklore.

Edward H. Bohlin personally engraved his Bisley Model Single Action Army and the accompanying accessories. (91.221.614; donated by Mr. and Mrs. Gene Autry)

SADDLEMAKER EDWARD H. BOHLIN'S CASED BISLEY MODEL SINGLE ACTION ARMY

Saddlemaker to the Stars

Edward H. Bohlin was the "saddlemaker to the stars." He designed and created the gear—saddles, spurs, buckles, gunbelts, and holsters—worn by countless screen cowboys. Bohlin's silver and leather creations can be seen to this day in numerous parades and festivals, most notably the annual Tournament of Roses Parade in Pasadena, California. Born in Sweden, Bohlin apprenticed as a cowboy in Montana before making his way to Hollywood, where he established one of the most important Western supply stores in American history. His clientele included screen royalty, working cowboys, and city slickers who simply wanted to look good. More than any other Western designer, his style helped define an age. Bohlin's impact on how cowboys dressed and the way the public expected them to appear, especially on-screen, cannot be overstated.

Bohlin's journey to Hollywood was the stuff of movie legend. Born Emil Helge Bohlin in a small village outside Örebro, Sweden, in 1895, the future saddlemaker supposedly saw William F. "Buffalo Bill" Cody's Wild West show as a child. He was captivated by the stylishly dressed cowboys and their beautiful equipment. Inspired to come to America, Bohlin immigrated and found work as a cowboy in Montana and Wyoming. Bohlin dressed like the cowboys he saw in the Wild West show, and his appearance caught the attention of a modeling agency that cast him in an advertising campaign for Camel cigarettes in 1918. Learning to carve leather and manipulate metal in his free time, Bohlin established a small shop in Cody, Wyoming, that catered to his fellow cowboys. After joining a vaudeville company, where he performed rope tricks and rode a bucking bronco onstage, he closed the shop and headed with the act to Hollywood.

Bohlin's performances in Hollywood were forgettable, but his clothing and gear made a dramatic impact. He resumed making leather products and quickly listed actors Tom Mix, Dustin Farnum, Douglas Fairbanks, and William S. Hart as clients. In the early 1920s, his success allowed him to open his own Hollywood shop selling all sorts of leather and silver goods to screen and working cowboys. His famous Western clientele expanded to include Buck Jones, Hoot Gibson, Tim McCoy, Ken Maynard, William "Hopalong Cassidy" Boyd, Roy Rogers, Clayton Moore, and Clint Eastwood.

His products were used on-screen and off. He even helped establish the Sheriff's Mounted Posse of Los Angeles County in the 1930s, and he naturally provided them with all their equipment. Bohlin's Hollywood shop was open for several decades, and the tradition continues today with the Bohlin Company based out of Dallas, Texas.

Bohlin's personal parade items in the Autry Collection, from his saddle to his cowboy boots, were some of his greatest masterpieces. Bohlin's revolver was the rare Bisley Flattop Target variation of the Single Action Army. Introduced in 1894, the model had adjustable rear and front sights and was produced primarily for marksmen and target shooters. Bohlin's Bisley, with mismatched serial numbers 239228 and 296248, is now part of the Autry Collection. The revolver was manufactured around 1903. Personally engraved by Bohlin, it has a blued finish with a silver border design on the barrel, ejector rod housing, and cylinder flutes. Silver-inlaid panels with floral and geometric designs are found throughout. The silver grips have a pink gold rope border and are heavily overlaid with gold floral and arabesque designs. The left panel has a pink and white gold bucking bronco and a yellow gold sheriff's badge. The right panel is decorated with a white and pink gold steer head and another sheriff's badge. The revolver is housed in a hand-tooled brown leather case with an opulently engraved silver cartridge board, cleaning rod, and accessory compartment.

200

Leo Carrillo carried a Single Action Army in his portrayal, on-screen and off, of Pancho, the trusted sidekick of the Cisco Kid. (90.152.1)

ACTOR LEO CARRILLO'S
SINGLE ACTION ARMY MODEL

Oh, Pancho

L eo Carrillo was an actor and conservationist. He is probably best remembered for playing the role of Pancho, the sidekick of the Cisco Kid. Carrillo first played the character on film, and in 1950, at the age of 70, he reprised the role for the popular *The Cisco Kid* television series. The actor's greatest passion was conservation. He served on the California Beach and Parks commission for 18 years and was instrumental in the state's acquisition of the Hearst Castle, the Los Angeles Arboretum, and the Anza-Borrego Desert State Park. He was also a key player in the establishment of the El Pueblo de Los Angeles State Historic Park. In honor of Carrillo's many contributions, countless places across California have been named in his honor, including the Leo Carrillo State Park, a stretch of beach west of Malibu, off the Pacific Coast Highway.

Carrillo's family had a long and distinguished role in the history of Southern California. His great-great-grandfather, José Raimundo Carrillo, was one of the first Spanish settlers of San Diego. His great-grandfather, Carlos Antonio Carrillo, served as governor of Alta California. José Antonio Carrillo, his great-uncle, was the alcalde of Los Angeles on three separate occasions and helped draft the Treaty of Cahuenga, which ended fighting in Alta California during the Mexican-American War. Pedro C. Carrillo, Leo's grandfather, served in many civic roles, including justice of the peace in Los Angeles and Santa Barbara's collector of customs. Leo's father, Juan José Carrillo, was acting mayor of Santa Monica for several years. Out of this noble lineage, Leopoldo Antonio Carrillo was born on August 6, 1881.

Carrillo began his acting career appearing onstage in Los Angeles, Chicago, and St. Louis before heading to New York. He was cast in 15 major productions, including several on Broadway. His most successful role was the lead in *Lombardi Ltd.*, a comedy that played for two years on Broadway and three years on the road. Carrillo made the transition to Hollywood, ultimately appearing in more than 80 films. In 1948, Carrillo appeared as Pancho, the trusted sidekick of Duncan Renaldo's Cisco Kid, in the film *The Valiant Hombre*. Carrillo reprised the role for four more films before

heading to television for six seasons and 156 episodes. He often wore a Single Action Army, such as serial number 283276 in the Autry Collection, on-screen and in parades. The nickel-plated revolver with stag grips was manufactured in 1906. While Renaldo's Cisco Kid was a classic Western hero of Mexican descent, Carrillo's bumbling Pancho was often criticized for its stereotypical characterizations.

Carrillo's critics, however, could not argue with his activities offscreen. Passionate about politics and mindful of his family's rich history, Carrillo contemplated running for governor of California in 1941. He deferred on account of his admiration for candidate Earl Warren. When Warren was elected, he appointed Carrillo to the State Park Commission in 1942. Carrillo spearheaded several notable campaigns in his position as commissioner. He pushed for the establishment of a historic monument recognizing Los Angeles's diverse cultural heritage. The city's center under Spanish, Mexican, and early American rule was ultimately commissioned as the El Pueblo de Los Angeles State Historic Park in 1952. Carrillo's personal relationship with the Hearst family helped the state acquire the exquisite Hearst Castle at San Simeon in 1957. He served as California's official ambassador of goodwill for several years, before passing away in 1961.

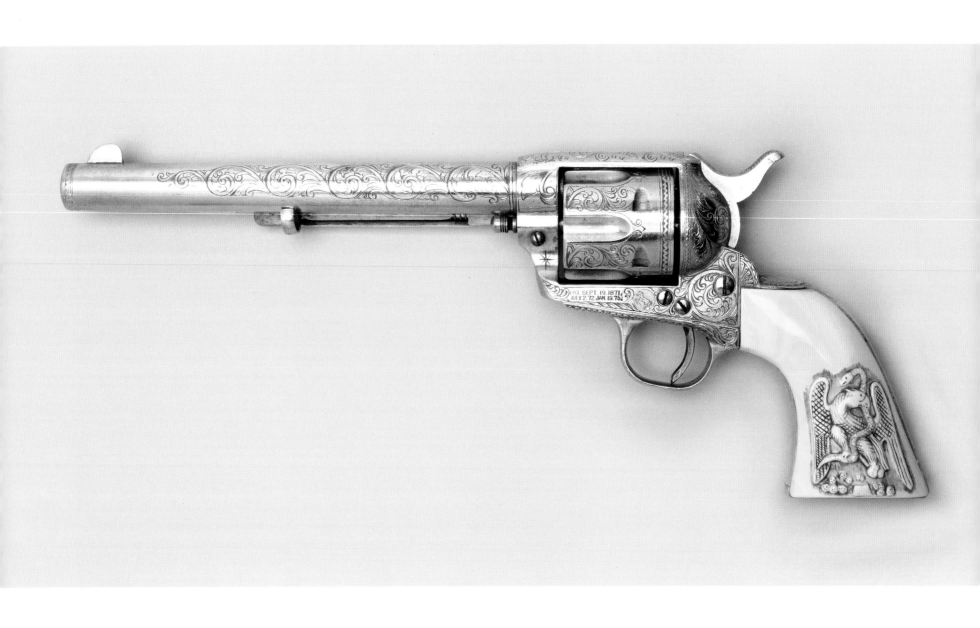

Buck Taylor, one of the first cowboy heroes, used this fancy Single Action Army as part of his Wild West show. (91.210.7; donated by Petra and Greg Martin)

WILD WEST PERFORMER BUCK TAYLOR'S SINGLE ACTION ARMY MODEL

The Original King of the Cowboys

I n the 19th century, cowboys performed important and difficult tasks on the American frontier. As the United States continued to expand westward, the demand for beef increased and cowboys became an absolute necessity. Unfortunately, cowboys had an unsavory reputation. They were blamed for a variety of offenses, from shooting up cow towns to participating in range wars. In the decades surrounding the turn of the 20th century, the image of the cowboy began to change. The popularity of dime novels and Wild West shows shifted the image of the cowboy from a violent outlaw to a hardworking, self-sufficient man of the people. An individual who played an important role in this transformation was Buck Taylor, the first "King of the Cowboys."

From the moment he was born in Texas in 1857, Taylor was groomed to be a cowboy. He was a distinguished rider and roper. He was so good at taming wild horses he was given the nickname "Buck." Sometime in his teens, he embarked on his first cattle drive from Texas to Wyoming, a task he repeated on at least one other occasion. When William F. "Buffalo Bill" Cody learned of Taylor's abilities as a cowboy, he hired him to run his ranch near North Platte, Nebraska. Buffalo Bill was so impressed with Taylor's work and presence on the ranch he convinced the cowboy to perform in his Wild West show. Billed as "King of the Cowboys," Taylor was one of Buffalo Bill's biggest stars for nearly 10 years.

The most remarkable aspect of Buck Taylor was his appearance. He stood around six feet, five inches, and weighed close to 300 pounds. He was extremely muscular with a well-proportioned frame. He had long, flowing hair and was always impeccably dressed. On a horse, Taylor was even more impressive. He performed a variety of tricks, including picking up coins and handkerchiefs off the ground while riding at full speed. Starring in various shows and reenactments, he often rode in to save damsels in distress. His exploits, real and imagined, were chronicled in several dime novels. This was the first time a cowboy was portrayed as

a hero in fiction, and soon thereafter, cowboy heroes were common in various forms of popular culture. Although he loomed large in and out of the saddle, Taylor was known to be especially kind and gentle. As the best-known cowboy in America, Taylor had a profound impact on how his fellow cowboys were perceived. His style and grace helped make the cowboy an American icon.

Taylor attempted to capitalize on his popularity by starting his own Wild West show after parting ways with Buffalo Bill. Like all Wild West shows, firearms were featured prominently in Taylor's exhibition. One of the revolvers he used was serial number 304972, which is now in the Autry Collection. Manufactured in 1908, it is silver plated and engraved with floral and scroll designs. It is stamped "Buck Taylor" under the ejector housing. The ivory grips feature a relief-carved Mexican eagle on the left side. Factory records state that it shipped with a custom two-and-a-half-pound trigger pull, indicating it was intended for exhibition and trick shooting. The revolver was acquired at some point by Jack Case, a champion cowboy who performed in various Wild West shows and rodeos. Given its association with one of the most important cowboys in history, Case cherished the revolver and often carried it while he performed.

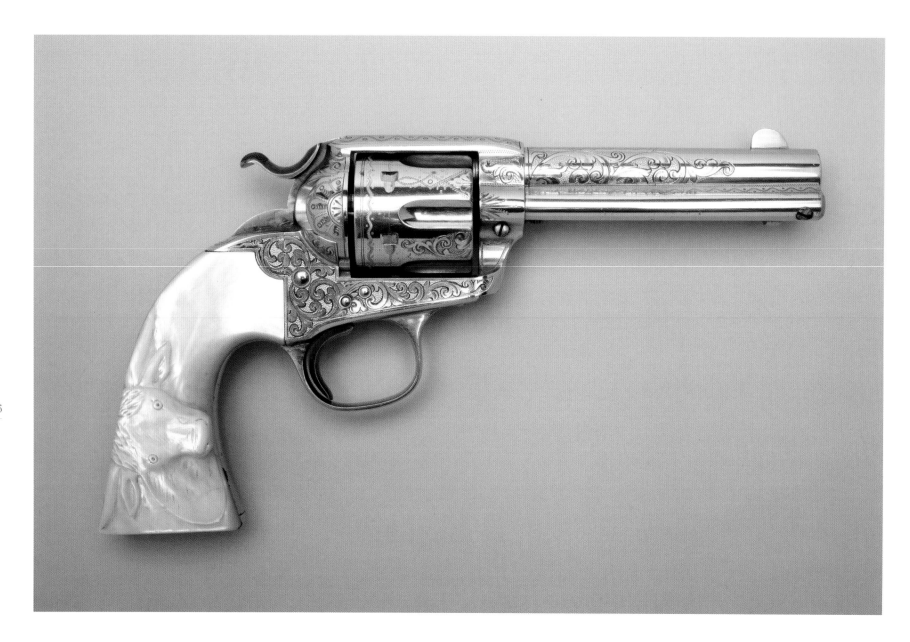

G. R. Tucker, the owner of this Bisley Model Single Action Army, was a hired assassin who took part in the infamous Johnson County War in Wyoming. (87.118.44)

GUNSLINGER G. R. TUCKER'S BISLEY MODEL SINGLE ACTION ARMY

An Invader

The Johnson County War, or the War on Powder River, was one of the last great range wars that took place in the American West in the 19th century. It was the basis or inspiration for countless Western movies, including *The Virginian* (1914), *Shane* (1953), and *Heaven's Gate* (1980). The war took place in Wyoming in the 1890s and was fought ostensibly over land. A group of powerful and well-connected cattle barons sought to monopolize the land and crush their competition. As more and more independent ranchers and homesteaders made claims on the land, the cattle barons decided it was necessary to take dramatic action. They hired a group of assassins to kill several independent ranchers whom they accused of rustling or stealing cattle.

Most of the land in Wyoming was owned by the federal government in the 1890s. It was considered public, and everyone technically had the same rights to the land. In reality, individuals who owned large herds of cattle controlled and monopolized the land in Johnson County. The Wyoming legislature officially sanctioned the actions of these cattle barons by passing laws that favored them over small, independent ranchers and homesteaders. Not satisfied, the cattle barons went even further by accusing the smaller ranchers of rustling. The cattle barons also asserted that these individuals were claiming unbranded calves as their own, a practice known as mavericking. While some individuals were guilty of such actions, the accusations were mostly baseless and merely an attempt to get harsher legislation passed. The tactic was often successful, but the smaller ranchers and homesteaders continued to resist the efforts of the cattle barons.

Claiming the local townspeople and law-enforcement officials were complicit in the illegal actions of the rustlers, the cattle barons decided to take matters into their own hands. They orchestrated the lynching of a few individuals they claimed were the most prominent rustlers. When this draconian action failed to strike fear in the hearts of the smaller ranchers and homesteaders, the cattle barons contracted a force of more than 40 assassins to come to Johnson County, mostly from Texas, and kill upwards of 70 of their opponents. These assassins called themselves regulators, but they came to be known as the Johnson County Invaders. While the assassins managed to kill a few people, the invasion was ultimately suppressed by the local townspeople. The invaders were arrested, but given their influential backers, no one was ever tried or convicted for the violence that took place. In the end, the Johnson County War exposed the social and economic divisions prevalent in the American West at the end of the 19th century. The war also contributed to the end of the open range system that was common throughout Wyoming.

G. R. Tucker was one of the Johnson County Invaders, and he was only 19 years old at the time of the incident. Arrested with the rest of the assassins, Tucker is clearly identified in a picture of the invaders that was taken at Fort D. A. Russell in Cheyenne, Wyoming, immediately following the bloodshed. It is unclear exactly what role Tucker had in the murders that took place, but like the rest of his companions, he was never tried for his involvement. Not a lot is known about Tucker, before or after the Johnson County War. Records indicate he later served on the other side of the law as a deputy United States marshal in Oklahoma. Sometime around 1910, Tucker acquired a Bisley Model Single Action Army, serial number 313648, with nickel plating and pearl grips. The engraving is the work of Cuno A. Helfricht. The right side of the grips features a relief-carved steer head, and the butt strap is inscribed "G. R. Tucker." Now part of the Autry Collection, the revolver is an interesting artifact from a mysterious figure who participated in an important chapter in the history of the American West.

The Bisley Model Single Action Army was a favorite weapon of Mexican revolutionary Pancho Villa. (85.1.1316; acquisition made possible in part by John E. Bianchi Jr.)

MEXICAN REVOLUTIONARY PANCHO VILLA'S BISLEY MODEL SINGLE ACTION ARMY

Viva Villa

Pancho Villa was a prominent figure who alternated between legitimate political pursuits and banditry during the Mexican Revolution. Villa helped overthrow Mexico's dictatorial President Porfirio Díaz in 1911. As the revolution raged on and a power struggle ensued, Villa commanded the *División del Norte* (Division of the North), the most feared and powerful army in Mexico. Villa and his troops faced off against various enemies, and they even went so far as to make a cross-border attack against the United States. Although he ultimately agreed to lay down his arms, Villa was assassinated in 1923. While Villa remains a controversial figure, many Mexicans considered him a national hero.

Born Doroteo Arango in San Juan del Río, Mexico, in 1878, Villa was the son of poor peasants. He became a sharecropper at a young age, and when he was 16, he killed the owner of the hacienda at which he worked, supposedly after the owner assaulted his sister. Villa fled to the mountains where he lived the life of a fugitive and bandit. After several run-ins with the law, he changed his name to Francisco "Pancho" Villa reportedly in deference to his paternal grandfather Jesus Villa. Around 1910, revolutionaries opposed to the rule of Mexican President Porfirio Díaz persuaded Villa to join the forces of revolutionary leader Francisco Madero. The rebels recognized that Villa's skills as a bandit and his knowledge of the land could be useful to their cause. Villa and the revolutionaries won several battles against the federal troops, and Díaz ultimately was forced into exile.

Francisco Madero became president in 1911. Pascual Orozco, one of his military commanders, eventually challenged his rule and began his own rebellion in 1912. Villa fought alongside Victoriano Huerta to quell the uprising, but Huerta became suspicious of Villa's intentions and had him arrested. Sentenced to death, Villa was given a stay of execution by Madero and instead was sent to prison. Villa escaped from prison and formed the *División del Norte* to combat Huerta, who was now in control of the country. Villa's forces won several key battles, and he became governor of the state of Chihuahua in 1913. When the United States supported one of Villa's rivals, he led approximately 500 men in an attack on the town of Columbus, New Mexico, on March 9, 1916. Nine American civilians and eight soldiers were killed and many others were wounded in the first foreign attack on American soil since the War of 1812. An American expeditionary force of 4,800 men was sent into Mexico in response, but they were unable to capture or kill Villa.

Villa used a variety of weapons throughout his life. His medium-range weapon of choice was the Bisley Model Single Action Army. Serial number 322053 in the Autry Collection, manufactured in 1912, is believed to have been one of Villa's revolvers. The Bisley has a five-and-a-half-inch barrel and is chambered in .44-40 caliber. It has a blued and case-hardened finish with mother-of-pearl grips. At one point, it was carried by General Jose Ruiz, a supporter of Villa who fought alongside him at the Battle of Columbus. Ruiz, like many others, ultimately became disenfranchised with Villa and his tactics. After losing several battles, Villa's power and prestige deteriorated. He agreed to a cease-fire with the Mexican government in 1920, but remaining a potentially disruptive force, Villa was assassinated in July 1923.

Ken Maynard, one of the most gifted equestrians in the history of Western film, owned this spectacular pair of gold-plated Single Action Armies. (91.221.613; donated by Mr. and Mrs. Gene Autry)

ACTOR KEN MAYNARD'S
SINGLE ACTION ARMY MODEL PAIR

Horse and Rider

Ken Maynard was arguably the greatest equestrian in the history of Western film. He often shared billing with Tarzan, one of the most gifted movie horses. Maynard made almost 90 films in the 1930s. Unfortunately, some of his films and conceivably his greatest moments have been lost to time. The films that do survive are a testament to his showmanship and daring. Besides his athleticism, Maynard is also credited with establishing the persona and style of the singing cowboy, a phenomenon that dominated Westerns for several years. Although Maynard was a fan favorite, he was difficult to work with given his explosive personality and fondness for alcohol. He had a rather short film career as a result.

Exactly how Maynard learned to ride is unknown. Studios filled his biography with countless tales, including spending time in the circus and winning a prestigious rodeo championship. While Maynard's early career was certainly embellished, he was a talented rider willing to perform dangerous stunts by the time he initially appeared on-screen in 1923. His first significant role occurred alongside Marion Davies in the film *Janice Meredith* in 1924. Although the film was not a Western, it led to a contract with an independent production company that cast Maynard in a series of Westerns. Featuring action and death-defying stunts, the films established Maynard's on-screen persona. Maynard quickly became a star, and his later films, some of which he produced, were backed by the more prestigious First National and Universal Studios.

Early on in his career, Maynard purchased a golden three-year-old palomino for $50. Maynard named the horse Tarzan after the Edward Rice Burroughs jungle hero. Often billed as the "Wonder Horse," Tarzan subsequently appeared in almost every one of Maynard's films. Although there were many talented and well-known horses in the formative years of Western movies, Tarzan stood out among the best. He was able to comprehend and obey the most difficult instructions, and he was exceptionally athletic. Most importantly, Tarzan looked great on-screen

and his chemistry with Maynard was obvious. Maynard's career was filled with exceptional highs and extreme lows, but the one thing he could always count on was Tarzan. The horse was a constant companion until his death in 1940.

Maynard's personal style was rather subtle, but his custom-engraved pair of Single Action Armies was quite spectacular. Now part of the Autry Collection, the gold-plated revolvers are serial numbers 321290 and 339789, manufactured in 1912 and 1920, respectively. They are engraved on the barrel, cylinder, back strap, trigger guard, frame, and ejector housing. The engraving appears to be the work of Texan Cole Agee. Agee was searching for a signature style while working on an earlier project, and it is believed that his wife suggested using Texas cattle brands. Agee thus turned to the book *A Century of Texas Cattle Brands* (1936) for inspiration. The final product, as evidenced on Maynard's revolvers, included numerous brands complemented with sprigs of scroll. Maynard's revolvers also include sterling-silver grips with 10-karat gold steer heads made by the shop of Edward H. Bohlin. Fellow singing cowboy Gene Autry was a longtime supporter of Maynard, and the revolvers were given to Autry as collateral for a loan. Autry did not want collateral, but Maynard insisted and consequently never paid back the loan or picked up his revolvers.

Tom Mix's flamboyant personal style was evident
in his fully engraved Single Action Army. (95.5.2;
donated by Ms. Mary Schoenfeldt)

ACTOR TOM MIX'S
SINGLE ACTION ARMY MODEL

The Flashiest Screen Cowboy

Tom Mix was an extremely influential figure in the history of the Western genre. He created the model, both in appearance and tone, that all screen cowboys followed for the next 50 years. Unlike his predecessor William S. Hart, who purposely appeared drab on-screen, Mix chose to wear fancy and ornate clothing in an attempt to stand out. A large white Stetson and shirts with flowers became his trademark. His gear, including his revolvers and spurs, was even more opulent. Mix's films focused on action and entertainment, and he chose not to address moral and social issues in a conscious effort to attract children. Along the same lines, his characters were extremely clean-cut and he only used a gun as a last resort. The persona Mix established dominated the genre until the rise of the antihero in revisionist Westerns of the 1960s and 1970s.

Mix was known to tell great tales of his early adventures before coming to Hollywood, and the studios and his early biographers were happy to reprint them. As the stories go, Mix was born in a log cabin in El Paso, Texas. He learned to ride by the age of four and was an expert shot by age 10. He bravely fought for various factions in the Boer War, the Boxer Rebellion, and the Spanish-American War. He served time as a Texas Ranger. As a United States marshal, he single-handedly captured a group of notorious cattle rustlers who terrorized New Mexico. He joined the famed Miller Brothers 101 Ranch and became a star attraction. He even found time to win a few rodeo championships. The stories were great, but with the exception of working at the Miller Brothers 101 Ranch, they were almost all untrue. In fact, his early life was not much different than countless other Wild West performers who worked long, hard hours for very little pay.

Mix's work in the Wild West arena brought him in contact with the Selig Polyscope Company around 1909. Initially hired as a laborer and consultant, Mix soon became a key player with the company. He starred in approximately 100 one- and two-reel films between 1911 and 1917. He served at various times as a writer, director, and producer. Mix signed with the more established Fox Film Corporation in 1917, and the quality of his films increased dramatically. By the mid-1920s, Mix was one of the most popular actors of the silent era. All of the studios tried to capitalize on his popularity, but no other Western actor could equal Mix's appeal and showmanship. He starred in more than 250 movies in his remarkable career. By the time sound revolutionized the film industry, Mix was past his prime. He only made a few talkies before dying in a car accident in 1940.

Mix's silver-plated Single Action Army, serial number 331793, was indicative of his lavish tastes. Cuno A. Helfricht's factory floral engraving fully covers every surface. "Tom Mix" is even engraved on the left side of the barrel. Manufactured in 1915, the revolver was originally shipped with pearl grips that had a carved ox-head motif on both panels. Mix replaced the factory grips with even more opulent examples from the shop of Edward H. Bohlin. The new sterling-silver grips are completely engraved and feature Mix's trademark brand on both sides. The right side also includes "Tom Mix" scripted in wire gold. "Texas Ranger" is inscribed on the back strap, and "Tom Mix" is inscribed on the butt strap. Now part of the Autry Collection, serial number 331793 perfectly represents one of the flashiest and most important cowboys in screen history.

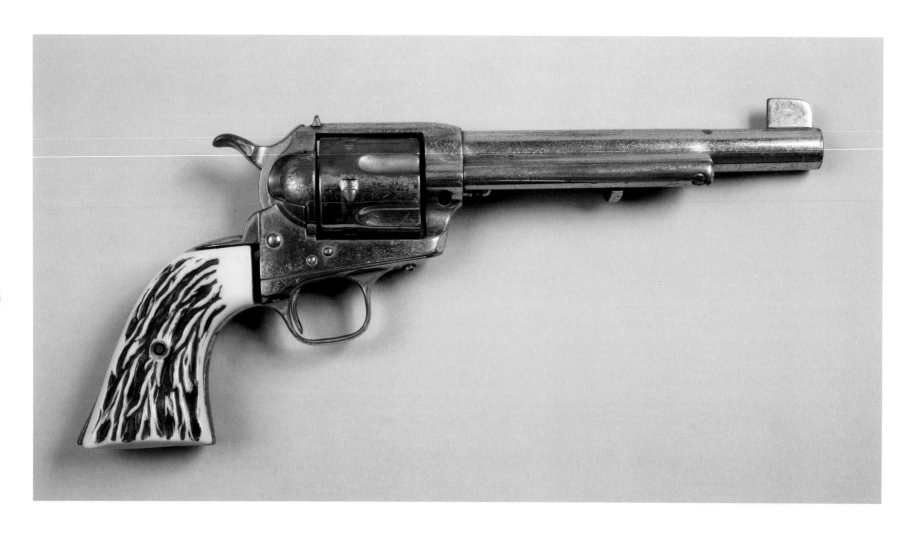

Used solely as a prop during personal
appearances, Roy Rogers's Single Action Army
was modified so it was no longer operational.
(88.285.14.1; donated by Roy Rogers and
Dale Evans)

ENTERTAINER ROY ROGERS'S SINGLE ACTION ARMY MODEL

All Hail the King

Roy Rogers was born Leonard Slye in Cincinnati, Ohio, in 1911. His father gave him a horse at a young age upon which he learned to ride and perform tricks. Around 1929, he bought his first guitar at a secondhand shop in Cincinnati. The family headed to California in 1930 during the Great Depression, and according to legend, Rogers played the guitar along the route at various campsites. Seeing the joy his music brought to others, especially those in need, Rogers was determined to become an entertainer. After arriving in California, he formed the Western musical group Sons of the Pioneers with Bob Nolan and Tim Spencer in 1934. The group was cast in several motion pictures, including *The Big Show* (1936) and *The Old Corral* (1936), which starred singing cowboy Gene Autry.

At that time, Autry was quarreling with Republic Pictures over his contract and other business dealings. Executives at Republic feared Autry would walk out of his contract, so they began searching for a new singing cowboy. Rogers auditioned on October 13, 1937, and was signed to a contract for $75 a week. He was still using the name Leonard Slye, or even the stage name Dick Weston, and the studio suggested changing his last name to Rogers (after Will Rogers). The first name of Leroy was also recommended, but Rogers objected and instead suggested just Roy. The studio liked the name, and Roy Rogers was born. When Autry finally did walk out of his contract, Rogers was chosen to replace him in a film tentatively titled *Washington Cowboy.*

Rogers needed a horse for the film, and a palomino stallion named Golden Cloud was chosen. Rogers's costar, Smiley Burnette, said the horse was so quick he should be called Trigger. Rogers's film was released in 1938 under the new title *Under Western Stars*. The film was successful, and with Trigger as his constant companion, Rogers quickly became the most popular Western actor in Hollywood. As a leading man, he appeared in approximately 100 movies for Republic Pictures, where he was advertised as "King of the Cowboys," a moniker that is associated with him more than any other figure in Western history.

From 1943 to 1954, *Motion Picture Herald* listed him as the top money-making Western star. Rogers saw little of the money made by his movies and personal appearances, but his contract stipulated that he owned his name and likeness. As a result, Rogers put his name on countless products. A pioneer in the field of licensed merchandise, he basically endorsed anything as long as it was not harmful, physically or morally, to children. Many of his products even included a pledge from Rogers to parents promising that the product was safe and his endorsement in no way increased its cost. It has been estimated that Rogers's name ultimately appeared on more products than any other name in history with the exception of Walt Disney.

When the popularity of the singing cowboy genre diminished, Rogers made the successful transition to radio and television. Besides Trigger, he was often accompanied by his wife, Dale Evans, the "Queen of the West." Rogers and Evans were vocal advocates of adoption and other children's charities. Rogers even went so far as to modify many of his personal appearance revolvers, such as serial number 334729 in the Autry Collection, so they could not fire or in any way inadvertently harm children. Manufactured in 1916, the grips on the revolver are made from Franzite, a plastic material designed to look like deer antlers. Rogers carried the revolver around the country for decades as he entertained countless fans of all ages.

216

Manuel Trazazas "Lone Wolf" Gonzaullas owned many elaborate firearms during his career as a Texas Ranger, including this fancy pair of Single Action Armies. (97.127.1-.2; donated by Mr. James R. McDade)

TEXAS RANGER CAPTAIN MANUEL T. GONZAULLAS'S SINGLE ACTION ARMY MODEL PAIR

The Lone Wolf

Manuel Trazazas "Lone Wolf" Gonzaullas was a lifelong Texas Ranger and the first ranger of Hispanic descent to rise to the rank of captain. Gonzaullas began his career in 1920 on horseback, combating bootlegging, bank robberies, narcotics trafficking, and prostitution. As Texas moved from its frontier past to a more urban future, Gonzaullas learned the modern techniques of scientific analysis and was instrumental in establishing one of the leading crime labs in the country at the Texas Department of Public Safety. After retiring from the Rangers in 1951, Gonzaullas moved to Hollywood and became a technical advisor to the entertainment industry. When he passed away in 1977, he was hailed as one of the finest Rangers in the history of the famed force.

Gonzaullas was born in Cádiz, Spain, in 1891. His father was a naturalized American citizen of Spanish descent who was visiting Spain with his wife at the time of Gonzaullas's birth. Gonzaullas grew up in Texas, where he was inspired by the Texas Rangers he saw roaming the streets on horseback. Desperate for action and adventure, he enlisted in the Mexican Army in 1911 and was appointed a major. He came back across the border a few years later and joined the United States Treasury Department as a special agent. In 1920, his childhood dream became a reality when he became a Ranger. Gonzaullas was given the nickname "Lone Wolf" or "El Lobo Solo" because he would enter into any confrontation, even if he was alone. It was said that Gonzaullas was often the only person who would come out of a dangerous situation alive or uninjured. During his 13 years of service, Gonzaullas earned a reputation as an honest and dedicated public servant.

A political battle in 1933 resulted in the dismissal of Gonzaullas and many other Texas Rangers. Two years later, the Rangers were reconstituted under the newly formed Department of Public Safety. Gonzaullas was hired as the superintendent of the Department of Public Safety's newly created Bureau of Intelligence. He helped the bureau establish a state-of-the-art crime laboratory that many considered to be second only to the Federal Bureau of Investigation's

lab in Virginia. When the opportunity to rejoin the Rangers arose in 1940, Gonzaullas resigned from the bureau to become captain of Ranger Company B in Dallas. He served admirably until permanently retiring from the Rangers in 1951. He moved to Hollywood and served as a technical advisor to the television series *Tales of the Texas Rangers* from 1955 to 1958. He ultimately returned to Texas and helped found the Texas Ranger Hall of Fame and Museum in Waco.

Throughout his career, Gonzaullas was known for his showmanship and style. One of the most striking aspects of his appearance was his custom-made firearms. A matching pair of Gonzaullas's Single Action Armies in the Autry Collection is emblematic of his tastes. The revolvers are serial numbers 332671 and 353753, manufactured in 1916 and 1929, respectively. The nickel plating is accentuated with a gold finish. Southwest cattle brands are engraved on the barrel, frame, and cylinder. Both revolvers have ivory grips with a relief-engraved steer head with ruby eyes on one side. A gold Texas Ranger badge is located on the grip of one of the revolvers, and a gold Texas state seal is located on the other. Both revolvers are inscribed "Capt. M. T. Lone Wolf Gonzaullas" on the back strap and "Texas Rangers" on the butt strap. Interestingly, the revolvers do not have triggers and are fired by cocking and manually releasing the hammers.

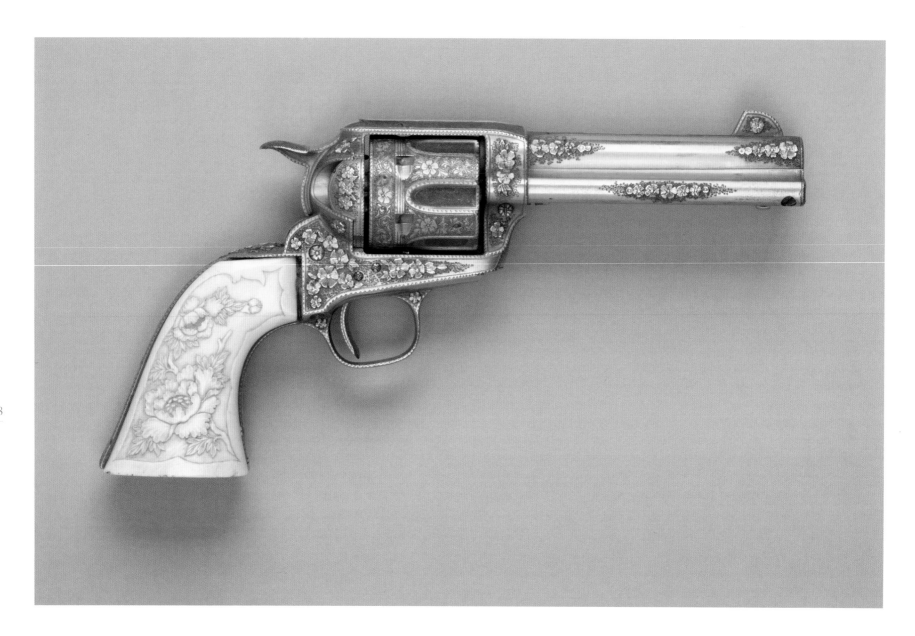

Gene Autry's Single Action Army was custom-designed for use on his personal appearance tours. (88.181.1; donated by the National Cowboy Hall of Fame and Western Heritage Center)

ENTERTAINER GENE AUTRY'S SINGLE ACTION ARMY MODEL

America's Favorite Singing Cowboy

The singing cowboy was one of the most important cultural figures to emerge out of the Great Depression. At a time when ordinary Americans faced a bleak and uncertain future, people took comfort in wholesome and heroic cowboys who expressed their emotion through song. Although there were several singing cowboys, none were as successful as Gene Autry, "America's Favorite Singing Cowboy." Autry's accomplishments in the entertainment industry were incredible. He starred in 91 feature films from 1935 to 1953, often sharing the billing with Champion, "World's Wonder Horse." Autry made 640 recordings and wrote or cowrote 300 songs, including the Christmas classic "Here Comes Santa Claus." He was one of the first recording artists to sell one million copies of a single record. *Gene Autry's Melody Ranch* radio show was broadcast from 1940 to 1956, and *The Gene Autry Show* aired on television from 1950 to 1956. The Gene Autry Rodeo began in 1939 and he continued to tour around the country until 1961.

Autry's unparalleled success in the entertainment industry gave him the distinction of being the only entertainer to have all five stars on the Hollywood Walk of Fame: one each for film, recording, radio, television, and live performance. Despite his accomplishments and hectic schedule, Autry always took time to acknowledge his fans. At the height of his popularity, he made personal appearances all over the country, visiting everywhere from veterans' hospitals to local theaters. Autry especially loved entertaining children, and he never denied a request for an autograph or picture. Autry took his responsibility as a role model seriously. He never drank, smoked, or used inappropriate language on-screen. He even established "Gene Autry's Cowboy Code" to help children of all ages lead a virtuous life.

On personal appearance tours, Autry carried a custom-made Single Action Army, serial number 355121, which is now part of the Autry Collection. Manufactured in 1934, the revolver is gold plated and engraved with floral designs. The frame is adorned with inlaid gold and silver flowers. The carved ivory grips also feature a floral design, and "Gene Autry" is scripted on the back strap. All of the embellishments were the work of Orville J. Kuhl of San Francisco, California. In addition to the revolver, Autry toured with another custom-made 45, a Martin D-45 guitar, the first such guitar ever made. Less than 100 of the model were manufactured during its initial production run from 1933 to 1942, and many guitar enthusiasts consider the Martin D-45 to be the Holy Grail of acoustic guitars.

Autry transitioned from entertainer to businessman in the 1950s. His company, Flying A Productions, produced several television Westerns, including *The Gene Autry Show*, *The Range Rider*, *Annie Oakley*, *Buffalo Bill, Jr.*, and *The Adventures of Champion*. He acquired Monogram Ranch, the filming location for countless Western movies and television shows, and renamed it Melody Ranch. Autry also owned hotels and radio and television stations across the country, including the Los Angeles television station KTLA. Autry's most visible company was the Angels Major League Baseball franchise. Autry was the team's principal owner from its founding in 1961 to his death in 1998. Autry's greatest professional accomplishment occurred with the founding of the Gene Autry Western Heritage Museum, now called the Autry National Center, in 1988. The museum allowed Autry to give back to the community that had contributed so much to his success.

Production on the Single Action Army ceased at the outset of World War II, but it resumed in 1956 with serial number 0001SA. (87.118.49)

THE FIRST SECOND GENERATION SINGLE ACTION ARMY MODEL

As Seen on TV

Colt's mass-produced the Single Action Army from 1873 to 1941. During that time, a total of 357,859 revolvers were manufactured, of which approximately 37,000 were ordered by the government. Minor changes were made to the model over time, including the addition of various calibers. This included .44-40 in 1878, .41 in 1885, .44 S&W in 1890, .45 ACP in 1924, and .357 Magnum in 1935. Two variations designed specifically for target shooters, the Single Action Army Flattop Target Model and the Bisley Model Single Action Army, were manufactured for a brief time. The Single Action Army was designated safe for smokeless powder in 1900. These changes and others were minor, as the Single Action Army remained rather consistent during its production run.

The company, however, went through extensive changes during the life of the Single Action Army. Seven individuals held the title of president, with Richard Jarvis, Samuel Colt's brother-in-law, serving the longest period, from 1865 to 1901. In 1877, revolvers employing the double-action mechanism, which allowed the user to fire the weapon simply by pulling the trigger, were introduced. Although single-action revolvers continued to be manufactured, no new single-action models were introduced thereafter. Revolvers with swing-out cylinders were introduced in 1889. Elizabeth Hart Jarvis Colt, Samuel's widow, sold the company to a group of outside investors in 1901. Most significantly, semiautomatic pistols, introduced in 1900, ultimately replaced revolvers as Colt's most important firearms.

Colt's was an innovator in the field of semiautomatic pistols just as it was in the arena of revolving handguns. A semiautomatic pistol, unlike a revolver, has a single chamber and the cartridges are stored in a magazine in the grip. When the trigger is squeezed, a live round is fired and a new round is chambered. (Colt's used the term "automatic" to describe its pistols, but since one shot is fired each time the trigger is pulled, they are technically semiautomatic.) Colt's was the first American manufacturer of semi-automatic pistols in 1900. The company's most successful semiautomatic

pistol was the Model 1911. The model and its variants was the primary sidearm of American forces in World War I, World War II, the Korean War, and the Vietnam War. The Model 1911 was so vital to the United States military that Colt's ceased production of the Single Action Army in 1941 at the outset of World War II to focus on it and other weapons deemed essential to the war effort.

Even with production halted, the Single Action Army remained popular and continued to be used around the world. In the 1950s, the Single Action Army could be seen almost every night on television. Westerns dominated the television industry in its formative years. At their peak, 26 Western series were airing on primetime, and eight of the Top 10 most-watched television programs were Westerns. The most commonly used firearm on these shows was the Single Action Army, and the exposure brought renewed attention to the model. As a result, beginning in 1956, Colt's reintroduced the Single Action Army to its production line. The new revolvers were made with the same quality of craftsmanship as the originals, and the only major difference was the addition of SA to the serial numbers of the newer models. Serial number 0001SA in the Autry Collection was the first production specimen of the second-generation or post–World War II line.

Colt's President Fred A. Roff presented this Single Action Army to Gail Davis, the first female lead in a television Western series. (91.221.612.2; donated by Mr. and Mrs. Gene Autry)

ACTRESS GAIL DAVIS'S PRESENTATION SINGLE ACTION ARMY MODEL

Girl Power

Gail Davis was the first female lead in a Western television series. Inspired by the legendary sharpshooter, Davis starred as the title character in *Annie Oakley* (1954–1957), a series spanning 81 episodes, all produced by Gene Autry's Flying A Productions. Davis also made countless personal appearances as Oakley. In an age when the entertainment industry was dominated by men, Davis was a strong female role model, on-screen and off, for girls of all ages. In honor of her contributions, Colt's President Fred A. Roff presented Davis with a Single Action Army, serial number 1568SA, in 1956. Inscribed "Gail Davis" in script on the back strap, this unique piece of Western entertainment is now part of the Autry Collection. (A matching revolver was also presented to Gene Autry in 1956, and it too is part of the Autry Collection.)

Born Betty Jeanne Grayson in 1925, Davis made her way to Hollywood after World War II with her then-husband Bob Davis. She was discovered by an agent and was signed to a contract with MGM. Because her married name was phonetically the same as star Bette Davis, she was given the stage name "Gail." Her first major role was in the Roy Rogers film *The Far Frontier* in 1948. Over the next few years, she appeared in more than three dozen movies, almost all Westerns. She worked alongside such Western luminaries as Allan "Rocky" Lane, Monte Hale, Charles Starrett, Johnny Mack Brown, Tim Holt, and Gene Autry. Davis also appeared in the Western television series *The Range Rider*, *The Cisco Kid*, *The Lone Ranger*, *The Adventures of Kit Carson*, *Death Valley Days*, and *The Gene Autry Show*. In 1954, Autry cast her in the lead role of Annie Oakley in the television series of the same name.

The show capitalized on the fame of sharpshooter Annie Oakley, but the name was where the similarities ended. Television's Annie lived in the fictional town of Diablo, Arizona, with her kid brother Tagg (played by Jimmy Hawkins). Annie was often accompanied by the handsome local sheriff Lofty Craig (Brad Johnson), who clearly had an affinity for her, but like other television Westerns designed for children, actual romance was never part of the show. Although she had pigtails and was quite feminine, Annie was the fastest and most accurate gun in town. She never shot to kill, but she did shoot the gun out of the hand of a bad guy on several occasions. Her handgun of choice on-screen was a Colt Police Positive .38 Model. The show featured all of the action of a Western with a male lead, and Davis performed most of her own stunts.

Aired in syndication, the show debuted in January 1954 in more than 100 markets, and it remained on air until 1957. While the show stands alone for its quality and content, it is remarkable for being the first Western series with a female lead. Especially popular with children, the show introduced firearms in a safe and responsible manner to countless young girls. Amazingly, *Annie Oakley* remained the only Western series with a female lead until Barbara Stanwyck played the matriarch of the Barkley family on *The Big Valley* almost a decade later, in 1965. Offscreen during and after the series, Davis appeared alongside Autry on his personal appearance and rodeo tours. Always in character, Davis performed stunts reminiscent of the real Annie Oakley, such as lighting matches with a revolver shot from the back of a galloping horse. Davis is remembered today as a pioneer in the history of Western entertainment.

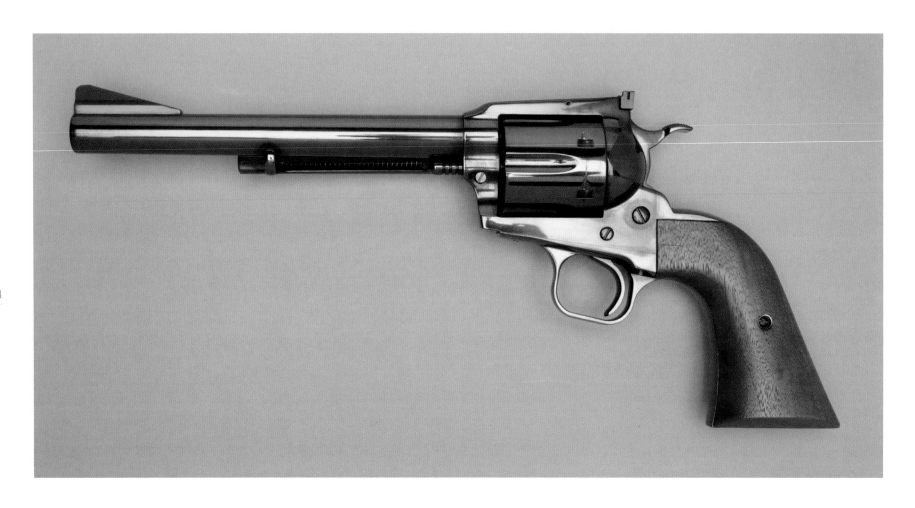

The only Single Action Army ever manufactured by
Colt's in .44 Magnum caliber was designed with a larger
frame, cylinder, and grips. (87.118.50)

.44 MAGNUM SINGLE ACTION ARMY MODEL

Do You Feel Lucky

But being as this is a .44 Magnum, the most powerful handgun in the world, and would blow your head clean off, you've got to ask yourself one question: 'Do I feel lucky?' Well, do ya, punk?" Clint Eastwood spoke these memorable lines in the 1971 action film *Dirty Harry* while wielding a Smith & Wesson Model 29. Introduced to the public in the 1950s, the .44 Magnum cartridge was a technical marvel. It was designed to deliver a large, heavy bullet capable of deep penetration. As Eastwood insinuated, it was the most powerful cartridge in the world when it was introduced. Unlike other handgun cartridges, the .44 Magnum was capable of taking down just about any animal in America at short range. However, it was so powerful it produced significant recoil and muzzle flash when shot from a handgun. The strain was such that repeat firing was difficult.

The cartridge was developed by Elmer Keith, a writer and outdoorsman who was also responsible for the development of the .357 Magnum. Keith took a standard .44 Special cartridge and "hotloaded" it, or loaded it beyond its specifications so it came out faster under higher pressure. Keith convinced Smith & Wesson to design a model specifically for the cartridge, with Remington manufacturing the cartridge itself. The .44 Magnum cartridge was introduced in 1955 with Smith & Wesson's Model 29 coming out the following year. A few months prior to the introduction of the Model 29, Sturm, Ruger & Company actually beat Smith & Wesson to the market with the Blackhawk, the first handgun designed specifically for the new cartridge. Exactly how Ruger learned about the ammunition is unclear. Some claim a Ruger employee stumbled upon discarded cartridges, while others contend an employee at Remington passed along the information. Regardless of what actually happened, the one company that was caught off guard was Colt's.

Colt's introduced the Python Model, chambered in .357 Magnum, around the time that Smith & Wesson and Ruger introduced their .44 Magnum revolvers. The Python quickly was hailed by many enthusiasts, from hunters to law-enforcement officers, as the pinnacle of Colt's revolver line. The Python was a natural choice for the .44 Magnum cartridge. Unfortunately, its frame was too small to accommodate the cartridge, and given its popularity, Colt's decided not to make changes to the model. No other model in production at that time could accommodate the cartridge, and believing the market for the .44 Magnum was rather limited, Colt's decided not to embark on a new model. As a result, Colt's went many years without a model capable of firing the .44 Magnum cartridge. Around 1972, Colt's reconsidered adding to its production line a revolver capable of firing this cartridge.

Because the Single Action Army remained one of the company's most popular models, experiments were undertaken to see if it could be converted to accommodate the cartridge. The standard Single Action Army was too small, so a new frame had to be enlarged and specially made. A longer, non-fluted cylinder was necessary, along with larger grips and a bigger grip frame. The finished product was serial number GX9234, which is now in the Autry Collection. Instead of the traditional case-hardened frame, serial number GX9234 was given a high-gloss royal-blue finish. Exactly how the revolver performed in tests is unknown, but the project appears to have been shelved with serial number GX9234 being the only Single Action Army ever manufactured by the company in .44 Magnum. As a result, it is a truly unique specimen in the history of the famed model. Finally in 1990, Colt's introduced the Anaconda, its first model capable of firing the .44 Magnum cartridge.

President John F. Kennedy tragically was assassinated prior to the completion of his presentation New Frontier Model Single Action Army. (87.118.52)

PRESIDENT JOHN F. KENNEDY'S PRESENTATION NEW FRONTIER MODEL SINGLE ACTION ARMY

A Tragic Reminder

Colt's has a long tradition of presentations to important military and political figures—including the president of the United States—that dates back to Samuel Colt. It is believed that the first sitting president to receive a presentation revolver from Colt's was Andrew Jackson. Other presidents known to have owned Colts, although not all of them were presentations, were Franklin Pierce, Ulysses S. Grant, Grover Cleveland, and Theodore Roosevelt. In modern times, the practice of presenting a revolver to the president resumed with Harry S. Truman, and many subsequent presidents have received one. Due to its history and popularity, the Single Action Army is often used for presidential presentations. Regardless of the model, presidential presentation revolvers are unique and interesting aspects of American history.

When John F. Kennedy accepted the Democratic Party's nomination for president of the United States in 1960, he declared that the nation was facing a "new frontier" of opportunities and challenges. Colt's sought to capitalize on the phrase and introduced a target version of the Single Action Army, the New Frontier Model, in 1961, the same year Kennedy assumed the presidency. Although he was only president for a few years, Kennedy's administration was filled with significant ups and downs. He initiated economic and social programs that initially were resisted but came to fruition in later years. He established the Peace Corps and challenged America to get to the moon by the end of the decade. He witnessed the failed Bay of Pigs invasion of Cuba and the successful standoff with the Soviet Union during the Cuban Missile Crisis.

Having already accepted a gold-plated M16 from Colt's sometime around 1962, the White House indicated that President Kennedy also would be pleased to accept a presentation revolver from the company. Not surprisingly, the New Frontier Model Single Action Army was chosen for the presentation. Alvin A. White was contracted to design and engrave the revolver. Approximately three prototypes were produced in 1963, with the design having been reviewed and revised as the prototypes were being completed. The prototypes were engraved, but to save time and money, a significant portion of the gold inlay intended for the actual presentation arm was left off. With Colt's acceptance of the final design, White began work on the actual presentation arm.

Appropriately given the serial number PT109 in deference to the boat Kennedy commanded in World War II, the presentation arm features deluxe engraving on the barrel, cylinder, and frame. Special emphasis was placed on the gold inlay. The cylinder features an image of the White House and the presidential seal executed in high-relief 18-karat gold. The initials "JFK" are scripted in flush gold inlay on the recoil shield. The rosewood grips are gold mounted. The back strap is inscribed "To John Fitzgerald Kennedy / 35th President of the United States / From Colt's Patent Fire Arms Mfg. Co. / 1963." Tragically, as the revolver was nearing completion, President Kennedy was assassinated on November 22, 1963. All work on the presentation was stopped, and it was soon polished and blued in an incomplete state. Now part of the Autry Collection, President Kennedy's presentation revolver is a powerful reminder that firearms can be beautiful works of art or devastating tools of evil, depending on how they are used.

The prototype for President Lyndon Johnson's Single Action Army features the same Texas theme found on the actual presentation revolver. (87.118.54)

PRESIDENT LYNDON JOHNSON'S PROTOTYPE SINGLE ACTION ARMY MODEL

White Hat/Black Hat

Around the turn of the 20th century, the American presidency became intertwined with the emerging image of the cowboy portrayed in art, literature, and popular culture. To many people, the image represented bravery, ruggedness, and a love of freedom, whereas others found it juvenile, reckless, and dangerous. Presidents used cowboy iconography to define themselves, their policies, and their opponents to America and the world. Journalists and cartoonists used cowboy imagery to commend or criticize politicians and their actions. The popularity of the cowboy image has ebbed and flowed with the politics of the time, but it remains one of the most persistent and recognizable of American political symbols. One politician who effectively used the image of the cowboy was Lyndon Baines Johnson, America's 36th president.

Johnson was born into poverty in central Texas in 1908. He worked his way through college and became a teacher. Johnson's compassion as a politician for the less fortunate was a result of his own upbringing and what he experienced while teaching the poor. In 1937, he successfully ran for Texas's 10th Congressional District as a New Deal Democrat. He represented Texas in the House of Representatives from 1937 to 1949. He received a Silver Star, the military's third-highest medal, during his brief tenure in the Navy during World War II. After six terms in the House, Johnson was elected to the Senate in 1948. He distinguished himself rather quickly, and in 1953, he was named the youngest minority leader in Senate history. The following year, the Democrats gained control of the Senate, and Johnson became the majority leader. Johnson got several key pieces of legislation passed, and by most accounts, he was the most effective majority leader of the 20th century.

In 1960, Democratic presidential nominee Senator John F. Kennedy of Massachusetts offered Johnson the vice-presidential nomination in an attempt to balance the ticket. The two were elected later that year in one of the closest races in presidential history. When Kennedy was assassinated in 1963, Johnson assumed the office of the presidency. Much like Theodore Roosevelt, Johnson capitalized on his Western heritage and his association with cowboys. Johnson spent many days of his presidency at his family's cattle ranch outside Austin, Texas. The ranch came to be known as the "Western

White House." He often entertained political allies and foreign dignitaries at the ranch, engaging in what one reporter called "barbecue diplomacy." Johnson was often portrayed as the white-hat hero who pushed through legislation that strengthened civil rights, fought poverty, and established Medicare. Conversely, he was also depicted as the black-hat villain that led America into the Vietnam War, a crisis at home and abroad. Johnson was elected to his own term in 1964, but he chose not to run again in 1968.

Following company tradition, Colt's received permission to present Johnson with a Single Action Army in honor of his presidency. Serial number LBJ1, now in the Autry Collection, is the prototype for the actual presentation arm. The revolver is engraved on the barrel, frame, and cylinder. The Texas state seal and the presidential seal are executed in high-relief 18-karat gold on the cylinder. Gold-inlaid Texas cattle brands are used throughout. The initials "LBJ" are scripted in bronze on the recoil shield. The grips feature the Texas state flag on one side and a steer head on the other. The revolver is inscribed "To Lyndon Baines Johnson / 36th President of the United States / From Colt's Patent Firearms Mfg. Co. / 1966." The decoration is the work of Alvin A. White. The actual presentation arm is in the collection of the Lyndon Baines Johnson Presidential Library and Museum in Austin, Texas. The layout of the two revolvers is the same, but there is more gold coverage on the actual presentation arm.

Specially designed for Colt Industries Chairman George Strichman, two of the finest Single Action Armies ever made feature a Western theme. (90.183.7)

SINGLE ACTION ARMY MODEL PAIR WITH GOLD INLAY AND "TIFFANY" GRIPS

The Best in the West

T he Single Action Army remains the most iconic and identifiable revolver ever manufactured. Although it has been used around the world since mass production began in 1873, it is commonly associated with the American West. The revolver was used by countless individuals on the American frontier, and the strong connection between the model and the West was strengthened by popular culture. The earliest accounts of the West, including dime novels and Wild West shows, prominently featured the Single Action Army. The association was taken to new heights with the advent of the film and television industries in the 20th century. Screen cowboys, both heroes and villains, relied on the Single Action Army more than any other firearm or prop.

A new generation of Western enthusiasts capitalized on the allure of the Single Action Army with the introduction of Cowboy Action Shooting (CAS) in the early 1980s. Designed to celebrate America's Second Amendment rights and to preserve the history of the Old West, the competitive shooting sport requires participants to use firearms that were available in the 19th century. While a variety of single-action revolvers are acceptable, the Single Action Army is by far the most popular. Authentic Single Action Armies are expensive, so Cowboy Shooters are allowed to use replicas and reproductions. Popular manufacturers include Uberti, Ruger, Beretta, and Cimarron Firearms. Participants are also required to dress in period costumes and select an Old West alias.

Countless commemorative revolvers and special orders have furthered the connection between the Single Action Army and the West. Commemorative revolvers often celebrate notable Western figures, such as Wyatt Earp, Pat Garrett, Bat Masterson, James Butler "Wild Bill" Hickok, John Wayne, and Gene Autry. Historic groups, such as the Texas Rangers, and important events, like the completion of the Transcontinental Railroad, are also honored. Commemorative revolvers released by Colt's are often the Frontier

Scout Model, a smaller version of the Single Action Army. Chambered in .22 rimfire caliber, the Frontier Scout is about nine-tenths the size of the standard Single Action Army. Countless custom-order Single Action Armies also feature spectacular examples of Western iconography. One of the finest pairs of Single Action Armies ever made employ a Western theme.

Now in the Autry Collection, serial numbers G. A. Strichman No. 1 and G. A. Strichman No. 2 were made circa 1965 for Colt Industries Chairman George Strichman. They feature gold-inlaid busts of Annie Oakley and William F. "Buffalo Bill" Cody on the recoil shields. Detailed scenes from the works of Western artists George Catlin, Albert Bierstadt, Frederic Remington, George Caleb Bingham, Harold Von Schmidt, and Frank Schoonover are featured in gold inlay throughout. Deluxe scrollwork is engraved on almost every part of the revolvers, and the "Tiffany" grips are made of silver and gold. Both revolvers are inscribed "G. A. Strichman / Chairman of the Board / Colt Industries." All of the embellishments were the work of noted engraver Alvin A. White. The revolvers are a testament to the craftsmanship and beauty of the Single Action Army and the model's strong connection to the American West.

Colt's manufactured a prototype Single Action Army
prior to embarking on the actual presentation arm for
President Richard Nixon. (87.118.55)

PRESIDENT RICHARD NIXON'S PROTOTYPE SINGLE ACTION ARMY MODEL

Overshadowed by History

President Richard Nixon was from the West, but he certainly was not a cowboy. Born and raised in California, Nixon's family struggled to survive. A brilliant student, Nixon used his intellect to escape poverty. He graduated from Whittier College in California and the Duke University School of Law in North Carolina. After college, Nixon returned to Whittier to join a law firm. He enlisted in the Navy during World War II and served as a lieutenant commander in the South Pacific Theater. Upon returning from the war, he successfully ran for the House of Representatives representing Whittier's district. Nixon made a name for himself in Congress as a member of the House Un-American Activities Committee (HUAC) investigating communist infiltration in America. He easily won a second term in 1948. Two years later, Nixon was elected to the United States Senate.

Nixon's anticommunist credentials made him a national figure, and in 1952, Republican presidential nominee General Dwight David Eisenhower chose Nixon as his vice-presidential running mate. Prior to the election, Nixon was accused of accepting cash and gifts in exchange for future favors. He denied the accusations on national television, and he promised to keep a black-and-white cocker spaniel named Checkers that had been given to the family as a gift. The "Checkers Speech," as it came to be known, was a brilliant political move that solidified his support within the party. Eisenhower and Nixon won the election in 1952, and during his two terms in office, Nixon elevated the visibility and stature of the vice presidency. In 1959, while representing the United States at the American National Exhibition in Moscow, Nixon deftly debated Soviet Premier Nikita Khrushchev on the superiority of American products, ideology, and military strength.

Nixon ran for president in 1960, losing a close election to Democrat John F. Kennedy. Nixon returned to California and was persuaded to run for governor in 1962. Nixon lost the race, and many believed his political career was over. After spending time practicing law and supporting various Republican causes, Nixon ran for president again in 1968. He defeated Vice President Hubert H. Humphrey and third-party candidate George Wallace to become America's 37th president. As president, he championed various domestic issues, such as environmental and criminal reform, but he is best remembered for his foreign policy achievements. He successfully negotiated the first strategic arms limitation pact between the United States and the Soviet Union. In 1972, he became the first American president to visit communist China. The Vietnam War was the most pressing issue of his presidency, and in 1973, he announced an accord to end American involvement in the region. Unfortunately, all of Nixon's accomplishments were overshadowed by the Watergate scandal.

In June 1972, five men associated with the Committee for the Re-Election of the President (CRP) were arrested after breaking into the Democratic National Committee headquarters in the Watergate office complex in Washington, D.C. Exactly what Nixon knew and when is still debated, but he certainly was involved in the attempted cover-up that followed. Facing the likelihood of impeachment, Nixon became the first president to resign from office on August 9, 1974. Prior to his resignation, Colt's prepared a presentation Single Action Army in honor of his presidency. Exactly what became of the revolver is unclear, as serial number RMN No. 1 in the Autry Collection appears to be the prototype of the presentation arm. Designed by Alvin A. White, it features detailed engraving and a gold-inlaid bald eagle on the recoil shield. The left side of the grip has a gold plaque inscribed "RMN," and the gold-plated butt cap features the presidential seal. The back strap is inscribed "Richard Milhous Nixon / 37th President of the United States / From Colt's Pt. Fire Arms Mfg. Co. / 1970."

Colt's prepared a Single Action Army in hopes of presenting it to President Gerald Ford, an individual who took a unique path to the presidency. (87.118.56)

PRESIDENT GERALD FORD'S PRESENTATION SINGLE ACTION ARMY MODEL

A Remarkable Journey

Gerald Ford's journey to the White House was unique and rather remarkable. He was the only individual to hold both the offices of president and vice president without having been elected to either. Born in 1913, Ford grew up in Michigan and graduated from the University of Michigan in 1935. Although he was later lampooned for his clumsiness, especially on shows like *Saturday Night Live*, Ford was a gifted athlete who played football on the University of Michigan's national championship teams in 1932 and 1933. He was offered two professional football contracts, but he turned them both down to coach and attend law school at Yale University. After graduating from law school in 1941, he served in the United States Navy during World War II, attaining the rank of lieutenant commander. He joined a law firm in Grand Rapids, Michigan, upon his return, and in 1948, he was elected to the House of Representatives.

Reelected 12 times, Ford served in the House from 1949 to 1973. He hoped to one day become Speaker of the House, so he rebuffed offers to run for Senate and governor of Michigan. Ford served on several powerful committees, including the House Appropriations Committee. In 1963, President Lyndon Johnson appointed him to the Warren Commission investigating the murder of President John F. Kennedy. Ford later cowrote a book on the assassination. He was appointed the House minority leader in 1965. Ford held the position until he was appointed vice president by President Richard Nixon in 1973. Spiro Agnew, Nixon's original vice president, resigned amid controversy after pleading no contest to charges of income tax evasion. Ford was a longtime friend and supporter of Nixon, but more importantly, Ford was someone with an impeccable record who had a long career of forging compromises in the House. Faced with his own troubles, Nixon needed someone with Ford's reputation.

When Nixon resigned from office in 1974 as a result of the Watergate scandal, Ford became the 38th president of the United States. A month into his tenure, Ford made the difficult decision to pardon Nixon for any crimes he may have committed as president. Ford knew the investigation into Nixon's activities would be a serious drain on the national psyche, so he issued the pardon hoping the nation would turn its attention to more pressing issues. The pardon was extremely unpopular, and it overshadowed the rest of Ford's administration. At home, Ford sought to confront the rising threat of inflation and boost the economy through a combination of tax cuts and stimuli. Internationally, Ford continued arms negotiations with the Soviet Union, and he oversaw the removal of the last American troops from Vietnam. Ford ran for his own term as president in 1976. He defeated challenger Ronald Reagan in a contentious battle for the Republican nomination, but he lost to Democratic nominee Jimmy Carter in the general election. The lingering suspicions over the pardon of Nixon played a significant role in Ford's defeat.

As was customary, Colt's planned to present President Ford with a Single Action Army while he was in office. For unknown reasons, the actual presentation never took place. As a result, it is unclear if the revolver in the Autry Collection, serial number GRF No.1, is a prototype or the actual presentation arm. The significant amount of gold inlay would seem to indicate that it is the actual presentation arm executed by Alvin A. White. The revolver features gold-inlaid initials "GRF" on the recoil shield, and a gold-inlaid banner on the barrel with the script "Special Bicentennial Model / 1776–1976." The Capitol Building and the presidential seal are relief engraved in gold on the cylinder. The Michigan state seal is featured in gold on one side of the grip, and a gold shield with the inscription "To / Gerald R. Ford / from / Colt Industries / Firearms Division / July 4th 1976" is on the other. The back strap is inscribed "Naval Officer / Congressman / Vice President / 38th President of the United States." The 18-karat gold butt cap has another image of the presidential seal.

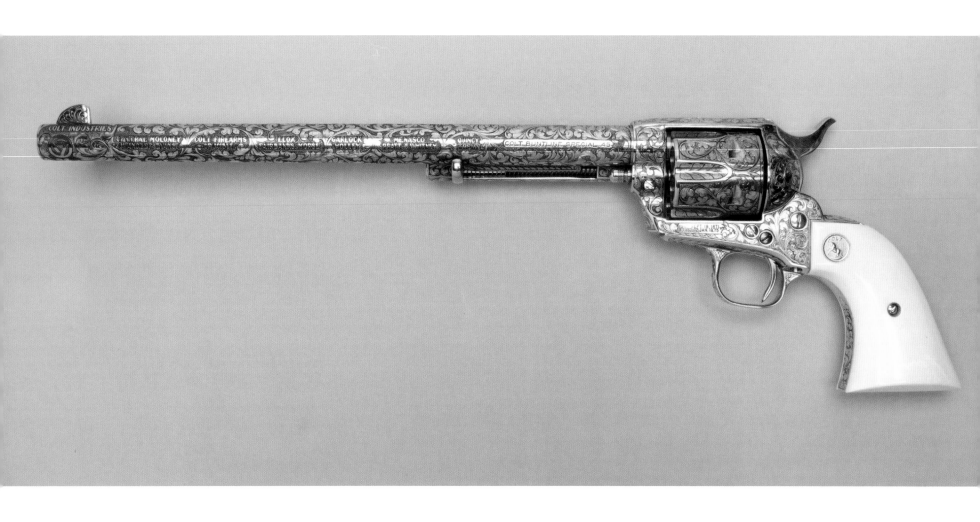

A gold-plated "Buntline Special" with ivory grips and full engraving was prepared exclusively for Colt Industries Chairman George Strichman, the individual who oversaw Colt's myriad business operations. (90.183.20.4.1)

MODERN "BUNTLINE SPECIAL" SINGLE ACTION ARMY MODEL

The Firearms Division

The "Buntline Special" was introduced in 1876, and at that time, Colt's was one of the leading firearm manufacturers in the world. A few years later, the company's position increased, as it offered a complete line of weapons ranging from derringers and double-action revolvers to hammerless shotguns and pump-action rifles. The company was also privileged to be the exclusive manufacturer of Dr. Richard Gatling's machine gun (commonly called a Gatling gun) for several decades. The introduction of the first semiautomatic pistol designed by the incomparable John Moses Browning in 1900 took the company in an entirely new direction. During all of that time, the company was controlled by the Colt family. Samuel Colt was the driving force until his death in 1862, and his widow, Elizabeth Hart Jarvis Colt, was an able successor. In 1901, Elizabeth sold the company to a group of outside investors.

The 20th century was a tumultuous time for Colt's. Production reached record levels during World War I, but orders decreased substantially after the war. Production slowed even further during the Great Depression. A bitter strike by employees and several natural disasters took a toll on the company in the 1930s. America's entrance into World War II revived the company's fortunes, but wartime production exposed poor management, antiquated machinery, and inefficient production techniques. The company was able to survive the first half of the 20th century due in large part to diversification that had began decades earlier, as evidenced by an 1892 catalog in the Autry Collection, in areas such as printing presses, dishwashers, and plastics. The various products manufactured by Colt's are popular with modern collectors, especially a line of tobacco-related products produced in the early 1930s. The humidor in the Autry Collection, made of Bakelite, has a molded leaf design on the lid, and a Rampant Colt is stamped on the bottom of the base.

Cycles of boom and bust continued into the second half of the 20th century. In 1955, the company was acquired by the Penn-Texas Corporation, a large conglomerate. Colt Firearms, based out of the city of New York, became a wholly owned subsidiary of the corporation. When the corporation struggled, a new group of investors took control in 1959 and the corporate name was changed to Fairbanks Whitney. The firearms division of the corporation was strengthened when it acquired the rights to the AR-15 Rifle in 1960. The fully automatic military version of the rifle, the M16, became one of the company's most important firearms with more than five million units sold. George Strichman became president and chairman of the board of Fairbanks Whitney in 1962, and two years later, he changed the corporate name to Colt Industries. The firearms subsidiary became Colt's Inc., Firearms Division. Strichman was instrumental in guiding the corporation and the firearms division onto sound financial footing.

Strichman also set about compiling one of the finest personal collections of modern engraved firearms. This included a set of four matched Single Action Armies featuring four different calibers (.357 Magnum, .44 Special, .44-40, and .45), barrel lengths (four and three-quarters inches, five and a half inches, seven and a half inches, and 12 inches), finishes (blue and case hardened, nickel plated, silver plated, and gold plated), grips (hard rubber, rosewood, walnut, and ivory), and coverage (A, B, C, and D). All of the revolvers are now part of the Autry Collection. The most striking example of the set is the modern "Buntline Special" engraved by Leonard Francolini. It is .45 caliber with a 12-inch barrel. The revolver is gold plated and engraved with D (or full) coverage. The grips are ivory. Engraved along the barrel are the names of the principal divisions of Colt Industries at the time of the revolver's manufacture, circa 1980. The revolver, serial number GAS-4/OSA, is arguably the finest "Buntline Special" ever made.

1856.

1892.

THIRD EDITION.

COLT'S

PATENT FIRE-ARMS MANUFACTURING CO.,

MANUFACTURERS OF

MILITARY, SPORTING, AND DEFENSIVE ARMS,

ALSO

BAXTER STEAM ENGINES,

COLT'S ARMORY PRINTING PRESSES.

ALL OF OUR WORK IS GUARANTEED, HIGHEST STANDARD ATTAINED.

HARTFORD, CONN., U. S. A.

10 FRONT ST.,
San Francisco, Cal. } · · DEPOTS · · { 26 GLASSHOUSE ST.,
London, W.,
England.

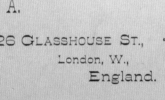

JANUARY, 1892.

238

Opposite:
As early as 1892, as evidenced by this catalog, Colt's was promoting the various products manufactured by the company. (87.118.170)

Right:
The "Jar," as it was officially known, was one of many popular Bakelite products manufactured by Colt's plastics division in the early 1930s. (87.118.160)

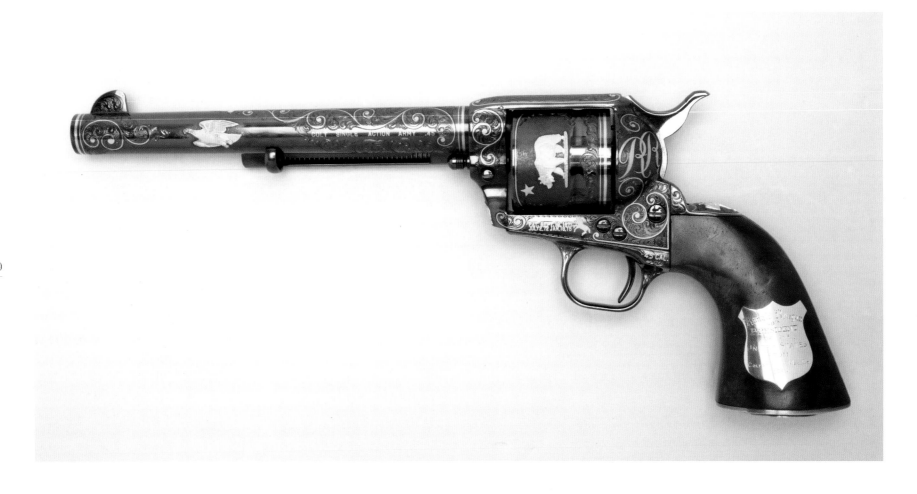

President Ronald Reagan's presentation Single Action
Army highlights his association with the American
West and California. (87.118.57)

PRESIDENT RONALD REAGAN'S PRESENTATION SINGLE ACTION ARMY MODEL

A Cowboy President

Ronald Reagan was born in Illinois in 1911. After graduating from Eureka College, he found work as a radio sports announcer. He traveled to Los Angeles in 1937 while covering the Chicago Cubs baseball team for a station in Des Moines, Iowa. Reagan used the opportunity to take a screen test, which led to a seven-year contract with Warner Bros. In a career that spanned more than two decades, Reagan appeared in more than 50 films. His roles varied dramatically, from George Gipp, "the Gipper," in *Knute Rockne, All American* (1940) to a man who has his legs amputated by a sadistic surgeon in *King's Row* (1942). Although he played the part in only a few films, Reagan made his biggest impression as a screen cowboy. His Western films included *Santa Fe Trail* (1940), *The Last Outpost* (1951), *Law and Order* (1953), *Cattle Queen of Montana* (1954), and *Tennessee's Partner* (1955). Reagan's association with cowboys continued with his work on the long-running Western television series *Death Valley Days* (1952–1975), where he served as both actor and host in 1964–1965.

Reagan's political career began in 1947 when he was elected president of the Screen Actors Guild. Reagan ran for governor of California in 1966, and he used his association as a screen cowboy to relate to voters. Reagan won the election and was reelected to a second term in 1970. After failing to secure the Republican nomination in 1976, Reagan easily defeated Democratic President Jimmy Carter in 1980. Reagan's election coincided with a wave of cowboy mania that swept the country throughout the decade. Cowboys seemed to be everywhere in the 1980s, from movies like *Urban Cowboy* (1980) to television shows like *Dallas* (1978–1991). Fancy boots, broad-brimmed hats, fringed jackets, bolo ties, and other Western garb became part of mainstream fashion. Riding mechanical bulls and two-stepping to Western music were popular activities for a brief period.

In August 1981, Reagan signed a sweeping tax reform bill at his ranch in California. Reagan's use of the ranch as his "Western White House" was an integral part of his administration. The main focus of Reagan's presidency was reducing the threat of nuclear war with the communist Soviet Union, and significant arms limitation treaties were signed during his administration. Many people liked Reagan's cowboy image, but it also proved to be an easy target for his detractors. His dismantling of government social programs and his aggressive foreign policy caused many critics to label him a reckless cowboy capitalist. Reagan nevertheless won a second term in a landslide in 1984, and he left office with one of the highest approval ratings in history. All subsequent presidents have attempted to use the cowboy image in one way or another, but none have been as effective as Reagan.

Reagan's Western background is one of several biographical elements highlighted in the presentation Single Action Army, serial number RR-1, that Colt's prepared for the president. The revolver was designed by Alvin A. White, and a gold-inlaid Western saddle is featured prominently on the top of the back strap. The White House is executed in gold inlay on the cylinder, along with a gold-inlaid bear and star from the California flag. The initials "RR" are scripted in gold on the recoil shield. A gold shield on the grip is inscribed "Ronald Reagan / 40th / President / of the / United States / From / Colt's Pt. FA Mfg. Co. / 1984." The presidential seal on the butt cap is executed in gold and surrounded with silver. The presentation revolver was never presented to Reagan for political reasons, and it is now part of the Autry Collection. Reagan and museum founder Gene Autry were friends, and when Reagan visited the museum, he always enjoyed seeing his revolver on display.

The first modern revolvers designed by the illustrious
Tiffany & Co. were a set of Single Action Armies
customized in 1982 with a nautical theme. (90.183.8)

SINGLE ACTION ARMY MODEL PAIR DESIGNED BY TIFFANY & CO.

The World's Premier Jeweler

Tiffany & Co. has a long and distinguished history of selling opulently embellished military wares. The company's entrance in the field dates to circa 1861 with the selling of elaborate presentation swords. It has been estimated that Tiffany made about 100 ornate swords and 30 extremely decadent swords during the Civil War period. The majority of these swords were presented to the leading military figures of the period, such as General Ulysses S. Grant, General William Tecumseh Sherman, and Rear Admiral David Farragut. Tiffany presentation swords are some of the finest and most beautiful examples ever made, and by the end of the Civil War era, the company was firmly established as a leader in the field.

Tiffany naturally transitioned from selling swords to selling firearms. In the 19th century, Tiffany sold and embellished firearms manufactured by Henry Deringer, Smith & Wesson, and Colt's. Tiffany had an exclusive arrangement with Philadelphia manufacturer Henry Deringer for many years, and it was the only company licensed to sell his pocket arms in the region. (Other companies got around this agreement by selling copies of Deringer's pistol that were purposely mislabeled "derringers," a name that continues to be used to this day.) Interestingly, none of the Deringers sold by Tiffany appear to have been embellished in any way with Tiffany silver. The company instead primarily embellished Smith & Wesson firearms. Clearly marked, these guns were used by Smith & Wesson for promotional purposes. Tiffany also embellished at least one Colt revolver, one Winchester rifle, and an L. C. Smith shotgun presented to sharpshooter Annie Oakley.

Unlike typical engraving, which cuts a design or pattern onto a steel surface, the craftsmen at Tiffany primarily fitted silver sheaths to firearms. These sheaths almost always completely encased the frame or grip. In some instances, the frame or grip was reshaped for decorative purposes. The silver was then relief stamped or hammered to form an embossed design. Tiffany also used acid etching to create floral and scroll motifs, and in a few rare instances, hand engraving was employed. Tiffany's busiest period of firearm embellishment was the 1890s. Choosing to focus on more profitable aspects of the business, Tiffany ceased all firearm adornment around 1916. The company returned to firearm design and decoration in 1982 with three Single Action Armies custom-made for retiring Colt Industries Chairman George Strichman. Two of the revolvers, serial numbers GAS-0/Tiffany and GAS-00/Tiffany, are part of the Autry Collection.

The revolvers feature relief-sculpted sterling-silver waves on the barrel, ejector rod housing, frame, cylinder, and hammer. Relief-sculpted sterling-silver dolphins and seashells are located respectively on the cylinder and the muzzle end of the barrel. The grips of cast and chased sterling silver have an image of Strichman's sailboat, the *Peacemaker*, on both sides. The sailboat's name on the bottom of the grip and Strichman's initials on the butt are scripted in vermeil. The grips are signed "Sterling," "Tiffany & Co.," and "U. Vitali" in the upper right panel. The back strap is inscribed "George A. Strichman / Chairman of the Board Colt Industries." The nautical theme includes the only time a rampant seahorse logo was used in place of the traditional Rampant Colt. The seahorse is executed in flush gold inlay along the top of the barrel along with the gold-inlaid marking "Designed by Tiffany & Co. for Colt Firearms Division." The revolvers are the result of the combined talents of designers Paul Epifanio and Larry Wojick of Tiffany and master engraver Leonard Francolini. Everything about the revolvers is truly worthy of the name Tiffany.

The Tiffany revolvers were made exclusively for retiring Colt Industries Chairman George A. Strichman, whose passion for collecting was inspired by his predecessor, Samuel Colt. (90.183.8.1)

The barrels of the Tiffany revolvers feature a gold-inlaid rampant seahorse, the only time it was ever used in place of the traditional Rampant Colt logo. (90.183.8.2)

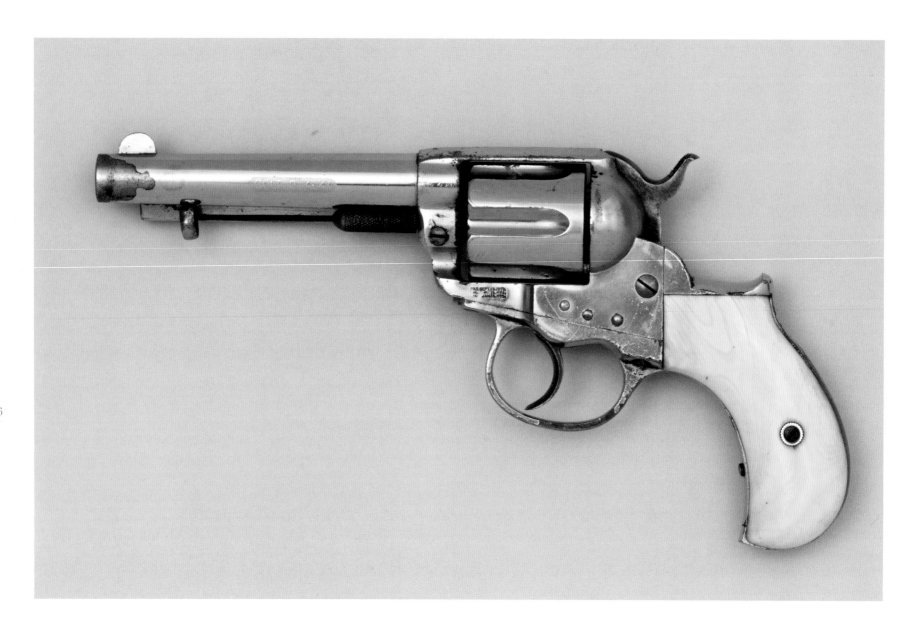

The favorite revolver of John Wesley Hardin, one of the deadliest guns in the West, was the Model 1877 Thunderer. (85.1.433; acquisition made possible in part by John E. Bianchi Jr.)

GUNSLINGER JOHN WESLEY HARDIN'S MODEL 1877 THUNDERER

Crime and Punishment

John Wesley Hardin was arguably the deadliest gunfighter in the history of the American West. He was exceptionally quick and accurate with a weapon. He claimed to have killed more than 40 men, although reports put the number closer to 20, before he was murdered at the age of 42. Named after the founder of the Protestant Christian movement, Hardin was only 15 years old when he killed his first man, a former slave, in 1868. Hardin left town to avoid prosecution, and he killed three soldiers who attempted to apprehend him. Hardin killed a few more men, including peace officers, before leaving in 1871 on a cattle drive along the Chisholm Trail to Abilene, Kansas. Hardin was forced to leave town shortly after his arrival when he shot and killed a man who was snoring in the hotel room next to him.

Hardin returned to Texas in 1872. Getting involved in the Sutton-Taylor Feud, a long-standing Texas range war, Hardin killed several men associated with the Sutton faction. Hardin was also involved, along with his father and brother, in the killing of Deputy Sheriff Charles Webb. Hardin managed to escape in the aftermath of the murder, and he fled to Florida, where he killed yet again. A posse of Texas Rangers tracked him down, and he was arrested in Pensacola in August 1877. Tried and convicted for the killing of Sheriff Webb, he was sentenced to 25 years in Texas's Huntsville Prison. His time served was difficult, as he was often beaten and forced into solitary confinement. He nevertheless used his time in prison to further his education and study law. He was released in 1894 after serving 15 years.

Hardin successfully petitioned for a pardon, and he passed the Texas bar exam in 1894. Hardin eventually made his way to El Paso, where he practiced law. One of Hardin's business cards is part of the Autry Collection. The majority of his time, however, was spent drinking and gambling. While his reputation struck fear in the heart of most, Hardin was also known to be charming and quite captivating. He often amused audiences with demonstrations of his shooting skills. His favorite trick was shooting faro cards thrown in the air, which he signed and passed out

as souvenirs. The example in the Autry Collection was shot multiple times at five paces. Hardin's weapon of choice upon being released from prison was a Model 1877 Thunderer. One of Hardin's revolvers, serial number 68837, is also part of the Autry Collection. Manufactured in 1888, it is nickel plated with a four-and-a-half-inch barrel and ivory grips. Chambered in .41 caliber, it clearly shows extensive use. Analysis supports the conclusion that serial number 68837 or another Thunderer was used by Hardin to shoot the souvenir faro cards.

On August 19, 1895, El Paso Constable John Selman Sr. killed Hardin at the Acme Saloon. Selman shot Hardin in the back of the head and three more times in the body. Two theories are given for Selman's actions. The first theory claims Selman was protecting his son, who was threatened by Hardin. The second theory speculates that Hardin contracted Selman and several other men, including George Scarborough, to kill the husband of Hardin's lover. Selman was upset with Hardin for some reason in the aftermath of the murder, possibly over money, so he killed Hardin. Interestingly, Scarborough killed Selman a few months later. Although the exact motivations for the two killings are unknown, the Hardin-Selman-Scarborough affair demonstrates the fragile balance of violence and justice on the American frontier.

JOHN W. HARDIN Esq.

ATTORNEY AT LAW

OFFICE:
200½ El Paso
Wells Fargo Bldg.

**PRACTICE IN
ALL COURTS**

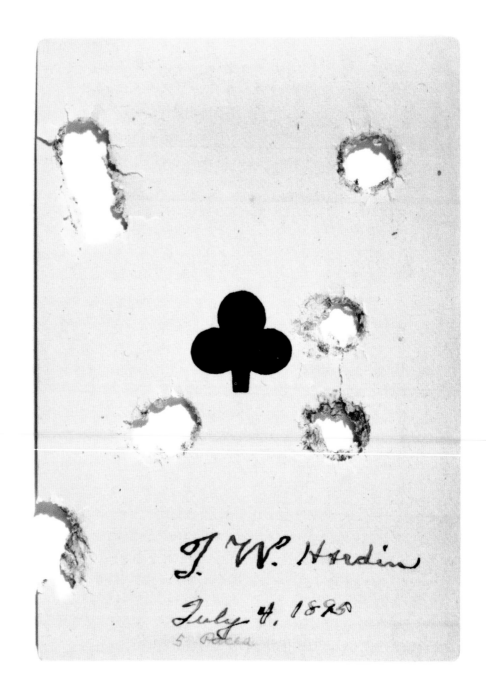

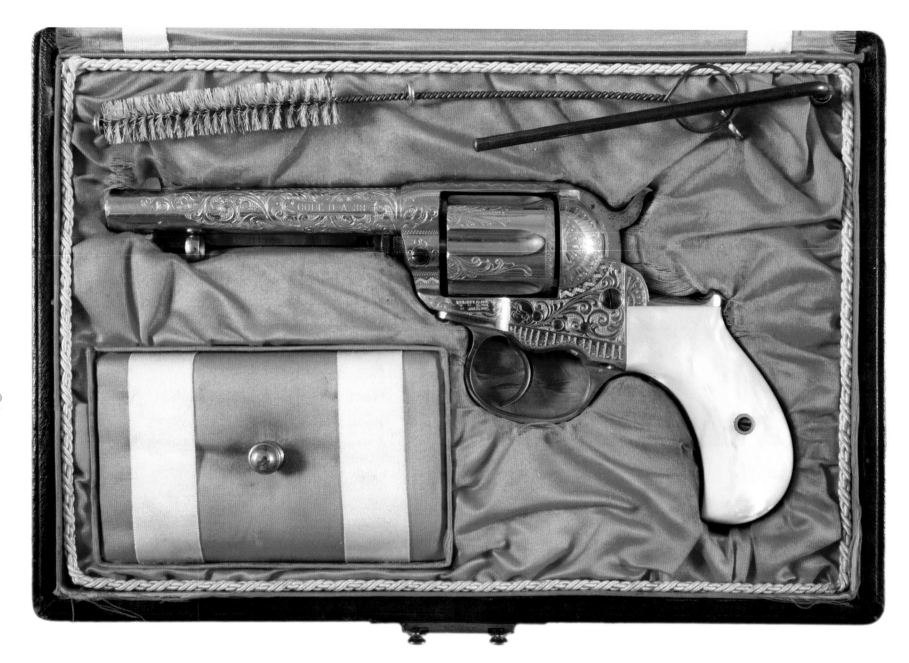

The Model 1877, including the Lightning chambered in .38 caliber, was the first double-action revolver mass-produced by Colt's. (2012.2.16; the George Gamble Collection)

HARTFORD CHIEF OF POLICE GEORGE F. BILL'S CASED PRESENTATION MODEL 1877 LIGHTNING

Pulling the Trigger

Colt's introduced its first double-action or self-cocking revolver in 1877. Unlike a revolver with a single-action mechanism, double-action revolvers can be fired simply by pulling the trigger. In other words, the double-action mechanism revolves the cylinder and cocks and releases the hammer. Double-action revolvers can be fired more quickly, but are often less accurate than their single-action counterparts. Double-action revolvers were common in Europe in the middle of the 19th century, but very few were produced by American manufacturers until the later part of the century. Samuel Colt never mass-produced a double-action revolver in his lifetime, and he even went so far as to publicly criticize the double-action mechanism. The introduction and efficiency of the self-contained metallic cartridge ultimately made the double-action revolver more appealing to American firearm manufacturers and users.

The Model 1877 was Colt's first double-action revolver. William Mason, the prolific designer of the famed Single Action Army, was instrumental in the development of the model. Interestingly, because the double-action mechanism had been in use for several decades, it was considered to be in the public domain by 1877. As a result, Mason's patents related to the model focus on different aspects of its design, such as the ejector system and cylinder features, as opposed to the double-action mechanism itself. Mason relied heavily on the design of the Single Action Army for the Model 1877. Given the Single Action Army's popularity and acceptance by the general public, it is not surprising that Mason and his employer both felt that a radical redesign was not necessary. The major difference between the Single Action Army and the Model 1877 was the smaller frame and the so-called bird's-head grip contour on the Model 1877.

The Model 1877 was manufactured from 1877 to 1910. During that time, approximately 167,000 were produced. All of the revolvers were six-shot, with most being either .38 or .41 caliber. The revolvers chambered in .38 are commonly called Lightnings and the revolvers chambered in .41 are called Thunderers. (A few were produced in .32, and these rare examples are called Rainmakers.) Barrel lengths typically ranged from a pocket-size two inches to a holster-size seven and a half inches. The revolvers featured a fixed cylinder and came with or without an ejector rod. Engravings were quite scarce, with only about 725 of the entire production run featuring factory engraving. A spectacular example of the 1877 Lightning is serial number 80220 in the Autry Collection. The nickel-plated revolver has a four-and-a-half-inch barrel. It has mother-of-pearl grips and features engraving by Cuno A. Helfricht. The revolver is contained within a leather-bound case lined with rose satin.

An inscription on the revolver's back strap reads "The Most Popular Policeman of Hartford, CT. Dec. 19, 1890." Although the recipient is not identified by name, it is believed that the revolver was presented to Captain George F. Bill. A longtime resident of Hartford, Bill was a member of the short-lived First Regiment of Colt's Revolving Rifles during the Civil War. Commonly called "Colt's Regiment," it was formed when Samuel Colt promised to train and equip a volunteer regiment from Connecticut if it was named after him. The regiment, however, was formally disbanded before ever leaving the city of Hartford. Bill fought in the war with a different regiment, and upon returning to Hartford, he became a police officer. He was appointed captain in 1873 and the city's chief of police in 1893. Bill served with distinction throughout his career, and, as noted in the inscription, he was a beloved member of the community.

The Model 1877 Lightning was one of many firearms Wells Fargo agents used to protect themselves and their cargo. (97.165.2; donated by Petra and Greg Martin)

MODEL 1877 LIGHTNING
WITH WELLS FARGO STAMPING

Riding Shotgun

Wells Fargo was one of the most important businesses in the history of the American West. The company was born out of the discovery of gold in California in 1848. Gold brought countless fortune seekers to the region, and businesses catering to their every need seemingly sprouted up overnight. Waiting a few years to make sure conditions remained stable, Henry Wells and William G. Fargo formed a joint stock association in 1852 called Wells, Fargo & Co. The business offered banking, express, and commission services. The banking operations included the collecting of deposits, the remittances and transfer of funds, and the extension of credit. The express side of the business included forwarding of gold, valuables, packages, parcels, letters, and other any form of merchandise. The filing of legal documents, collecting bills to make payments, and even purchasing goods were examples of the commission services offered.

The company flourished, and after the Financial Panic of 1855, Wells Fargo was the dominant firm in the region. Initially relying on others to move its cargo, Wells Fargo was associated with the Pony Express during its brief tenure in 1860 and 1861. Beginning in 1866, Wells Fargo expanded rapidly into the staging business. The operation of stagecoaches and stagecoach lines was a new source of revenue. It also assured the company a secure and speedy transportation network that helped facilitate its banking and express operations. Wells Fargo stagecoaches often carried high-value cargo, so they were prime targets for highwaymen and robbers. As a result, Wells Fargo agents carried a variety of firearms. Armed personnel often supplied their own weapons, so firearm purchases were usually made locally.

The weapon of choice was often a double-barrel shotgun, as it was both effective and intimidating. Shotguns were so ubiquitous on Wells Fargo and other stagecoaches they were commonly called coach guns. Armed agents or shotgun messengers usually sat to the stagecoach driver's right, and even to this day, the front seat passenger in a car is said to be "riding shotgun." Wells Fargo agents also used revolvers. Firearms with Wells Fargo stampings are popular with collectors, and, as a result, many are faked. In fact, fake Wells Fargo firearms greatly outnumber authenticated examples. A bona fide Wells Fargo firearm in the Autry Collection is an 1877 Lightning, serial number 91267, manufactured in 1893. It has a four-and-a-half-inch barrel, and the checkered black rubber gribs have Rampant Colt emblems on each side. The revolver is stamped "W.F. & Co. EX. 91" on the back strap. While Wells Fargo agents were commonly known to carry Single Action Armies, documented Lightnings are exceptionally rare. The example in the Autry Collection can be traced directly to a Wells Fargo employee who worked in the vicinity of Laramie, Wyoming.

Wells Fargo went through significant changes in the 20th century. The railroad decreased the need for stagecoaches, and Wells Fargo adapted by reaching an agreement with the Central Pacific Railroad. The express business was consolidated with other companies during World War I and was eventually acquired by the American Express Company. When a prominent eastern financier took control of Wells Fargo in 1905, he divested the company of its banking operations, which went through several mergers and acquisitions in the first half of the 20th century. In 1969, a direct continuation of the banking business acquired all rights to the Wells Fargo name. As a result, Wells Fargo & Company, the financial service business that exists today, is a direct descendent of the original company started in 1852.

254

Three variations of the Model 1878 Double Action Frontier are displayed in this case, along with parts, gauges, stamps, and other related artifacts. (87.118.75)

MODEL GUNS FOR THE MODEL 1878
DOUBLE ACTION FRONTIER

A Unique Display Case

T he Model 1878 Double Action Frontier was Colt's first heavy-frame, double-action revolver. More than 51,000 of the fixed-cylinder revolvers were manufactured from 1878 to 1905. Like the Model 1877, its double-action predecessor, the 1878 Frontier was based on the design of the popular Single Action Army. The Single Action Army and the 1878 Frontier shared common barrel lengths and many of the standard calibers. The calibers included .32-20, .38-40, and .44-40. The Colt Lighting Rifle and the Winchester Model 1873 Rifle were also chambered in these calibers. As a result, individuals often carried some variation of these guns, especially on the American frontier. The dual chambering for both handgun and rifle was convenient and eliminated any safety concerns over accidentally loading the wrong cartridge, a mistake that could be deadly.

Tested by the Ordnance Department in 1878–1879, the 1878 Frontier was deemed unacceptable for military use. Despite the model's larger size and sturdier interior parts, at least in comparison to the Model 1877, the 1878 Frontier was prone to accidental discharges and a high rate of misfires. A weak mainspring allowed the model to fire simply by pulling the trigger, but it also caused the misfires. The government nevertheless ordered approximately 4,600 specially designed 1878 Frontiers chambered in .45 Colt caliber in 1902. The military revolvers differed in several aspects from those mass-produced for the civilian market. They all had six-inch barrels, a large trigger guard (twice the normal size), and a correspondingly bigger trigger. It is believed that the larger trigger guard was intended for use by individuals wearing gloves in cold climates such as Alaska. In actuality, the government version saw use in the Philippines. As a result, it is often referred to by collectors as the Philippine or Alaskan Model.

Civilian users of the 1878 Frontier were critical of the model for the same reasons as the Ordnance Department. Simply put, the revolver's double-action mechanism would not stand up to heavy use. The shape of the grip was also criticized. The introduction of swing-out cylinder Colt revolvers in 1889 ultimately made both the Model 1877 and the 1878 Frontier obsolete. As a result, the 1878 Frontier was the last fixed-cylinder double-action revolver manufactured by Colt's. Despite its poor initial reception, the model has increased in popularity with collectors in the past few decades. Antique revolvers made prior to 1898 are highly collectible, along with engraved specimens and those with unique features. Examples owned by historic figures, many of which are associated with the American West, are also prized.

A unique display case in the Autry Collection contains rare model guns of three variations of the 1878 Frontier. Manufactured circa 1878, all of the revolvers lack serial numbers and are instead marked "M" for model on the butt. The top revolver in the case is one of only two known Flattop Target versions of the 1878 Frontier. The revolver is unfinished or "in the white," and the front sight has a steel blade insert. The center revolver is one of approximately four known 1878 Frontiers in a hammerless design. The hammer is concealed beneath a machined steel plate, and the side plate on the left frame of the revolver is partially cut away. The bottom revolver is the Sheriff's Model 1878 Frontier, the only variation of the three that was mass-produced. The display case also includes parts, gauges, stamps, and other related artifacts from Colt's Inspection Department, Model Room, and Production Department. The entire set is quite unique and a testament to the evolution of a poorly received model.

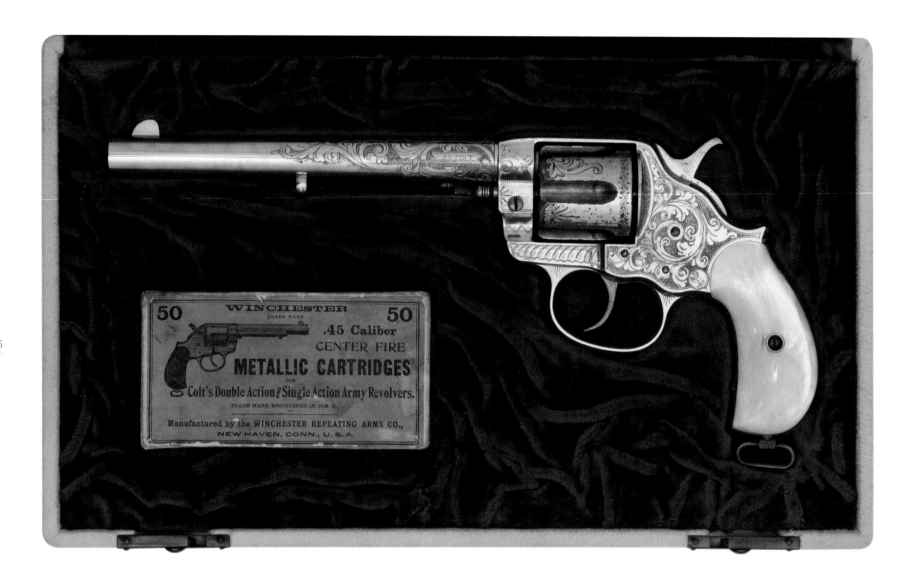

Colt's presented a beautifully engraved Model 1878 Double Action Frontier to Captain Jack Crawford, a nationally renowned figure. (2012.26.1; the George Gamble Collection)

CAPTAIN JACK CRAWFORD'S CASED PRESENTATION MODEL 1878 DOUBLE ACTION FRONTIER

The Poet Scout

Although he is not as well known today as many of his contemporaries, Captain Jack Crawford, the "Poet Scout," was one of the most colorful figures in the history of the American West. Crawford was born in Ireland in 1847 and immigrated to America in his teens. The first great adventure in his life came when he fought as a volunteer for the Union Army during the Civil War. Wounded at Spotsylvania and Petersburg, he learned to read and write while recovering in a hospital from the first wound. Crawford clearly understood the power of words, and unlike any other individual who roamed the American frontier, he wrote about his experiences in a dramatic style that was fully intended for the general public. Whether it was a newspaper article or poem, Crawford's words captivated audiences across the United States.

After the Civil War, Crawford was one of the first miners to enter the Black Hills of the Dakotas in the mid-1870s. As a scout for the Black Hills Rangers, a unit organized to protect miners from the Sioux, he came to be known as Captain Jack, a moniker he used for the rest of his life. He joined the Army as a civilian scout, eventually replacing William F. "Buffalo Bill" Cody as chief scout for the Fifth Cavalry. He worked for the Army until 1886, and during his tenure, he continued to explore mining opportunities. He even spent time in 1878 in the Cariboo gold mines in British Columbia. He vividly described all of his experiences as a scout and miner for publications in cities across the country, including New York. He also shared his adventures in seven books of poetry, four plays, and more than 100 stories.

Prior to the advent of the elaborate Wild West show, Buffalo Bill and others starred in frontier melodramas, commonly called combinations, which featured frontier heroes in adventurous situations. Buffalo Bill convinced Crawford to join his combination in 1876, and the two toured the West into 1877. Disagreements over finances and publicity came to a head when Buffalo Bill accidentally stabbed Crawford during an appearance in Virginia City, Nevada. Crawford left Buffalo Bill's company and formed his own. The Captain Jack Combination was a financial disaster that disbanded in 1878 after performing for less than a year. Returning to show business in 1885, Crawford joined Doc Carver's Wild West show before finding success on the lecture circuit. For more than 30 years, Crawford traveled around the country entertaining audiences with a combination of stories, poems, and dramatic re-creations. Crawford's tours brought him further national acclaim.

Crawford was an avid collector of firearms. One of his finest was a Model 1878 Double Action Frontier, serial number 33233, which is now part of the Autry Collection. The revolver has a nickel-plated frame and a gold-plated cylinder. Manufactured in 1894, the engraving appears to be the work of Cuno A. Helfricht. The two-piece bird's-head grips are made of pearl. The back strap is inscribed "Presented to Capt. Jack Crawford / by the Colts Patent Fire Arms Mfg. Co." The suede-covered presentation case is lined with purple velvet. A ribbon on the top of the case reads "This handsome revolver was presented to Capt. Jack Crawford, / 'The Poet Scout' by the Colt's Patent Fire Arms Mfg. Co., it / being his favorite make of revolver, and the one he recommends / above all others for durability and effective work." Colt's clearly hoped the presentation would serve as a powerful advertisement as Crawford toured around the country.

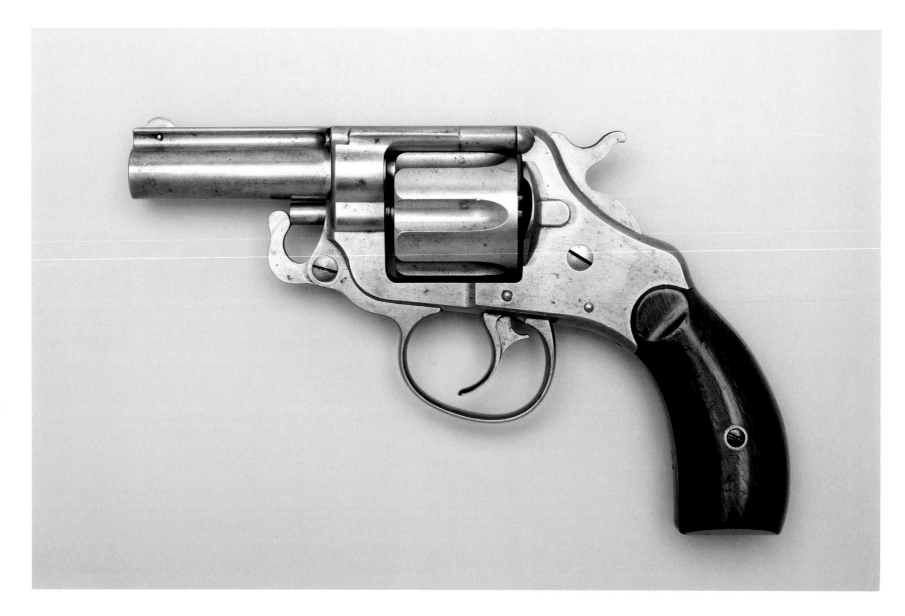

Lacking any sort of markings, this experimental revolver
was one of the first Colts with a swing-out cylinder.
(87.118.77)

EXPERIMENTAL DOUBLE ACTION WITH SWING-OUT CYLINDER

The Latest Innovation

All of Colt's revolvers prior to 1889, whether single or double action, had fixed cylinders or cylinders that were firmly attached to the frame. This made reloading very difficult. During the percussion era, a revolver could be reloaded by changing out cylinders or the components had to be added individually to each chamber. Metallic cartridge revolvers usually had a loading gate at the rear of the cylinder that allowed an empty casing to be ejected one at a time and a new cartridge loaded. Either way, reloading a fixed-cylinder revolver was slow and labor-intensive. Beginning in the late 1860s, swing-out cylinders began to emerge in Europe. One of the earliest British patents, taken out in 1869, swung the cylinder out to the right of the frame and employed an ejector star to push all of the empty casings out simultaneously.

In America, the Winchester Repeating Arms Company was one of the first manufacturers to experiment with swing-out cylinders. Winchester was the dominant manufacturer of rifles and other longarms in America, and in the 1870s, it contemplated entering the highly competitive handgun market. The motivating factors were the allure of large sales to the American and Russian governments, coupled with the notion of making companion pieces to its longarms for the civilian market. Winchester's final handgun design, based on the work of Hugo Borchardt and S. W. Wood, was a single-action revolver with a swing-out cylinder and a cylinder pin that extracted all of the spent casings at one time. Patents related to the design covered various devices for ejecting spent casings, but not the swing-out cylinder itself. The revolvers were submitted to the United States Navy in 1876 and to the Russian Ordnance Department soon thereafter. The revolvers were rejected, and Winchester subsequently abandoned its attempts to enter the handgun market.

Colt's began experimenting with swing-out cylinders at a time when the company was shifting its focus primarily to double-action revolvers. The prolific William Mason was the leading designer behind Colt's efforts. His first patent related to swing-out cylinders was number 249,649 granted on November 15, 1881. He obtained an additional patent on December 6 of that year. Mason's patents covered such things as the swing-out cylinder, the mechanism on which the cylinder is swung out, the ejector star, and the thumb-operated cylinder latch. Additional patents were taken out by Horace Lord and C. J. Ehbets. Lord's patent of August 5, 1884, number 303,172, simplified and strengthened the way the cylinder swung out and returned into place. Lord's patent was deemed so significant that it was stamped on almost every Colt swing-out cylinder revolver for the next 50 years. Based partially on Lord's design, the first swing-out cylinder revolver mass-produced in America was Colt's Model 1889 Navy.

An experimental double-action revolver in the Autry Collection shows the evolution of the swing-out cylinder. It was manufactured circa 1884, approximately five years before the introduction of the 1889 Navy. The unmarked revolver is chambered in .38 centerfire with a three-inch barrel and rosewood grips. It is unfinished or "in the white." Research indicates that it was based on patents taken out by C. J. Ehbets and Horace Lord. To swing the cylinder out, the trigger guard is pulled down and forward, then pivoted clockwise. All of the empty casings are ejected simultaneously by pushing the trigger guard forward. Unlike the swing-out cylinder revolvers eventually mass-produced by Colt's, the cylinder on the experimental revolver swings out on a crane that pivots from the top of the frame as opposed to the bottom. Only three of these experimental swing-out cylinder revolvers are known to exist. Each one is slightly different, but they all show the efforts Colt's put forth to once again be a pioneer in the field of firearm manufacturing.

John T. Thompson, an ordnance officer and the inventor of the Thompson Submachine Gun, was awarded this Model 1903 New Army and Navy for a government competitive prize. (87.118.80)

BRIGADIER GENERAL JOHN T. THOMPSON'S MODEL 1903 NEW ARMY AND NAVY

The Ordnance Department

Military patronage has and continues to be essential to the success of Colt's. The United States government's condemnation of all the revolvers produced by the Patent Arms Manufacturing Company proved to be a major factor in the permanent closing of Samuel Colt's first company in 1842. Military orders for the Walker Model ultimately revived Colt's fortunes as a gunmaker in 1847, and continued patronage allowed his second company to flourish in the second half of the 19th century. Substantial government orders in the 20th century helped the company survive difficult periods. Recognizing the significance of military patronage, Colt's has submitted countless firearms to the Ordnance Department (later renamed the Ordnance Corps) for government testing. A variety of other Colt-related products also have been manufactured with the military in mind.

Two rare Colt accessories in the Autry Collection are the Bridgeport Rig and a Colt toolkit. The Bridgeport Rig, patented in 1882 by Texas Sheriff Louis S. Flatau, was designed to mount a revolver directly to a belt so it could be fired quickly. The belt consisted of a two-pronged steel clip and the revolver was attached by a large customized hammer screw that protruded from the frame. Because the revolver was exposed to dirt and moisture, it was deemed unsuitable for military use. It was nevertheless popular wtih many on the American frontier. An even rarer object in the Autry Collection is a toolkit manufactured by Colt's that was intended to help soldiers do repair work on revolvers while on the battlefield. Although the idea seemed promising, it proved to be impractical, and the toolkit in the Autry Collection may be the only surviving example.

A notable Ordnance Department officer who was involved in the testing of several Colt firearms and related products was John Taliaferro Thompson. A graduate of the United States Military Academy, Thompson was assigned to the Ordnance Department in 1890. During the Spanish-American War, he was instrumental in the formation of a unit armed with Colt's Gatling gun. In the years that followed, he oversaw the development and adoption of Colt's Model 1911 Pistol and its .45 ACP cartridge. Retiring from the Army with the rank of brigadier general, Thompson formed the Auto-Ordnance Corporation in 1916. The company developed the

Thompson Submachine Gun, and a manufacturing contract was signed with Colt's in 1920. (A submachine gun is an automatic shoulder weapon that fires pistol-caliber cartridges.) The weapon was intended for the military, but unfortunately it gained notoriety in the hands of Prohibition-era gangsters. Dismayed by the negative publicity, Colt's discontinued its association with the gun, but its use by Allied militaries during World War II redeemed its reputation.

Prior to his invention of the weapon that bears his name, John T. Thompson was awarded a Model 1903 New Army and Navy, serial number 201070, for a government competitive prize. The revolver, now part of the Autry Collection, was shipped directly to Thompson in August 1903. It is of the highest quality, indicating that Colt's recognized the significant position the recipient held within the Ordnance Department. The revolver is .38 caliber with a six-inch barrel, blued finish, and checkered ivory grips. The profuse and intricate engraving on the barrel, cylinder, and frame is believed to have been executed by Cuno A. Helfricht. Ordnance Department inspector markings are located on the left side of the frame above the grip and on the breech end of the cylinder. Engraved arms inspected and stamped by Ordnance Department officials are exceedingly rare. Given the revolver's appearance and association with an important historical figure, it is a prized specimen.

Above:
Produced outside the factory, the Bridgeport Rig was designed to facilitate quick firing of a Colt revolver, but it was deemed unsuitable for military use. (90.120.6)

Opposite:
The military also did not adopt a special toolkit manufactured by Colt's that was intended to facilitate the repair of revolvers by soldiers while on the battlefield. (87.118.79)

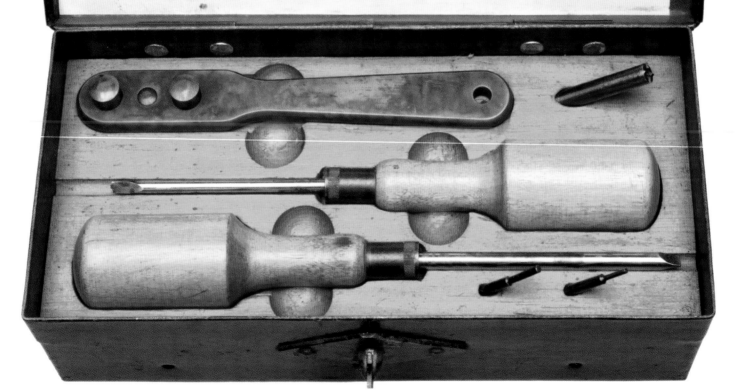

Albert Fall owned this New Service prior to becoming the first former cabinet officer to go to prison as a result of misconduct in office. (85.1.1332; acquisition made possible in part by John E. Bianchi Jr.)

POLITICIAN ALBERT FALL'S
NEW SERVICE MODEL

Rocked by Scandal

Albert Fall was a prominent Western politician who is best remembered for his involvement in one of the biggest political scandals in the first half of the 20th century. Born in Kentucky in 1861, Fall had very little formal education and was primarily self-taught. A respiratory problem plagued him most of his life, and he eventually headed west in search of a more forgiving climate. He tried prospecting and mining for a time and finally ended up in Las Cruces in the New Mexico Territory. Fall practiced law and became active in local politics. He was elected to the territorial legislature in 1890. He also served time as an associate justice of the New Mexico Supreme Court and briefly as solicitor general. Fall was an effective, albeit controversial, politician.

Initially a Democrat, Fall was estranged from the party due in part to his defense of a group of Texas cattle rustlers accused of killing a fellow politician. Fall was also involved in the controversial defense of a few notable characters, including Constable John Selman, the killer of gunslinger John Wesley Hardin, and Wayne Brazel, the man who killed legendary lawman Pat Garrett. Fall's legal and political activities garnered him many enemies. He once claimed he was the target of an assassination attempt, and he often traveled with bodyguards. It was rumored that he always carried a gun.

Fall owned several revolvers in his lifetime, including the New Service Model in the Autry Collection, serial number 17639. The revolver was manufactured in 1907. It is .45 caliber with a six-inch barrel, blued finish, and checkered walnut grips with Rampant Colt medallions. On one occasion, Fall and his supporters actually got into a gunfight with a rival, but no one was killed. At the outbreak of the Spanish-American War, Fall tried to take his warrior's mentality to the actual battlefield. He abandoned politics to serve as a captain of an infantry company from New Mexico. Despite his great desire to distinguish himself in battle, his company never left the United States.

Fall made his way back to politics, and as a Republican, he was named one of the first United States senators from the state of New Mexico in 1912. He was reelected in 1918. Fall believed that New Mexico benefited greatly from outsiders who capitalized on the state's natural resources, so he was a vocal advocate of corporate interests and an opponent of conservation. Fall was also a prominent supporter of the women's suffrage movement. During his tenure in the Senate, he served on the prestigious Foreign Relations Committee and the Public Lands Committee. He was regarded by many of his colleagues as the leading voice on Mexico and Mexican affairs at a time when the Mexican Revolution and the country's involvement in World War I were pressing concerns for all politicians. Fall served as an advisor to the presidential campaign of Republican Senator Warren G. Harding in 1920.

When Harding was elected president, he appointed Fall as Secretary of the Interior. Fall's time in office was rather inconsequential. However, in 1922, Fall became embroiled in a huge political scandal. Harding's administration transferred control of several key oil fields in California and Wyoming from the Navy to the Department of the Interior. Fall subsequently leased the fields, which had previously been held in reserve, to oil companies headed by his friends. Fall was given cash and gifts in return, including a "loan" of $100,000. The details of the leases became front-page news, and it was called the Teapot Dome scandal in reference to a unique rock formation at the site of one of the oil fields in Wyoming. Forced to resign, Fall was found guilty of conspiracy and bribery. He was required to pay a $100,000 fine and serve one year in prison. The scandal came to epitomize all that was wrong with politics and politicians. It was arguably the single biggest political scandal of the 20th century until Watergate in the 1970s.

A customized New Service Model was one of Colonel Charles Askins Jr.'s favorite weapons, and he used it around the world. (85.1.1335; acquisition made possible in part by John E. Bianchi Jr.)

COLONEL CHARLES ASKINS JR.'S NEW SERVICE MODEL

A Modern-Day Gunslinger

Colonel Charles "Boots" Askins Jr. was a colorful figure in the 20th-century American West. Askins spent his early years fighting fires for the U.S. Forest Service and serving as a park ranger. He joined the U.S. Border Patrol in 1930 and the U.S. Army in 1941. Throughout his career, Askins won numerous shooting competitions, including the prestigious National Matches at Camp Perry, Ohio. Askins used many firearms in his life, but one of his favorites was a specially modified New Service Model, now in the Autry Collection. The revolver, serial number 339755, has a relief-carved steer head on the right side of the grips and "CA / 1936" is carved on the left side. The revolver accompanied Askins everywhere, from the border of Mexico to the banks of Germany's Rhine River.

Askins was born in Nebraska in 1902. His father was an Army officer and writer whose books on shotguns are still considered some of the best in the field. Askins's father taught him how to shoot, and when he was only 15, he spent a summer hunting in Africa. He got a temporary job with the U.S. Forest Service fighting fires in the Flathead Forest in Montana, and by 1929, he was a full-time forest ranger stationed with the Vaqueros Ranger Division in the Kit Carson National Forest. Askins used his time as a ranger to perfect his shooting skills. He nevertheless found the job rather boring, and in 1930, he joined the U.S. Border Patrol. In his autobiography, Askins boasted that he was in a gunfight every week. While Askins never let the truth or a grandiose claim get in the way of a good story, he certainly saw extensive action on the border during the lawlessness of the Great Depression and Prohibition.

While with the Border Patrol, Askins began participating in competitive shooting contests on behalf of the agency and the Texas National Guard, which he joined in 1930. He won numerous state and national championships over the next few years. In 1937, Askins won the first aggregate pistol and revolver championship at the National Matches competition at Camp Perry. The competition required the shooter to fire .22, .38, and .45 calibers. Askins's first-place finish was awarded with a medal and a cash prize of $8.56. Askins later learned that accepting the money made him a professional, and he was never allowed to compete for a spot on the United States Olympic pistol team. It was reported that Askins won more than 534 medals and 117 trophies during his competitive shooting career. His shooting prowess eventually led to his appointment as instructor of firearms for the entire Border Patrol. At his insistence, the agency adopted the .38 Special caliber New Service as its standard sidearm. Following in his father's footsteps, Askins also wrote several books and more than 1,000 articles on firearms, shooting, and hunting.

When the Texas National Guard was called to active duty in 1941, Askins asked for and received a commission as a first lieutenant in the Ordnance Department. Stationed in North Africa, Askins was assigned as a battlefield recovery officer tasked with finding and overhauling equipment abandoned in the field. During the Allied invasion of Sicily, he was promoted to an executive officer of an ordnance battalion. He served in that capacity during the invasion of continental Europe. Askins was discharged from the Army as a major after the war, and after a brief tenure as field editor for *Outdoor Life* magazine, he returned to the Army as a paratrooper. He was stationed in Spain for several years, tasked with studying Spanish munitions capabilities, and in 1956, he was sent to Vietnam as chief instructor of firearms. Prior to retiring from the Army in 1963, he was instrumental in the founding of an Army pistol shooting team. Askins continued to write, and given his reputation as a modern-day gunslinger, his autobiography was aptly titled *Unrepentant Sinner*.

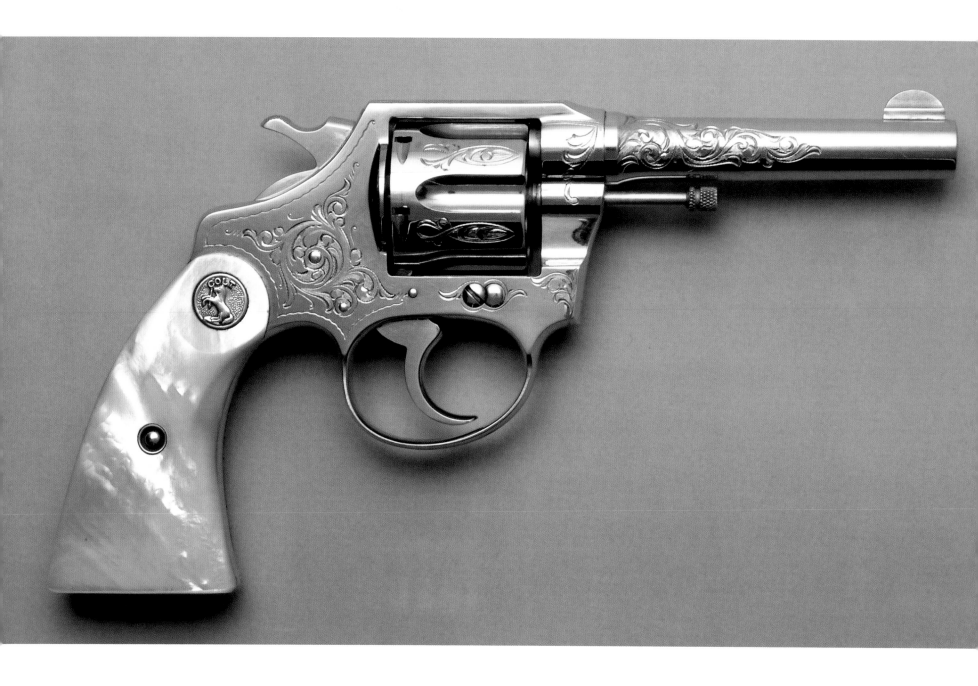

Abercrombie & Fitch, a company with a long and distinguished history that dates to 1892, originally sold this Police Positive Model. (87.118.99)

ABERCROMBIE & FITCH
POLICE POSITIVE MODEL

Not Your Grandfather's Company

Abercrombie & Fitch is a retail clothing chain that caters to young adults and the casual American lifestyle. The company is probably best known for its lurid advertising that features scantily clad young models in extremely provocative positions. While Abercrombie proudly markets itself as "authentic American clothing since 1892," the company that exists today was really started in 1988 when The Limited, a large apparel corporation that includes such brands as Victoria's Secret and Lane Bryant, purchased the company name and operations from Oshman's Sporting Goods, a Houston-based retailer. Abercrombie was transformed at that time from a sporting goods store to a high-end apparel merchandiser focusing on the teen market. The new Abercrombie was extremely successful and spun off as a publicly trading company in 1996. Today, Abercrombie has more than 300 locations in the United States. Firearms are no longer sold by Abercrombie, but they played an important part in the company's history.

David T. Abercrombie originally founded the Abercrombie Company in the city of New York in 1892. Abercrombie was a former miner, prospector, and railroad surveyor, and the store sold a variety of camping equipment. Ezra H. Fitch, a lawyer, was one of Abercrombie's best clients, and in 1900, he purchased a major stake in the business. The name was officially changed to Abercrombie & Fitch in 1904. The two owners eventually disagreed over the future direction of the business. Abercrombie wanted to continue selling gear to professional sportsmen, but Fitch wanted to broaden the company and position it as a general retailer. The quarreling finally came to a head, and in 1907, Abercrombie sold his interest in the company he originally founded. Under Fitch's ownership, Abercrombie & Fitch became one of the first New York retailers that catered to both men and women. In 1909, the company mailed out its first catalog, an expensive but highly effective marketing tool. It continued to expand, and in 1917, the retail operations were moved into a 12-story building on Madison Avenue. By the time Fitch sold his interest in the company in 1928, Abercrombie & Fitch was a market leader.

For decades, firearms were some of the company's most popular and best-selling items. The store and catalog listed a variety of shotguns, rifles, pistols, and revolvers. Manufacturers included Winchester, Parker, Remington, Smith & Wesson, Iver Johnson, and Colt's. The seventh floor of the Madison Avenue store was dedicated solely to firearms, and a shooting range was located in the basement. The company's inventory of firearms was one of the largest and most valuable private collections in the United States. In 1939, guns accounted for 40 percent of the store's sales. The company continued to sell firearms and a variety of sporting goods as the company expanded in the middle of the 20th century, but clothing eventually became the main focus. Firearms slowly disappeared from the shelves, and they were completely removed when The Limited purchased interests in the stores and the corporate name in 1988.

An exceptional example of a firearm that was originally offered by Abercrombie & Fitch is the Police Positive Model, serial number 314785, in the Autry Collection. The revolver is chambered in .32 caliber, but built on a .38-caliber frame. It features nickel plating and pearl grips. The grade A engraving was the work of Wilbur A. Glahn. The revolver was shipped to Abercrombie & Fitch on September 2, 1930. Abercrombie's firearm catalog in 1930, an example of which is part of the Autry Collection, listed Police Positives starting at $27, but the engraving and pearl grips on serial number 314785 would have increased the selling price significantly. The individual who ultimately purchased the revolver appreciated its craftsmanship and beauty, as it has never been fired and thus appears exactly as it did the day it left the Abercrombie store.

GUNS

Abercrombie & Fitch Co.

MADISON AVENUE & 45TH ST.

New York

"POLICE-POSITIVE," DOUBLE ACTION REVOLVER
Jointless Solid Frame, Simultaneous Ejection

For the Following Cartridges:

.32 Colt Police Positive, .38 Colt Police Positive.

SIX SHOTS..

LENGTH OF BARRELS: Cal. .32, 2½, 4, 5 and 6 inches. Cal. .38, 4, 5, and 6 inches.

FINISH: Full Blued or Full Nickel Plated. Checked Walnut Stocks. Checked Trigger.

WEIGHT: With 4-inch Barrel, 20 ounces.

LENGTH OVER ALL: With 4-inch Barrel, 8¼ inches.

No. F5..Price $27.00

BANKER'S SPECIAL (Same as above) 2-inch Barrel...............Price $27.00

Opposite:
Prior to focusing exclusively on clothing, Abercrombie & Fitch depended heavily on firearm sales, as evidenced by their distribution of a dedicated gun catalog. (T2012-118-1)

Above:
In 1930, a standard Police Positive Model was sold by Abercrombie & Fitch for $27. (T2012-118-1)

Dr. Charles H. Wilson, the owner of what may be the finest Police Positive .22 Target Model G ever made, was a national shooting champion. (2010.1.1; the George Gamble Collection)

SHOOTING CHAMPION
DR. CHARLES H. WILSON'S POLICE
POSITIVE .22 TARGET MODEL G

Rapid Fire

Colt's introduced Police Positive Models in 1905. The pocket revolver was originally chambered in .38 caliber, and it was designed to provide a powerful successor to the Model 1877 Lightning, which was soon to be discontinued. A similar model was already on the market, the New Police, but it was only chambered in .32 caliber. The Police Positive was very successful, and in 1907, a .32-caliber version was manufactured to replace the New Police. The Police Positive .32 was equipped with a "positive lock" between the face of the hammer and the frame. It was designed to engage only when the trigger was pulled. Because the firing pin only came into contact with the cartridge during use, the "positive lock" prevented the revolver from accidentally discharging. A target version of the Police Positive .32 was released in 1925.

Additional target models, chambered in .22 caliber, were also introduced. The Model G was manufactured from 1910 to 1925, and the heavier-framed Model C was produced from 1925 to 1941. A combined total of approximately 45,000 were manufactured for both models. The models came with a standard barrel length of six inches and a weight ranging from 22 to 26 ounces. Grips were initially made of hard rubber and were later replaced by checkered walnut. Only about 10 Model G revolvers were engraved, and only one or two featured any sort of gold inlay. A superb example of a Police Positive .22 Target Model G is serial number 11400 in the Autry Collection. It may be the finest Model G ever produced.

The revolver was custom ordered and features several special features. It has a blued finish with a high polish. The profuse oak leaf and acorn engraving is the work of Rudolph J. Kornbrath, one of the foremost arms engravers in the history of American gunmaking and a contract engraver for Colt's from around 1910 to 1937. Engraving is found on the barrel, cylinder, frame, top strap, and trigger guard. The areas of the barrel where markings would normally be stamped are also engraved, as are the normally unembellished areas of the front sight base, the recoil shield, and the cylinder thumb release. The revolver has an exceptionally long 10-inch barrel and target sights. The factory ivory grips have inset Colt medallions on each side. The right panel has a relief-carved American eagle and shield motif. The name "Chas. H. Wilson" is stamped in black ink on the inside surface of the grips, and "CHW" is executed in gold inlay on the butt strap.

The revolver was custom-made for Dr. Charles H. Wilson in 1914. Wilson was a distinguished general practitioner in Pittsburgh, Pennsylvania, and the surgeon for the Baltimore & Ohio Railroad in the early 20th century. He was also a hunter and an expert competitive shooter. He won numerous shooting competitions with pistols and revolvers. In 1912, Wilson won the United States pistol championship, and the following year, he set the indoor pistol shooting record of the world with a score of 488 out of a possible 500. The indoor record was set with a pistol that Wilson personally manufactured. Wilson also owned several beautiful engraved Colt revolvers, including the Police Positive .22 Target Model G in the Autry Collection. The revolver shows signs of use, but like most target shooters, Wilson took excellent care of his equipment. As a result, the revolver remains in superb condition.

The Python Model is considered by many to be the finest Colt revolver ever manufactured, and this pair is arguably the best of the best. (90.183.18)

PYTHON MODEL PAIR WITH GOLD INLAY

The Capstone

Samuel Colt founded Colt's Patent Fire Arms Manufacturing Company with the sole intent to mass-produce revolvers. The company expanded its product line beyond revolvers while Colt was still alive, and in the century following his passing in 1862, the company developed a complete line of weapons. By the time Colt's Inc., Firearms Division, was established as a subsidiary of Colt Industries in 1964, revolvers were only a small part of the company's annual sales. In the 1960s and 1970s, the M16 Rifle was the company's most successful firearm. Adopted as the United States military's standard service rifle by 1969, the M16 played a crucial role in the Vietnam War. Other governments around the world also adopted the rifle, and it is estimated that more than 25 million M16-style weapons have been manufactured since its introduction. Despite the success of the M16, the decline in government orders following America's exit from Vietnam once again put the company in a precarious financial situation.

Colt Industries attempted to revive its fortunes by partially shifting its focus to sporting weapons and special orders placed through the newly established Custom Gun Shop. Despite the changes, the company struggled as government contracts continued to dwindle. Further problems were caused by increased competition in the law-enforcement market and a long, bitter strike by company employees. The strike ended when the company was sold to a coalition of private investors, the state of Connecticut, and the union employees in 1990. The company was renamed Colt's Manufacturing Company after the sale. With its debt increasing, the company filed for Chapter 11 bankruptcy protection in 1992. Emerging out of bankruptcy in 1994 under the primary ownership of New York investment firm Zilkha & Company, Colt's Manufacturing returned to profitability in the 21st century under the capable leadership of William M. Keys, a retired lieutenant general in the United States Marine Corps. Today, the company is once again a leader in the field of firearm manufacturing for the military and civilian markets.

Throughout its history, the one constant for Colt's has been the revolver. Sales of other firearms have been more substantial at times, but the company's identity and heritage will forever be associated with Samuel Colt's original invention. For many enthusiasts, from hunters to law-enforcement officers, the pinnacle of Colt's revolver line was the Python Model. Introduced in 1955 and discontinued entirely in 2005, the Python was hailed for its accuracy, balance, and smooth trigger pull. The superior finish, royal blue or nickel, was also praised. The revolver came in barrel lengths ranging from two and a half to six inches, all chambered in .357 Magnum caliber. The standard grips were two-piece walnut with inset gold-plated Colt medallions. The Python came in several variations, including the Python Hunter. It had an eight-inch barrel, neoprene grips, and an elaborate, factory-installed telescopic sight. The Python Hunter also came standard with an aluminum carrying case made by Halliburton.

Only a small number of Pythons were engraved. A pair made circa 1965 for Colt Industries Chairman George Strichman is by far the most deluxe examples ever produced. They are the work of master engraver Alvin A. White. The relief gold-inlaid images on the barrel, cylinder, and frame depict products manufactured by Colt Industries, along with a few key items relating to Samuel Colt. The ivory grips have gold-plated Colt Industries medallions in place of the standard Rampant Colts. The 18-karat gold butt caps feature a portrait of Samuel Colt and the inventor's coat of arms. The revolvers, serial numbers GAS-0 and GAS-00, are the perfect examples of Colt's continued dedication to quality and aesthetics. A far cry from the first prototypes Colt produced in the 1830s, the Pythons are a fitting capstone to the Autry National Center's fabulous Colt collection.

Samuel Colt, depicted on one of the revolver's 18-karat gold butt caps, would certainly take pride in the Python Model and the company that manufactured it. (90.183.18.1)

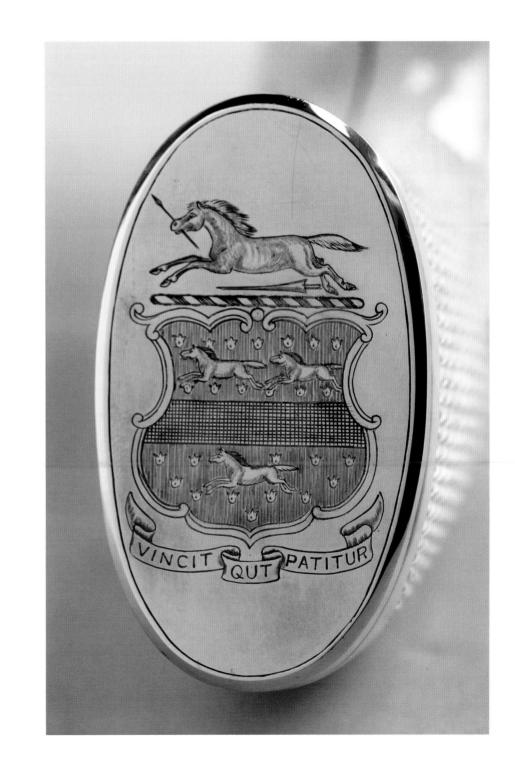

Originally appearing on the Colt coat of arms, the Rampant Colt remains a powerful symbol for the company more than 150 years after it was first introduced. (90.183.18.2)

BIBLIOGRAPHY

Adler, Dennis. *Colt Single Action: From Patersons to Peacemakers*. Edison, NJ: Chartwell Books, 2007.
———. *Guns of the American West*. New York: Chartwell Books, 2009.
———. *Guns of the Civil War*. Minneapolis, MN: Zenith Press, 2011.
Anderson, Andy. *Wells Fargo and the Rise of the American Financial Services Industry*. New York: Simon & Schuster, 2002.
Askins, Charles. *Unrepentant Sinner: The Autobiography of Colonel Charles Askins*. Boulder, CO: Paladin Press, 1985.

Barnard, Henry, ed. *Armsmear: The Home, the Arm, and the Armory of Samuel Colt; A Memorial*. New York, 1866.
Barra, Allen. *Inventing Wyatt Earp: His Life and Many Legends*. Edison, NJ: Castle Books, 2005.
Black, Conrad. *Richard M. Nixon: A Life in Full*. New York: Public Affairs, 2007.
Blake, Michael F. *Hollywood and the O.K. Corral: Portrayals of the Gunfight and Wyatt Earp*. Jefferson, NC: McFarland, 2007.
Boorman, Dean K. *Guns of the Old West: An Illustrated History*. Guilford, CT: Lyons Press, 2004.
Brinkley, Alan. *John F. Kennedy*. American Presidents Series. New York: Times Books, 2012.
Brinkley, Douglas. *Gerald R. Ford*. American Presidents Series. New York: Times Books, 2007.

Carpenter, Charles Hope Jr. with Mary Grace Carpenter. *Tiffany Silver*. New York: Dodd, Mead, 1978.
Carrillo, Leo. *The California I Love*. Englewood Cliffs, NJ: Prentice-Hall, 1961.
Carter, Joseph H. *Never Met a Man I Didn't Like: The Life and Writings of Will Rogers*. With an introduction by Jim Rogers. New York: Avon Books, 1991.
Carter, Robert A. *Buffalo Bill Cody: The Man behind the Legend*. New York: Wiley, 2000.
Chandler, Robert J. *Wells Fargo*. Images of America. Charleston, SC: Arcadia, 2006.
Clum, John. *Apache Days & Tombstone Nights: John Clum's Autobiography*. Edited by Neil B. Carmony. Silver City, NM: High-Lonesome Books, 1997.
Clum, Woodworth. *Apache Agent: The Story of John P. Clum*. Boston: Houghton Mifflin, 1936.
Cox, Mike. *The Texas Rangers: Wearing the Cinco Peso, 1821–1900*. New York: Forge, 2008.
———. *Time of the Rangers: Texas Rangers from 1900 to the Present*. New York: Forge, 2009.

Dallek, Robert. *Lyndon B. Johnson: Portrait of a President*. New York: Oxford University Press, 2004.
———. *An Unfinished Life: John F. Kennedy, 1917–1963*. Boston: Little, Brown, 2003.
Dalton, Emmett with Jack Jungmeyer. *When the Daltons Rode*. Garden City, NY: Doubleday, Doran, 1931.
Davis, John W. *Wyoming Range War: The Infamous Invasion of Johnson County*. Norman: University of Oklahoma Press, 2010.
Desinger, Bernd and Matthias Knop, eds. *Treasure of Silver Lake: The Myth of the American West in Germany*. Düsseldorf: Filmmuseum Düsseldorf, 2011.
D'Souza, Dinesh. *Ronald Reagan: How an Ordinary Man Became an Extraordinary Leader*. New York: Free Press, 1997.

Edwards, William B. *The Story of Colt's Revolver: The Biography of Col. Samuel Colt*. Harrisburg, PA: Stackpole, 1957.
Eisenhower, John S. D. *So Far from God: The U.S. War with Mexico, 1846–1848*. Norman: University of Oklahoma Press, 2000.
Etcheson, Nicole. *Bleeding Kansas: Contested Liberty in the Civil War Era*. Lawrence: University Press of Kansas, 2004.

Everson, William K. *The Hollywood Western: 90 Years of Cowboys and Indians, Train Robbers, Sheriffs and Gunslingers, and Assorted Heroes and Desperados*, rev. ed. New York: Carol, 1992.

Fenin, George N. and William K. Everson. *The Western: From Silents to Cinerama*. New York: Orion Press, 1962.
Ford, Gerald R. *A Time to Heal: The Autobiography of Gerald R. Ford*. New York: Harper & Row, 1979.
Fradkin, Philip L. *Wells Fargo and the American West*. New York: Simon & Schuster, 2002.

Garavaglia, Louis A. and Charles G. Worman. *Firearms of the American West: 1803–1865*. Niwot: University Press of Colorado, 1998.
———. *Firearms of the American West: 1866–1894*. Niwot: University Press of Colorado, 1997.
Gatto, Steve. *The Real Wyatt Earp: A Documentary Biography*. Edited by Neil B. Carmony. Silver City, NM: High-Lonesome Books, 2000.
George-Warren, Holly. *Public Cowboy No. 1: The Life and Times of Gene Autry*. New York: Oxford University Press, 2007.
Goodwin, Doris Kearns. *Lyndon Johnson and the American Dream*. New York: Harper & Row, 1976.
Graham, Ron, John A. Kopec, and C. Kenneth Moore. *A Study of the Colt Single Action Army Revolver*. Dallas, TX: Taylor, 1976.
Grant, Ellsworth S. *The Colt Legacy: The Colt Armory in Hartford, 1855–1980*. Providence, RI: Mowbray, 1982.
Green, Douglas B. *Singing in the Saddle: The History of the Singing Cowboy*. Nashville, TN: Vanderbilt University Press, 2002.
Guinn, Jeff. *The Last Gunfight: The Real Story of the Shootout at the O.K. Corral—And How It Changed the American West*. New York: Simon & Schuster, 2011.

Hardin, John Wesley. *The Life of John Wesley Hardin: From the Original Manuscript / As Written by Himself*. Seguin, TX, 1896.
Hart, William S. *My Life East and West*. Boston: Houghton Mifflin, 1929.
Haven, Charles T. and Frank A. Belden. *A History of the Colt Revolver and the Other Arms Made by Colt's Patent Fire Arms Manufacturing Company from 1836 to 1940*. New York: Bonanza Books, 1978.
Henderson, Timothy J. *A Glorious Defeat: Mexico and Its War with the United States*. New York: Hill & Wang, 2008.
Herring, Hal. *Famous Firearms of the Old West: From Wild Bill Hickok's Colt Revolvers to Geronimo's Winchester, Twelve Guns that Shaped our History*. Guilford, CT: TwoDot, 2008.
Horan, James D. *The Gunfighters: The Authentic Wild West*. New York: Crown, 1976.
Hosley, William N. *Colt: The Making of an American Legend*. Amherst: University of Massachusetts Press, 1996.
Houze, Herbert G. *Samuel Colt: Arms, Art, and Invention*. Edited by Elizabeth Mankin Kornhauser. New Haven, CT: Yale University Press, 2006.

Johnson, Marilynn S. *Violence in the West: The Johnson County Range War and the Ludlow Massacre*. The Bedford Series in History and Culture. Boston: Bedford/St. Martin's, 2009.

Ketchum, Richard M. *Will Rogers: His Life and Times*. New York: American Heritage, 1973.

Lake, Stuart N. *Wyatt Earp: Frontier Marshal*. Boston: Houghton Mifflin, 1931.

Levy, Shawn. *Paul Newman: A Life*. New York: Harmony Books, 2009.

Loy, R. Philip. *Westerns and American Culture, 1930–1955*. Jefferson, NC: McFarland, 2001.

———. *Westerns in a Changing America, 1955–2000*. Jefferson, NC: McFarland, 2004.

MacDonald, J. Fred. *Who Shot the Sheriff? The Rise and Fall of the Television Western*. Media and Society Series. New York: Praeger, 1987.

Malsch, Brownson. *"Lone Wolf" Gonzaullas, Texas Ranger*. Norman: University of Oklahoma Press, 1998.

McGilligan, Patrick. *Robert Altman: Jumping off the Cliff*. New York: St. Martin's, 1989.

McLynn, Frank. *Villa and Zapata: A History of the Mexican Revolution*. New York: Carroll & Graf, 2001.

Mercer, A. S. *The Banditti of the Plains, or the Cattlemen's Invasion of Wyoming in 1892*. Cheyenne, WY, 1894.

Metz, Leon Claire. *John Wesley Hardin: Dark Angel of Texas*. El Paso, TX: Mangan Books, 1996.

Meyer, William R. *The Making of the Great Westerns*. New Rochelle, NY: Arlington House, 1979.

Miller, Darlis A. *Captain Jack Crawford: Buckskin Poet, Scout, and Showman*. Albuquerque: University of New Mexico Press, 1993.

Mitchell, James L. *Colt: A Collection of Letters and Photographs about the Man, the Arms, the Company*. Harrisburg, PA: Stackpole, 1959.

Moore, Clayton with Frank Thompson. *I was that Masked Man*. Dallas, TX: Taylor, 1996.

Morris, Edmund. *Dutch: A Memoir of Ronald Reagan*. New York: Random House, 1999.

———. *The Rise of Theodore Roosevelt*. New York: Coward, McCann & Geoghegan, 1979.

Nordyke, Lewis. *John Wesley Hardin: Texas Gunman*. New York: Morrow, 1957.

Nottage, James H. *Saddlemaker to the Stars: The Leather and Silver Art of Edward H. Bohlin*. Photography by Susan Einstein. Los Angeles: Autry Museum of Western Heritage, 1996.

Ogle, John. *The Book of Colt Paper, 1834–2011*. Minneapolis, MN: Blue Book, 2011.

Pegler, Martin. *The Thompson Submachine Gun: From Prohibition Chicago to World War II*. Oxford: Osprey, 2010.

Phillips, Philip R. and R. L. Wilson. *Paterson Colt Pistol Variations*. Dallas, TX: Woolaroc Museum by Jackson Arms, 1979.

Rainey, Buck. *The Life and Films of Buck Jones: The Silent Era*. Waynesville, NC: World of Yesterday, 1988.

———. *The Life and Films of Buck Jones: The Sound Era*. Waynesville, NC: World of Yesterday, 1991.

Rogers, Roy with Carlton Stowers. *Happy Trails: The Story of Roy Rogers and Dale Evans*. Waco, TX: Word Books, 1979.

Rosa, Joseph G. *The Taming of the West: Age of the Gunfighter*. New York: Smithmark, 1993.

———. *They Called Him Wild Bill: The Life and Adventures of James Butler Hickok*, 2nd ed. Norman, OK: University of Oklahoma Press, 1974.

———. *Wild Bill Hickok, Gunfighter: An Account of Hickok's Gunfights*. Norman: University of Oklahoma Press, 2003.

Rothel, David. *The Roy Rogers Book*. Madison, NC: Empire, 1987.

Serven, James E. *Colt Firearms Since 1836*. La Habra, CA: Foundation Press, 1972.

Sharp, Lewis I. *John Quincy Adams Ward, Dean of American Sculpture: With a Catalogue Raisonné*. Newark: University of Delaware Press, 1985.

Silva, Lee A. *Wyatt Earp: A Biography of the Legend*. Santa Ana, CA: Graphic, 2002.

Smith, Robert Barr. *Daltons! The Raid on Coffeyville, Kansas*. Norman: University of Oklahoma Press, 1996.

Smokov, Mark T. *He Rode with Butch and Sundance: The Story of Harvey "Kid Curry" Logan*. A. C. Greene Series 13. Denton: University of North Texas Press, 2012.

Stratton, David H. *Tempest over Teapot Dome: The Story of Albert B. Fall*. Norman: University of Oklahoma Press, 1998.

Taffin, John. *Gun Digest Book of the .44*. Northfield, IL: Gun Digest Books, 2006.

Tefertiller, Casey. *Wyatt Earp: The Life behind the Legend*. With a foreword by Angus Cameron. New York: John Wiley & Sons, 1997.

Tuska, Jon. *The Filming of the West*. Garden City, NY: Doubleday, 1976.

Van Hise, James. *The Story of the Lone Ranger*. Las Vegas: Pioneer Books, 1990.

Virgines, George E. *Saga of the Colt Six-Shooter and the Famous Men Who Used It*. New York: F. Fell, 1969.

Welsome, Eileen. *The General and the Jaguar: Pershing's Hunt for Pancho Villa; A True Story of Revolution and Revenge*. Lincoln: University of Nebraska Press, 2007.

Wilkins, Frederick. *The Legend Begins: The Texas Rangers, 1823–1845*. Austin, TX: State House Press, 1996.

Wilson, Gary A. *Tiger of the Wild Bunch: The Life and Death of Harvey "Kid Curry" Logan*. Guilford, CT: TwoDot, 2007.

Wilson, R. L. *The Book of Colt Engraving*. Los Angeles: W. Beinfeld, 1974.

———. *The Book of Colt Firearms*, 3rd ed. Minneapolis, MN: Blue Book, 2001.

———. *Colt: An American Legend*. New York: Abbeville Press, 1985.

———. *Fine Colts: The Dr. Joseph A. Murphy Collection*. Doylestown, PA: Republic, 1999.

———. *The Paterson Colt Book: The Early Evolution of Samuel Colt's Repeating Arms*. Palo Alto, CA: Strutz-LeVett, 2001.

———. *The Peacemakers: Arms and Adventure in the American West*. New York: Random House, 1992.

———. *The Rampant Colt: The Story of a Trademark*. Spencer, IN: T. Haas, 1969.

———. *Theodore Roosevelt: Outdoorsman*. New York: Winchester Press, 1971.

Wilson, R. L. with Greg Martin. *Buffalo Bill's Wild West: An American Legend*. New York: Random House, 1998.

Worman, Charles G. *Gunsmoke and Saddle Leather: Firearms in the Nineteenth-Century American West*. Albuquerque: University of New Mexico Press, 2005.

Yoggy, Gary A. *Riding the Video Range: The Rise and Fall of the Western on Television*. Jefferson, NC: McFarland, 1995.

Zuckoff, Mitchell. *Robert Altman: The Oral Biography*. New York: Knopf, 2009.

Inspiring | Educating | Creating | Entertaining

Brimming with creative inspiration, how-to projects, and useful information to enrich your everyday life, Quarto Knows is a favorite destination for those pursuing their interests and passions. Visit our site and dig deeper with our books into your area of interest: Quarto Creates, Quarto Cooks, Quarto Homes, Quarto Lives, Quarto Drives, Quarto Explores, Quarto Gifts, or Quarto Kids.

This edition published in 2018 by Chartwell Books,
an imprint of The Quarto Group,
142 West 36th Street, 4th Floor,
New York, NY 10018, USA
T (212) 779-4972 F (212) 779-6058
www.QuartoKnows.com

© 2013 Autry National Center

Preface © 2013 William M. Keys
Foreword © 2013 Beverly Haynes

Chartwell Books titles are also available at discount for retail, wholesale, promotional, and bulk purchase. For details, contact the Special Sales Manager by email at specialsales@quarto.com or by mail at The Quarto Group, Attn: Special Sales Manager, 401 Second Avenue North, Suite 310, Minneapolis, MN 55401, USA.

Project Editor: Candice Fehrman
Book Design: Aldo Sampieri
Text: Jeffrey Richardson

All objects in this book are from the collection of the Autry National Center. Photographs of objects from the Autry Collection are by Susan Einstein Photography, Los Angeles; David Benitez, Autry National Center; and Carmel France, Autry National Center.

p. 156: Original © Colt's Patent Fire Arms Manufacturing Co.
p. 157: Original © Warner Bros. Pictures Inc.
p. 270: Original © Abercrombie & Fitch Co.

10 9 8 7 6 5 4 3 2 1

ISBN: 978-0-7858-3694-0

Printed in China

ACKNOWLEDGMENTS

The author would like to thank the dedicated staff of the Autry National Center, especially the collections department and photography personnel, and the individuals at Rizzoli who contributed to the publication. The book also would not be possible without the generous support of George Gamble, Greg Martin, and Dennis A. LeVett.